Charles Martin Newell

Kaméhaméha, the conquering king: the mystery of his birth, loves and conquests

Charles Martin Newell

Kaméhaméha, the conquering king: the mystery of his birth, loves and conquests

ISBN/EAN: 9783743313293

Manufactured in Europe, USA, Canada, Australia, Japa

Cover: Foto ©ninafisch / pixelio.de

Manufactured and distributed by brebook publishing software (www.brebook.com)

Charles Martin Newell

Kaméhaméha, the conquering king: the mystery of his birth, loves and conquests

KAMÉHAMÉHA

THE CONQUERING KING

THE MYSTERY OF HIS BIRTH, LOVES, AND CONQUESTS

A ROMANCE OF HAWÁII

BY

C. M. NEWELL

KNIGHT COMPANION OF THE ROYAL ORDER OF KAPIOLANI; AUTHOR OF
"KALANI OF OAHU," "PEHE NU-E," ETC.

NEW YORK & LONDON
G. P. PUTNAM'S SONS
The Knickerbocker Press
1885.

COPYRIGHT BY
C. M. NEWELL
1885
All rights reserved

Press of
G. P. Putnam's Sons
New York

Iolani Palace
Honolulu
January 14. 1885.

Sir,

I am commanded by His Majesty the King to inform you that Her Majesty the Queen has been pleased to accept the dedication of Dr. Charles. M. Newell's Hawaiian romance, "Kamehameha" to be published shortly in New York.

I have the honor to be
Sir,
Your most Obedient Servant
Edward W Purvis
H. M's. Vice-Chamberlain.

TO

HER MAJESTY

QUEEN KAPIOLANI

THIS ROMANCE OF THE RENOWNED KING IS DEDICATED

BY ROYAL PERMISSION, WITH KIND

ALOHA!

TO HERSELF AND HER SUNNY ISLES

BY THE AUTHOR

PREFACE.

THE greater part of this Romance is a truthful narration of the real history of this most remarkable of Polynesian kings. The account of the destruction of Keoúa's army by means of Pele's volcanic eruption is trustworthy, both as to the number destroyed and as to the terrible circumstances of their death ; and equally historical are the dramatic incidents of the assassination of the brave king, together with seven of his royal chiefs. Truly, history repeats itself, for this was a repetition of Pompey's death on the Egyptian shore.

None of the battles described, or of the personal combats of Kaméhaméha, are fictitious, though the historian has depended for his details upon the traditions of the priests and the chants and *meles* of the ancient bards, each of whom seized upon the most dramatic epochs of his theme, to the exclusion of all intermediate incidents —these being left for the modern narrator to conceive.

Thus, while we have freely romanced with one of the many legendary stories of Kaméhaméha's birth and boyhood, we have held strictly to all known records of history, making a connective narrative as best we could. What the still unknown secret of the " Iron Mask " was to the reign of Louis XIV., the romantic and yet unsolved mystery of our hero's birth—fathered by a trio of kings—was to the contemporary historians of Hawáii. For half a century prior to his birth prophets had predicted the coming of a great chief, and bards had sung of a renowned warrior who should conquer the "Eight Isles," and forever end the cruel wars between the six kingdoms.

Of the several traditional birth-stories related to us by the bards and chiefs forty years ago, we have chosen the most romantic, if the least authentic. Our chosen version of this long-disputed question has the merit of showing why Kalaniopuu, the ruling king, came to divide his kingdom between his known and his unknown heirs —Kiwalao and Kaméhaméha.

It is but fair to state that the legend which found most favor half a century ago was told in this wise: One stormy night a famous chiefess gave birth, in the war-camp of King Alapai's army, to a lusty boy. Priests, prophets, and bards at once pronounced the young *Alii* to be the coming man. Tempted by this belief, Naeóle, a great chief, stole the babe that night from the sleeping mother's side, and secreted him for five years. Then Alapai ordered the chief to bring the boy to court. In fear lest the king meant to kill him, Naeóle delivered the wrong child, still keeping the real one secreted until he was twenty years old. Some years after Alapai secretly killed prince Keoúa. This led Kalaniopuu to think the king would soon make away with the boy, and he made an attempt by force of arms to take the youth from court. A severe battle was fought, and Kalaniopuu was beaten without rescuing the boy. This "wrong boy" gave rise to the erroneous story that the high-born Kaméhaméha was of low origin.

A glossary of Hawáiian names and phrases will be found at the close of the book.

THE AUTHOR.

BOSTON, *May*, 1884.

CONTENTS.

	PAGE
I—WAIMÁNU VALLEY	1
II—WAILÉLE: THE ROMANCE OF HER BIRTH	9
III—THE MYSTERY OF A HUNDRED YEARS	14
IV—THE PERILOUS DESCENT INTO WAIMÁNU	24
V—PRIEST-GIRLS ANOINTING THE DOGS	34
VI—HOW TO WOO A PROUD WOMAN	47
VII—MYSTERIOUS SACRIFICE BY MOONLIGHT	60
VIII—MOON-SPIRITS IN THE VALLEY	66
IX—LAST INTERVIEW OF THE LOVERS	70
X—WOOED AND WON, AND PARTED FOREVER,	75
XI—UMI, THE GOD-BORN CHIEF	86
XII—BOYHOOD DAYS OF UMI, NOW KAMÉHAMÉHA	95
XIII—HUMAN SACRIFICE IN THE TEMPLE	105
XIV—MIDNIGHT INCANTATIONS AMONG THE GHOSTS	116
XV—KAMÉHAMÉHA'S PILGRIMAGE TO THE GODS,	126
XVI—THE KING AND HIS COURT AT WAIPIO	141
XVII—THE FEAST OF THE WARLIKE KINGS	150
XVIII—THE MAN-KILLERS ON THE CHIEF-BOY'S TRACK	161
XIX—PEPEHI REBUKED BY THE GODDESS OF MUKÍNI	172
XX—KAMÉHAMÉHA VISITS WAIPIO TO CLAIM HIS BIRTHRIGHT	180
XXI—COMMOTION AT WAIPIO	187

		PAGE
XXII—LIFE OR DEATH FOR THE KING'S SON		191
XXIII—COMBAT WITH SPEARS BETWEEN THE PRINCES		197
XXIV—THE COURT AT WAIPIO		203
XXV—QUEEN NAMAHANA'S TRAGIC STORY		209
XXVI—VIEW OF WAIPIO VALLEY FROM THE PÁLI		215
XXVII—SATAN CONFRONTING THE YOUNG PRINCE		222
XXVIII—KAAHUMANU INTRIGUES FOR A THRONE		233
XXIX—THE WAR WITH MAUI		240
XXX—THE COMING AND DEATH OF CAPTAIN COOK		251
XXXI—THE QUARREL OF THE PRINCES		268
XXXII—HAWAII'S NEW KINGS		273
XXXIII—ROYAL LOVERS ON THE MOONLIT SHORE		285
XXXIV—WAR WITH THE KINGS OF HILO AND KAU		292
XXXV—THE CONQUEST OF MAUI		302
XXXVI—BRILLIANT NAVAL VICTORY OF KOHALA		315
XXXVII—THE TRAGEDY OF KEOÚA AND HIS ARMY		321
XXXVIII—THE TIME OF THE GOOD VANCOUVER		334
XXXIX—THE INVASION OF OAHU		347
XL—THE BATTLE OF NUUANU: KAIANA SLAIN		353
XLI—BATTLE OF THE PÁLI AND DEATH OF KALÁNI		367
XLII—CONCLUSION		378

KAMÉHAMÉHA THE GREAT.

I.

WAIMÁNU VALLEY.

WHEN approaching the great island of Hawáii from the sea, one is enchanted by the mystery and majestic beauty of its three gigantic mountains, one of which often bursts upon the delighted vision of the weary wanderer while yet he is a hundred and fifty miles away. Thus they appeared to their discoverer, Juan Gaetano, when approaching "La Mesa Islas" from New Spain.

Coming from the eastward, bowling down before the strong trade-wind, with every white-breasted sail exulting in the breeze, the coast line is usually shut out from view by dark nimbus clouds, until the vessel sails quite near in to the land. But the nimbus is an earth-loving cloud, which never rises even to a mile's height, and one must look for the mountain tops above even the fleecy-white cumuli, which often creep joyfully up the mountain side two and a half miles high, and there lie slumbering in the sun, like sheep in a fold.

Mauna Kéa is generally the first of the trio of mountains to appear. How impatiently we wait the joyful cry of "Land O!" on that eventful day! With what thrills of delight we at length behold the snow-crowned mountains, looming clear and distinct above a sheeny-white cumulus, and glowing like the silver dome of some temple of the gods in the morning sun!

Silently we gaze upon the mountain crest, awed by its vastness and sublimity, and made humble and prayerful by its look of majestic repose.

How softly the hoary-headed monarch lies pillowed against the exquisite turquoise of the tranquil sky, brooding like some fabled god of the enchanted isle in divine reverie!

Drawing near to the windward shores of Hawáii, one is amazed at the countless streams, cascades, and gigantic waterfalls that tumble seaward; threading the evergreen slopes, leaping the cliffs, and supplied by the exhaustless reservoirs of mountain snows. The tiny rivulets blend in streams; these seek companionship in torrents, and they in turn become formidable rivers. One and all run wildly upon devious courses, seeking outlet through the numerous ravines that are riven deeply in these rockbound shores.

These deep, dark gorges, originally rent by earthquakes through the enormous cliffs of the iron-bound coast, have widened with time, and deepened by the constant attrition of floods, until some of them have become beautiful valleys.

One of these, the charming valley of Waipio, or "Captive Waters," had been the seat of empire for the ruling chiefs and kings for a thousand years. It is still the garden-land of this ever fruitful island of Hawáii, where flowers and fruits blossom and ripen throughout the year.

But it is not to the Eden-land of Waipio that I would now draw the reader's attention. There is another valley, deeper, darker, and more inaccessible, which we must see: the Valley of Waimánu, where the heroic subject of our story came upon the scene and passed his boyhood days. There he acquired from the old war-chiefs of the valley such mastery of weapons as to astonish the island world. Very few of its people had ever heard of such a person as Kaméhaméha * until he stalked proudly into their midst at a mighty tournament of kings, and took rank as a knight-errant against all competitors of his own age.

This romantic and inaccessible valley of Waimánu—the opening scene of our story—is one of the numerous river-washed ravines on the windward coast of Hawáii, and is undoubtedly the most remarkable human abode in the knowledge of man; the deepest, greenest, weirdest valley in the world. It is one of the sixty profound chasms originally rent by the primal earthquakes during the parturient throes of the embryo island. An amazing fissure, cleft into the basalt a half mile deep, extending three miles back into the coast-flank of Mauna Kéa. Walled in as it is on three sides by a stupendous *páli* (precipice) of gray lava-rock—grown gray by the fret of ages—with a perpendicular height of from two to three thousand feet above the valley, surely none but winged creatures, or some desperate adventurer, would seek to pass its barriers, either from the land above, or from the vale below.

Yet these rocky battlements are not bereft of vegetation, for, strange to say, from every chink spring hardy grasses and tender ferns, while from out the deeper clefts in the precipitous walls grow stunted shrubs, and occa-

---

* This name, often mispronounced, is to be sounded Kah-may-hah-may-hah: it is thus pronounced by the islanders themselves.

sionally stout trees, like the silvery *kúkúi* or candle-nut tree, and the gnarled pandanus or screw-pine, whose hundred aërial roots serve well to brace and support the venturesome tree. It grows where no other plant of its size could cling.

The narrow water-front of Waimánu Valley opens through gigantic crags upon the blue Pacific. Here its scant mile of pebbly beach and frequent boulders is strongly barricaded by sharp black lava rocks, threatening destruction to all comers from the sea. And as if to make the strong valley doubly secure, the most gigantic surf of the whole rock-bound coast thunders angrily against these caverned cliffs, its billows floundering like hungry demons on the black-pebbled shore.

It is indeed a strange habitation for man; it is a darkly beautiful sight, whether we look down from its highest *páli*, four thousand feet above its numerous villages of neat grass houses, showing small as beehives from the cliff, and built along the flowery banks of the smooth-flowing river or embowered among the shrubbery, or whether we peer into the deep cool valley from the hot sunshine of the wave-rocked ocean.

From the sea how cool and inviting are the dark shadows of the *páli!* Looking through the long, drooping fronds of the palms that grow thickly along the shingly beach, the reedy banks of the shallow river are seen clothed in brightest verdure. The rich meadow-lands and thrifty taro patches reach back to the cliff. The river-houses are embowered among dark-leaved bread-fruit, the red-leaved *ohia* and flowering *hau* trees; the houses back in the fields are almost hidden from view by the dense growth of bananas, guavas, and sugar-cane. And still other houses of the lordly chiefs

Waimánu from the Sea. 5

are surrounded with clusters of palms, and groves of fruit-laden orange and papaya trees, the last two being exotics brought hither a century since by Spanish voyagers from other tropic lands.

Seen thus from the sea, the profile view of the towering precipice along the valley sides seems everywhere green with tenacious grasses and hardy shrubs; while tough vines, strong as cables, hang pendent over the cliff, swaying in the wind five hundred feet from where they are rooted deep in the crevices, for a century's growth. It is but an unsatisfying glimpse one catches while thus sailing by this enticing solitude, but it is all-sufficient to arouse one's deepest curiosity in the weird, wild mysteries of by-gone ages which have been enacted here! It now becomes our province to search out the most romantic of these old histories, and impart them to the world.

With reference to the narrative, a knowledge of the extreme upper valley of Waimánu, with its marvellous surroundings, is most needful for a clear understanding of coming events.

Standing on the mountain side three miles inland, we look down upon five **stupendous cataracts,** leaping over the black *páli* into the wooded vale below,—three thousand feet of unimpeded fall. So high are these magnificent falls, that they seem rather to burst headlong from the clear blue sky, than to flow from the snows above that veil the seven eternal snow-crests of Mauna Kéa.

Waimánu is the scene of the first Spanish wreck upon these islands. Many a wreck strewed the rock-bound shores of Hawáii when adventurous men began their traffic between the gold mines of Mexico and the spice isles of the East Indies.

Here the old Spanish priest, Pàáo, was shipwrecked

on Waimánu rocks, during the stormy year of 1527,* and was the only survivor of a numerous crew. The quaint galleon had belonged to the famed navy of Spain, and was one of three stout vessels selected to bear the costly shrines, images, and cathedral decorations of gold sent from Acapulco to Manila. Two of the three treasure vessels were lost upon these yet unknown islands.

Finding himself the sole survivor—with the exception of several hogs and dogs, which, not being weighted with bullion, reached the river mouth in safety—the wise old priest set about making himself popular with the hospitable people of this unknown land. His first act of importance was to induce his followers to build a strong-walled *heidu*, the first heathen temple of its kind built on Hawáii.†

This temple, called *Mukíni*, was of great strength. It had walls twenty feet thick, and was built ostensibly for a "City of Refuge" in times of war—and when was not war raging in this turbulent land?

Assuming control of this sacerdotal castle from the first, and daily increasing his authority over the superstitious people by a display of occult arts and by foretelling astronomical events, Páào gave his own glittering shrines, altars, and sacred images to the fabulous gods of the Hawáiians.

Thus, with artful dissembling from the outset, this crafty old priest also adopted the vile *Tabu* rule of the country—then too revolting to bear description by a

---

* The Hawaiian Islands were subsequently discovered in 1555 by Juan Gaetano, of Spain. The vessel wrecked in 1527 was the "Santa Iago," one of Don Alvaro de Saavedra's fleet. See "Spanish Archives."

† The more ancient Heiáus were flat-topped pyramids, not walled enclosures.

Christian pen.* Modifying its lustful tenets, and ennobling its heathenish rites, Pàáo restrained the frightful practice of *kápu káne* or human sacrifices. And, as much as a foreigner dared, he endeavored to bring the chiefs to use greater humanity toward their inferiors, and more courteous language and affability of manner among themselves. And that Pàáo attained to a considerable degree of success in all these delicate innovations, shows that he was of no common order of man.

Marrying a royal chiefess of great rank among her people, and of rare wisdom and beauty, Pàáo, the clerical celibate in his own country, begot children as famous as himself. Among the most noted of his progeny was Opili, whose descendants have ever since presided over the *Mukíni*,† and many other *heidus* in distant parts of the island.

It was this noble line of chief-priests that eventually ennobled their class. They raised it from the standing of the vile magicians and sorcerers who ranked below

---

* The antiquity of the Tabú system is coëval with the superstitions of Polynesia. A more cogent religious despotism could not have been devised by heathen ingenuity. Unless powerful friends interfered, the slightest breach of these ecclesiastical restrictions was punished with death. Some were burned, strangled, or despatched with clubs or stones; others were sacrificed in a more dreadful manner by scooping out the eyes, breaking their limbs, or other exquisite torture, inflicted for days before the final stroke was given. Jarves' "History," p. 57; Ellis' "History," p. 367.

† While traditions agree that Pàáo landed on Hawáii before the reign of Umi, they differ as to where he was wrecked. Some native historians assert that he first landed in Púna; but while the majority agree that the wreck occurred on Kohála coast, they differ as to the exact spot. Most authorities fix it at Puuépa, rather than Waimánu. But we have assumed the author's right in matters that are indifferent, and have chosen the latter place as best answering the purpose of our story.

the petty chiefs, to the high caste of the *Alii Kapu*, or *tabú* chiefs, who were second only to the members of the royal family. Among the most famous of all this long line of *kahína maóle*—high-caste priests—none were ever more deservedly popular than Wailéle, the beautiful Priestess of Mukíni, the prophetess and spiritual adviser of wise old kings from all the islands.

II.

WAILÉLE—THE ROMANCE OF HER BIRTH.

WAILÉLE, the Priestess of this famous temple of Hawáii, was the child of her father's old age. Born an *Alii pio nui*, she was of the highest possible rank, with one exception. Only an *Alii Niaupio*—*i. e.*, one born of a married brother and sister who were themselves of the highest rank, was yet more exalted. Wailéle was reared in pious seclusion and with the utmost tenderness during her adolescent years.

The story of the Priestess' birth is a romance in itself, and so well illustrates the strange customs of the times that it is well worth relating. So exalted was the rank of this tabued chiefess, that the sun was never permitted to shine upon her. Nor was she allowed to wander in the fields, unless the sun was too low to touch her sacred head, lest its beams should blemish her exquisite complexion.

Though the real mystery of Wailéle's birth was known to but few in her day, yet the most famous bards of her time learned enough of her history to compose chants and weave charming legends about her wisdom and beauty. One of these enthusiastic poets has given her a euphonious name in one of his melodious *meles*, a name containing as many letters as the English alphabet.*

---

* Before Kalola became the wife of Keoúa, and the queen of Kalani-

Wailéle's father, Wahupu, the great High-Priest of the temple of Mukíni, was a lineal descendant of Pàáo, and the highest high-caste priest of Hawáii. His prophecies were much sought after by old and young throughout the islands. Kings, chiefs, and most noble chiefesses made frequent pilgrimages to Waimánu, seeking some divination from Wahupu's auguries, or marvellous prediction from his occult art; for he alone of all the land could predict the coming occultation of a star, or an eclipse of the sweet-faced moon.

It was an age of great gallantry at all the island courts. Blood-rank was esteemed above all other worldly possessions. The noble-born of both sexes visited from court to court, accompanied by their household bards to chant their family *Náne*, or pedigree, seeking to secure the noblest mate, thus to exalt their children a degree higher in rank. For it was an irrevocable rule of the great *Ahu Alii*—"Council of Nobles,"—that a chief, whatever station in life he might acquire by meritorious deeds, could assume no higher rank among them than that to which he was born. But the most singular feature of the Hawáiian system was the following: A child took rank from its mother, rather than its father. A chiefess was therefore privileged to pay court to whomsoever she would. It was by no means deemed indelicate for a noble lady of royal family to "prospect" for a husband in a foreign court.

The most beautiful princess of her time was Kalola, the highest *tabú* chiefess of the Maui court. She was a descendant, through her mother, of a long line of Ha-

---

opuu, she became mother of a girl (no parentage given) named *Kalanikauikikilokalaniakua*, one of the highest *tabú* chiefesses, on whom the sun was not permitted to shine.—Fornander's "Polynesian Races," vol. II., p. 212.

wáiian queens, chiefesses who ruled in their own right, or were coördinate with a king of less rank than themselves. Kalola's father was the great king Kekaulike; her mother was Queen Kekuiapoiwa Nui, a daughter of Keawe, of Hawáii. The princess was also sister to the famous Kahekili.

Her father's court was thus much frequented by gallants from the other islands, who came to seek her hand. Being of a religious turn of mind, and having scruples about marrying either of her brothers—the usual method of imparting exalted rank to the progeny,—Kalola left Maui and came to Waimánu, seeking a *wanána* or prophecy—from the venerable Wahupu of Mukíni.

Wise and beautiful, Kalola wished a good husband, that she might rear a chieftain imbued with her own noble qualities; one who could redeem his country from useless wars and the cruel persecution of the people.

Solemnly entering upon his auguries, after profound deliberation with the princess, Wahupu uttered this divination:

"The chiefs of Maui are brave and warlike, but they are far too treacherous and cruel ever to better the condition of their country. Alas! I foresee that the dynasty of Maui will end within the memory of living men. Wed not with the princes of the doomed house of your father. There are noble chiefs of Hawáii with whom Kalola may beget children. In the second generation, their progeny shall rule over all the Eight Isles; and their posterity shall rule for a century of time."

In further talk with Kalola, the priest advocated Kalaniopuu and his handsome brother Keoúa as suitors offering the best qualifications for good husbands,—as princes by whom it were possible to bear children that the gods would bless with redeeming qualities.

It is well known that in her ardor for a hero Kalola did subsequently marry each and both of these royal chiefs.

Many days passed in these pious deliberations at the great *heiáu* of Mukíni. The marvellous beauties of the historic valley of Waimánu, together with the saintlike gentleness and purity of Wahupu's holy life at the temple, completely captivated this high-born princess, until, most strange to tell, she lost her young heart to the priest, and demanded—as was her birthright—that the holy man should himself take her to wife, and beget the child of promise which she so ardently desired.

The result of this romantic marriage was a high-born girl, afterwards a *tabú* chiefess, named Kekuiapoiwa after Kalola's queen mother, Kekuiapoiwa. The Christian name, Wailéle (water-fall), was subsequently added to the family name because of the proximity to the vast cataracts, which Kalola loved so well.

So great were Kalola's regrets that her pious marriage had not been blessed with a chief, that with the tenderest affection, Wahupu admonished his loved young wife to leave the temple and seek in the gay court of the brilliant Alapai Nui a husband more fitted to be her mate. There Keoúa and Kalaniopuu had been established from their youth. Alapai married their mother, and usurped their kingdom; and having killed Keoúa's father in battle, a weakling king, not hardy and warlike enough for the rough-handed times in which he lived, the monarch now sought to cherish the royal boys.*

Putting Wailéle in the care of a *káhu*—guardian—who had been her own nurse, and receiving the farewell

---

* Or, perhaps, to spy upon their political ability, for Keoúa was subsequently poisoned at Alapai's court. Fornander's "Polynesian Races," p. 142.

blessings of her noble priest-husband, Kalola departed for the Hawáiian court, at Waipio, ten miles away. There she wedded the noble prince Keoúa. But again the beautiful princess was doomed to disappointment; she bore a chiefess, and named her Liliha. Again assuming the right of her high rank, she left Keoúa and married Kalaniopuu, who, at the death of Alapai soon after, became king of Hawáii.

Years passed before Kalola bore another child, the frivolous and petulant Kiwalao, who was far removed from a hero and a conqueror. But the methods of the gods often accomplish their ends in indirect ways. Kalola lived to see her two daughters bear progeny who in turn became the future king and queen of the united kingdoms.*

Liliha became the mother of Keopuolani, the future state queen of Kaméhaméha, and the mother of two kings. Wailéle bore the long-looked-for hero, whose praises bards had sung in many an epic chant before he was born. The prophecy of many a venerated priest had foretold his coming.

Thus in an indirect way, the famous *wandna* or prophecy of Wahupu proved a faithful prediction, when he declared to Kalola: "A conquering hero shall be born to you, *in the second generation*, who shall rule over the "Eight Isles" and better the condition of the people.

---

* Queen Kalola fled to Molokai after the battle of Iao, in which Kaméhaméha destroyed the Maui army and took possession of the kingdom. There Kaméhaméha sought an interview with the queen, and begged that she and her daughter, Liliha, and her granddaughter, Keopuolani, would go back to Hawáii. Kalola consented, but was taken sick and died before she could leave Molokai. Her family and followers returned with Kaméhaméha to Hawáii, where Keopuolani became the state queen, and bore the two kings that succeeded Kaméhaméha.—" Polynesian Races."

III.

THE MYSTERY OF A HUNDRED YEARS.

THE rosy dawn of a tropic day was fast nearing the mountain isle of Hawáii. The summer moon, now nearly at her full, had gone down over Mauna Kéa's lofty snow-crest, fringing the snow peaks of the gigantic mountain with a halo of violet, crimson, and palest gold.

A reflection of this weird lunar light shone upward into the purple sky above the mountain, showing verily like some half-disclosed vision of glory in the realm beyond the stars.

Just at the opportune moment before the waning moonlight was quenched in the east, the tall figure of a gigantic chief suddenly appeared on the southern brink of the precipice which walls in the upper valley of Waimánu. This *páli* was made dreadful by its stupendous height—nearly a half mile of perpendicular cliff,—but yet more so by its cruel *tabú* law of *Death to all comers* below the rank of *tabú* chief. This ban was promulgated two hundred years before the date of our story, by the arrogant high-caste priests of the temple of Mukíni, in the vale below.

The well-defined outline of this adventurous person was only seen for a moment in the moon-setting ere he was again hidden from view by that mysterious hour of darkness which ever preludes a tropic dawn. Yet, alas, even such a moment of disclosure had cost many a common

The Tabued Páli.

man and petty chief his life, for thus spying down upon this most ancient of all the tabued *heiáus* of Pele. The upper valley was hedged in by a dreadful *kapu e make* (death tabu). But the penalty for spying down upon it was not simply death; it was death accompanied by tortures too fiendish to relate.

Some historians have claimed that even a *tabú* chief, being exempt from the ban of the *tabú*, would not have risked prowling about the verge of a frightful precipice in the darkest of all darkness, an hour before dawn; and it is well known that few common Kanakas have sufficient courage to risk the *kapu e make*, when prompted by mere curiosity. Moreover, this superstitious class not only knew of the *páli's* being guarded by the *pepehi káne* —men-killers—of the priests; they also believed that there was a yet more dreadful enemy to contend with in the lynx-eyed Invisibles in the service of the gods. These were malicious creatures who delight in cruelty to man. There was also, so they believed, a black demon, made up of darkness and lava fire, having eyes lurid with consuming flame; a demon so noiseless in movement, that he would steal upon the spy and hurl him headlong over the cliff before he could glance into the sacred vale.

The natives also knew that if they should escape the boding watch-fiends of the *páli* they were sure to be detected by the dreadful *kilo*, or sorcerers, who are never content but when praying people to death. They discovered the guilty ones by the trick of *wai-halulu*, the "shaking waters," or by roasting some beast-offering over fires of poisonous wood.

The stranger on the *páli* came from the direction of Waipio, ten miles away. There Kalaniopuu held his barbaric court, and gathered about him his most notable chiefs, after the cunning custom of other kings, lest some of the most turbulent of the haughty nobles should find time to plot against his peaceful rule.

Who was this chieftain that had taken a two-hours' walk from Waipio in the moonlight, and had timed his arrival upon the brink of a dangerous precipice just before dawn? This has been a grave matter of dispute among native historians for a century past.

That he was among the noblest of chiefs and most gallant of men, all have agreed. For he alone successfully descended the tabued precipice of Mukíni, and succeeded in winning the vestal love of the beautiful Priestess, so famed throughout the land.

Numerous other chiefs had visited the noted *heiau*, ostensibly to procure oracles in matters of state. Their visits had ended in prayers of love to the maiden Priestess; but without once touching her obdurate heart. Among the host of the wooers, three at least of the gallants were kings, one of whom, it is now universally believed, was the successful wooer of this most charming celibate of Mukíni.

The new-comer was evidently a stranger to the perilous path that he secretly traversed. He groped watchfully and warily along the dizzy brink, lest he should be discovered from below. But his manner of grasping his huge war-spear, and occasionally clutching the hilt of his long dagger, as he glanced sharply about him at the rustling of the wind, or a falling stone, was that of a man who feared neither visible nor invisible foes, if only he were warned of their coming.

Planting the polished staff of his curiously carved war-spear against the crumbling lava-rock before him, he felt his way cautiously through the stunted fern bush and scanty growth of hardy grasses that found precarious life on the barren verge of the cliff.

The point sought by the wary chief was evidently a huge pandanus or screw-pine, which marks the lowest part of the precipice along the whole three miles of southern *páli*. A remarkable tree was this great pandanus, for it had already grown a long century of perilous years, thus leaning out over the frightful gulf. Among the few daring spirits in the past ages who had descended to the valley, here two thousand feet deep, many had found their well-earned graves, now marked by a darker green and a thriftier growth of flowers.

As it was yet too dark for a stranger to grope about in search of a particular object, the majestic chief came to a stand beneath a small *kúkúi*, or candle-nut tree, and leaning thoughtfully on his stout spear, looked down with eager eyes and swelling bosom upon the wondrous vision of beauty in the vague half-light below.

Sombre and silent the stalking shadows crouched over the whole sweep of this priest-ridden valley. Its funereal stillness was everywhere peopled with the dark-boding spirits of disembodied souls. They had been sacrificed by the murderous priests of Pele, the supreme but vengeful goddess of the isles.*

The Hawáiians believe there are dual souls; and there is a universal belief that after death one soul flies to its abode in *Akea*, the land of the blessed, where spirits feed on lizards and butterflies; or, if it is a bad soul, its abode is in *Po*, the place of night, where they are forever cooked and eaten by the gods; while the ghost of the second soul always lingers on earth, gently ministering to

---

* The Hawáiians cherish the idea of the *Au Makua*—ghost-spirits of dead ancestors—ever being present.

the loved ones. But more especially does this ghost delight to haunt dark places and sepulchres, stealing abroad at night to strangle the enemies of the dead during sleep, and to inflict all manner of harm on those who speak evil of the dead.*

Well might the superstitious chief shudder with awe, as he peered down into the ghoul-haunted valley at this unseasonable hour. It was strange to think of thousands of innocent human beings slumbering in the unearthly stillness below, all unmindful of the spirit-peopled gloom about them; sleeping as peacefully as the countless dead slept who were sepulchred in the black caverns high upon the *páli* walls, sealed up in rocky tombs hidden behind the curves of the plunging cataracts. The ceaseless rumble of the falls serves well to drown the wails of these unwilling dead, these murdered victims of the altar, secreted there by priestly hands in unhallowed graves.

Directly beneath the stranger lay the Mukíni, half veiled in the gloom, the far-famed temple built in past centuries by the Spanish priest, Pàáo.

The *tabú* grounds belonging to Mukíni were about a mile square, highly cultivated with gardens and taro patches, and adorned with the rarest of flowering shrubs, and the largest and most thrifty fruit-trees known in all the land. These consecrated grounds are shut in from

---

* Dibble relates a case in point. "The following may serve as an instance of this belief. One dark night I heard a horrid shriek in the street. A strong, athletic man was running with all speed, both hands clutching at his throat, endeavoring to tear some imaginary ghost away. He reached our house, burst through the door, and fell on the floor terrified to faintness and insensibility. He said the ghost of a dead chief had a grip on his throat, and was trying to strangle him."—"Sandwich Islands," p. 99.

intrusion of the outer world by a half-mile belt of impenetrable forest, which reached from cliff to cliff across the whole width of the valley.

The only accessible entrance through this dense everglade of forest-trees and tangled vines is by wading up the shallow waters of the gently running river. But even this inviting water-gate is guarded by a dread line of tabued flags planted on the river banks at the forest edge, and out in mid-stream, a warning of "Death to All."* So that below the rank of *Alii Kapu*—tabu chief —none of all the ten thousand people of Waimánu dared ascend the sacred water-path.

There are times, however, when this extreme restriction is modified so as to permit chiefs of a lower rank, with their families, to attend during feast-days, and on the *Makahiki*—the New-Year's festival at the *heiáu*.

The one sublime object which most attracts the stranger on the *páli*, as he gazes into the deep, dark vale, is the fivefold cataract plunging like a milky-way from the starlit sky. The glassy curves of the water-falls reflect the starlight so brightly that they illuminate the ghostly gloom. Like the white hand of an avenging God, its five shining fingers clutch downward through the darkness toward the ghost-spirits of the inhuman priests, who are said still to haunt the unhallowed scenes of their long-past crimes.

At length day dawned upon the cheerful upper world, revealing the statuesque figure of the chief. Spear in hand, he stood on the sun-gilded verge of the precipice; a large grand-looking man of fifty well-kept years, of noble mien and most commanding presence. His long

---

* The priests used small white flags to tabu property and places.— Jarves' "History," p. 56.

black hair waved gently in the cool damp breeze that welled upward from the depths of the *páli*. His only insignia of rank were a *lei* and *niho palaoa*, worn about his neck. These ornaments, wrought from one large and two small whale teeth, were of great value in those days; they were enough to turn the tide of battle, in a coming year when king met king at Keei, contending for a kingdom. He was armed with a stout spear and a long *Koa*-wood dagger, edged with sharks' teeth. A gay-colored garment of *tapa* was flung carelessly across his left shoulder, and knotted loosely beneath the right arm, deftly arranged so as to conceal his insignia. His only other article of apparel was that worn by all men, the *malo*, a strip of bark cloth girded about the loins, and passed between the thighs. This served also for a belt for a dagger nearly two feet long.

Nothing was visible in the simple garb of the stranger to denote whether he were priest, chief, or king; yet in his haughty bearing there was evidence enough of rank. But a humble man dared not, on peril of his life, wear even the *kihei*, or *tapa* cape, which clothed him.

Though he lacked the golden-yellow *mamo*, or feather cloak,[*] the state robe of the Hawáiian kings, or even the red *mamo* of high-priest or lordly chief, yet in the half-nude Hawáiian before us, we behold a man of mark in the state, a mighty warrior in the hour of battle. He was a man who carries his nobility in his right arm and in his

---

[*] Some of the gorgeous war cloaks of kings, sun-gold in color, required nine generations to fabricate. But two tiny feathers are found beneath each wing of the *O-o*, and the *Iiwi*. The birds are caught by smearing their perches with a gum from the bread-fruit tree, and are given their liberty after the feathers are plucked. The stems of the rare feathers are woven into the fine network of a previously formed cape.

The Huge Pandanus.

handsome face, and who does not need even his much prized *lei* and *palaoa* as proof of his exalted rank.

Skirting cautiously along the edge of the precipice in search of the pandanus which marks the only possible place of descent into the valley, the chief's countenance expressed satisfaction when at length he stood confronting the gigantic tree. Evidently something in its perilous position aroused his admiration, and perhaps served to awaken his contempt for the danger of the descent, so much vaunted in the traditions of Waimánu.

No other tree could have sustained itself so long in such a place. Springing from a sapling, its adventurous taproots had burrowed deep down into the rich soil of a crack in the lava-rock. Then a storm had bent the tree out over the cliff, where it had grown for a century; yearly sending new aërial roots down the precipice, where they spread out fan-like, and laid hold with countless fingers upon every shelf and crevice for thirty feet below. And now the veteran tree reposed upon its hundred strong supports, and watched over the passing generations of men below. The chief strode fearlessly out upon the level roots of the pandanus and seated himself against the gnarled trunk, where, unobserved, he could watch the dawn-light slowly sinking into the valley, and quietly bide his time.

As yet, sombre shadows remained untouched in the mystic vale. Not a gleam of sunshine had enlivened the steel-gray surface of the fog-covered river, as it winds sleepily along among the green lawns; running lazily to meet the surly breakers of the in-rolling sea, where it foams and flounders on the valley shore.

The half-awaking valley is full of exquisite vistas. Blue mists rise languidly above the silent forest, as if about to take wing in search of the far-off day. Stealing up from the soft-flowing river, among the overarching trees, the mists cringe and crouch like timid ghosts among the tree-tops. The weight of night-gathered spray from the cataracts has made them too heavy to rise from their haunts without the warmth of the coming sun.

Not a sluggish mortal has yet stirred in the valley. A small hairless dog creeps out from among his human bedfellows in one of the riverside houses. Stretching his cramped legs, and wondering at his own temerity in rising so early, the dog runs to the river to drink. While lapping, he often stops to peer into the white fog midway out in the stream; he laps and looks, and sniffs at the ghostly creatures he smells in the mist. Then he runs home barking furiously at imaginary dangers; though he is quite unconscious of a real danger that is imminent—that of being roasted and eaten.

His bark awakened the bark of a thousand dogs, though half of the dog-voices which welled up from the valley were but the echoes and re-echoes, resounding from cliff to cliff. Thus awakened, a few of the lazy denizens of the valley began to grope about in the shadowy gloom. Some ran to the river for a morning plunge, too scantily apparelled to have aught to disrobe. Some might now be seen swimming back and forth across the half-awakened river. They were neighborly women, alert for a sweet morsel of Waimánu gossip to enliven the new-born day. All clapped their hands and mumbled their morning prayers like good heathen, as they ran. Dogs, also, were crossing the water to greet some favored cur. Even grunting pigs were seen running in long procession to the stream; scenting perhaps a breakfast afar off through the mist, where other creatures, human and canine, had disappeared. They, too, plunged in, seeking the happy porker whose thrifty mistress had gathered store of over-ripe guavas for her own petted swine.

Up the stream above the village, where the river widens out into quiet pools, dozens of young girls were wading waist-deep in the lucid water, trying warily to entrap the tiny shrimp, in scoops made of broad green leaves. Merry was the girlish prattle, and gay the happy laughter, welling up like bird-songs to the listening chief on the *páli*, as he lay watching the pretty group of nude foragers, making frolic of finding sweet morsels for their morning meal. A dull rhythmic thud echoed from *páli* to *páli*, like the muffled beat of a funeral drum. If you had sought its cause you would have discovered a number of bustling old male housewives making *poi* from cold baked *kalo* roots, and zealously pounding the moist blue mass with huge stone pestles, on the ancient hollow stone ever standing for that purpose at the homestead door.

IV.

THE PERILOUS DESCENT INTO WAIMÁNU.

THE sun was already an hour high, but only its reflected light, gleaming from the higher cliff of the opposite *páli*, had yet illuminated the dark crags beneath the watchful chief.

What was the motive of his coming to such a place at such an unseemly hour? It was evident that the fearless if not foolhardy man contemplated a descent into the valley, and was now only waiting for sufficient light to accomplish his purpose. But the motive for risking such a peril could not even be guessed at.

Peering eagerly down over the *páli's* edge the chief scanned the foothold of each tree and shrub and long pendent vine, searching down the sheer side of the ragged crag as far as the yet deep shadows would permit. But if he sought to make the perilous descent, and wished to accomplish it unseen, he had no time to lose, and this he seemed to realize.

Again and again the impatient man scanned the frightful task before him, weighing the chances along every foot of the awful abyss down to the green meadows in the far-away valley.

Would his courage sustain him in the daring undertaking that he contemplated? Well he knew that when once midway down, though yet a thousand feet from the valley, there could be no return. He must complete the descent in his downward path, or perish while perched like a wounded bird in mid-air.

In the heart of man there are but two emotions sufficiently frenzied to prompt to such a peril as this. Was it love or hate that could thus impel a man in the wise maturity of his life? Either the one or the other might well be the motive; for at fifty love can become the most loving, and hate more bitter than at any other period in life.

Without a moment's hesitation the resolute chief stood up and flung both his spear and his dagger far out into the valley, and folding his bare and brawny arms, watched a long and breathless moment to see them fall. Neither of the weapons was broken in the descent. Both of them plunged point foremost into the moist green turf below.

It was deemed a good omen, for a brave smile lit up the manly face of the heroic chief, radiant as the rosy sun-tints just glinting upon the upper arc of the waterfall. Henceforth we may know him for a lover. Forgetful of all danger, he is seeking a noble and beautiful woman that he loves. None other could inspire a brave man with such love as his.

Grasping one of the long pendulous roots of the pandanus, which reached thirty feet down the face of the precipice, the agile chief swung himself sheer out over the cliff, and slid down hand over hand to the lowest roots of the friendly tree. Clinging there a brief instant, before he parted with this last strong fibre that linked him to the upper world, as if testing his courage, or weighing the frightful peril against the sweet emotion that prompted him, he gazed coolly down the two thousand feet of cliff below, and unclasping his hands from the root, dropped down ten feet into a strong shrub that was well rooted into the face of the crag. Landing with a crash among the tough branches, he sat calmly a moment to catch his breath, perching there like a bird on its bough.

He now came to that which had most encouraged him to undertake the task,—three hundred feet of tough vines, reaching downward, strong as a network of cables, in the direction he wished to go. Assuring himself with the utmost precision that the roots were well grounded in the rock, the chief sprang out from his perch and caught the vine, clambering downward to its lowest limits.

But here he found himself hanging in mid-air, swaying in the treacherous wind just out of reach of another and much longer vine, which a puff of wind had blown ten feet away. His own weight prevented him from swinging in the same direction, though previous to his descent the two vines had swayed in the wind together.

He could now only cling to his own support and wait with impatience for the vine that had betrayed him to blow back within his grasp. Half an hour passed, and minutes became hours from that moment. His brave hands grew tired; his sweet hopes grew pallid with fear as he looked down with dizzy eyes upon the certain doom below. Ten minutes more he hung dangling in the wind. Then his hands grew numb, and his fingers began to relax their iron grasp. Blood rushed to the brain as if it would burst its bounds; a dark mist came over his eyes, until all grew black as midnight. Calling upon Pele, and preparing himself to die, the blinded chief made ready to fall, as he had flung his spear and dagger and watched them plunge down to the far-away valley below.

One hand now lost its grasp and fell exhausted at his side. As he hung by the other hand and stretched his left arm out endeavoring to recover his strength, the wind from a new direction blew in his face, and the treacherous vine swung back within his blind grasp, and he was saved!

He secured himself firmly among the strong lateral branches of the new vine, where his hands could be left at liberty, and sat securely holding by his legs. With rest a reaction soon took place, and sight and hope and new life came back to the daring chief once more.

When fully recovered he slipped easily down five hundred feet on the ponderous vine, and yet another hundred feet on roots and trees and shrubs, until he came to a broad shelf in the cliff which offered complete repose. He now found himself but a thousand feet from the coveted valley, with shrubs and vines becoming more numerous as he descended.

When fully rested he again tried the downward path. Dropping from tree to tree, and clambering down from one strong vine to another, a brief half hour more of daring leaps and dangerous descents found the courageous chief standing tired, but unharmed, amidst refreshing fruits and grateful flowers in the thrifty valley of Waimánu.

Plucking spear and dagger from out the moist earth, he skirted along the friendly woods until he reached the river, where it ran embowered through the forest into the tabued valley of Mukíni. Here he bathed himself in the cool waters, gathered fruit for refreshment, and rested on the flowering bank.

Thus far he had purposely avoided meeting the people of the valley, whose homes were nestled about everywhere among shrubbery and fruitful trees. A thousand houses, large and small, in clusters few and many, lay between the tabued forest and the rock-bound shore two miles away.

Now his path lies either through the dense and difficult jungle of the woods or up the river. The old warrior concluded to take to the easier pathway in the stream, and defy all comers.

Just where the dark foliage of the primeval forest met the green fields of grass, sugar-cane, and taro patches, a huge flat rock stood in the middle of the river. It had attracted the chief's attention as he lay hidden by the stream. Hither came canoes from the lower valley, to deposit their daily tributes of food, mats, or *tapa*, designed for the priesthood of Mukíni. At least twenty canoes had come quietly up the river to make their sacred offerings to the gods, some of them leaving baked pigs, dogs, and fowls; others bringing *poi* and fruit, and baskets of fresh-caught shrimps, which they hung in the water securely attached to the rock.

All of these people bringing tribute were below the rank of even petty chiefs, being of the class called *Kanáka wále*, or freemen, whether farmers, fishermen, or private citizens; in distinction from the servant class, the *Kaúwa*, or even the *Kaúwa maóli*, the actual slaves. Thus the working class in Hawáii, as elsewhere, had to provide both for chiefs and priests, as well as for their own families. They held their land in fief to one harsh extortioner or another. None dared omit, on peril of his life, to bring his begrudging gifts. Their fear of the *tabú* priests, and of the whole sacerdotal class, was seen in the dreadful aversion with which the Kanákas approached the Tribute Rock, the upper part of which lies over the dreadful *tabú* line of small white *tapa* flags.

With wild eyes and apprehensive looks, each native brought his allotted tribute, and departed silently, with many a furtive glance up the embowered river toward the much-dreaded *heidu*. There his plebeian fathers and grandsires had for ages been sacrificed on the altar of Pele. Yet the common Hawáiian believed to a much greater extent than the chief class that the *kahúna* or priest was the necessary intermediate between the gods and the people, and had power of daily communing with the deities for the spiritual welfare of the nation.

Where the flowering vines lock arms from top to top of the giant trees, across the river, there also flaunt the *tabú* flags, a warning of death to all who are not of sufficient rank to entitle them to pass. This restriction applies to all below *tabú* chiefs, priests, and reigning kings.

Whether in cool derision of this dreadful ban against all comers, or perhaps with wise intent to finally disclose his own rank—thus far carefully concealed—in case he should be refused admittance to the *heidu*, the proud chief plucked up one of the *tabú* flags from mid-river and attached it to his spear, as he waded through the wood beneath the green arcade above the river.

When the chief had fairly entered the forest, the outer world was shut out by the winding river through which he passed. At times even the blue sky was obscured by the interlacing boughs of the large-leaved *ohia* trees, their crimson apples and vermilion blossoms spangling the green foliage like the red-fish in the water and the red-birds in the trees.

Yellow gleams from the noonday sun darted down through the emerald leafage, serving to enliven the cool dreamy seclusion about the chief; falling like flashing spears or winged arrows of gold among the everglade, where the song of the rustling leaves and the soft music of the flowing river were the only sounds.

The whole upper valley soon becomes a dense jungle of forest- and fruit-trees, together with a network of clambering vines. The vines run to the tops of the tallest trees, where, aided by some friendly wind, they toss their exultant tendrils across the stream, festooning the peaceful river until their flowers trail in the murmuring tide. But most beautiful of all these forest climbers is one which leaps heavenward over parasite and tree-top, the proud mauve-colored morning-glory which lifts her tendril hands skyward like an appealing spirit.

An hour of wading brought the chief into the clearing at the head of the valley, where a yet more bewitching scene burst upon his gaze. The weird stillness and cathedral gloom of the forest now gave place to the hoarse melody of the colossal waterfalls, whose five torrents leaped down in sunlit curves as from out the summer sky. No wonder the barbaric chief stayed his footsteps in the river, and stood pensively leaning on his spear, half bewildered with the varied beauty of the scene.

Before him rose the vine-covered walls of the most famous *heidu* upon the islands, the heathen temple presided over by Wailéle, the virgin Priestess, of highest rank and of supremest beauty.

The high walls of lava rock built round about the ancient temple enclosed, perhaps, an acre of land. Huge stone pyramids, built upon raised stone terraces, towered above the enclosure, together with a graceful bamboo temple containing the altar of sacrifice and the shrine of prayer.

About the walled *heidu* were clustered various outhouses: on the one side were houses for storage of *tapa* and provisions, and numerous neat grass-house dwellings for the minor priestesses connected with the temple; while on the side remote from the forest were the cook-houses and buildings where *tapa* cloth was made, and luxurious mats for bedding and carpeting constructed.

Still other grass houses, of a less tasteful character, were scattered from the back wall of the *heidu* to the cliff. They were built for the **Kaúwa maóli** (slaves), a class selected by the former priests from among prisoners of war, and considered as surplus food for their human sacrifices. But once enslaved, these *Kaúwa* remained in bondage, they and their progeny, forever. It was death for one of them to enter a chief's house. They dare not even approach a chief, or his house, except upon all-fours. Held in such contempt were these poor bondsmen, that a *Kandka wále*—a freeman—strikes the bottom of his foot with scorn to express the degradation of a slave. And yet they have shown their love for a kind master by taking the front of the most savage battles; as in the case of the two Leapuni, slaves who fought with such superhuman courage for their king Keliiokaloa, that they came near killing the opposing king in battle.

In front of the gray old walls of the ancient *heidu* rose a large bamboo dwelling, airy and neat, thatched with *lauhála* leaves, and having a broad, cool veranda about three sides of it. This, with its well-kept grounds, was a more sumptuous abode than the palace at Waipio.

Here dwelt Wailéle who had consecrated her vestal life to the worship of Pele. Here she endeavored to interpret the hidden mysteries of that dim and ghostly interval lying between the visible and the invisible world,

—the spirit-land of the gods, which borders so near upon mortal domain.

The palace garden around three sides of the dwelling, together with the green lawn, reaching down to the river, was enclosed by a thrifty hedge of *kí* plant, having an opening on the river bank, and another at the back of the palace, leading through the high wall into the *heidu*.

The veranda of this charming abode was half buried in pendent vines trailing coyly down from its thatched roof, and all aglow with tropical blossoms. The numerous supports of the veranda were thickly festooned with climbing trumpet plants, their yellow, waxy flowers prettily contrasted with the purple morning-glories, the crimson hibiscus, and the varied colors of the mountain hollyhock.

Clusters of graceful papaya trees, thirty feet high, with large indented leaves and long symmetrical foot-stalks, grow plentifully about the grounds, every tree laden with rich, melon-shaped fruit. Masses of bread-fruit trees, with their dark, quaint-shaped foliage, skirted the river bank, loaded with fruit ready for the housewife's hand. Here grew *ohia* trees to enormous size, refreshed by the spray that was ever drifting from the cataracts; these were loaded with rose-colored apples, made yet more brilliant by the crimson tinge of their young leaves.

But most graceful of all the growths, in field or forest, were the long feathery foliage of the *algaroba* trees, and the clusters of magnificent bamboo that shot up eighty feet in the air. Pretty fan-palms and the silvery-sheened *kúkúi*, or candle-nut trees, were numerous, their foliage adding grace to their more stately fellows.

As yet, no vestige of human life had become visible to the pondering chief, as he stood by the bank of the river, gazing on the bewitching landscape before him. Not even a voice reached his listening ear, only the twitter of gay-colored birds, with plumage brighter than the odorous flowers.

It soon became evident to the watchful chief that even the birds knew him to be a stranger, as they entered their noisy protest against his intrusion into their precinct. Constituting themselves the outpost guard of the sequestered place—the sanctuary of priesthood,—they flocked about him in countless numbers with their warning cries. But as he remained motionless for a time, and as no notice was taken of their alarm at the palace, the indignant creatures grew more quiet, yet they continued to follow the intruder until he disappeared from view.

Charmed by the floral beauty about the dwelling of the Priestess, and awed by the suggestive mysteries of the gray old *heidu* walls, the chief now grasped his spear and waded across the river to the entrance in the hedge. Though resolute to enter the temple and discover its occupants, yet there was less arrogance in his bearing, and less pride in his majestic walk as he entered the mystic solitude, for the proud man had here met two things that often serve to divest the human heart of its vanity and bring it into closer kinship with nature.

V.

PRIEST-GIRLS ANOINTING THE DOGS.

LEAVING the river, the chief entered the aborescent enclosure of *kí* hedge surrounding the Kahúna's palace and garden grounds. Crossing the green lawn over the path of large smooth pebbles brought from the river mouth, he passed on unchallenged through a floral archway leading to the veranda, where he heard the singing of lullabies by a number of rich voices.

What a strange sight was that which met the gaze of the intruder man, as he stood, spear in hand, peering through the vines, unseen by the fair occupants of the veranda. Seven dark-haired priest-girls were discovered, sitting upon the soft mats and singing liquid melodies, while several half-grown hairless dogs were being nursed by fat slave women. They were *Ilio poli* (breast-nursed dogs*), consecrated to Pele, and about being anointed for sacrifice upon her altar; in lawful substitute, upon minor occasions, for human victims.

Six of these charming *wahines* were from fourteen to

---

* The Hawáiians were great epicures in dog meat. The kinds raised for feasts were small and easily fattened. Dogs suckled at the breast were called *Ilio poli*, their flesh being tender and deliciously flavored (Jules Remy's "Venerable Savage," p. 53). Children were not much valued, and were so frequently given away that they seldom knew their real parents; dogs were better fed, and were often nursed at the mother's breast in preference to her own offspring (Jarves, p. 94).

The Beautiful Priestess. 35

sixteen years old. All were plump and pretty chiefesses from the best families of Waimánu; girls piously devoted to the sacred duty of fattening puppies for the altar of their loved goddess.

The seventh was Wailéle, High-Priestess of Mukíni, a person of remarkable presence. A large, tall, graceful woman of twenty, in a tropical climate where girls mature at twelve. Dark lustrous eyes that could languish with love or wither with scorn. She was grand and beautiful as the full-orbed night when adorned with a hemisphere of stars.

Abundant masses of long raven hair were sweeping about her bare shoulders and full attractive form, like a midnight pall draped on a statue of bronze. The soft tones of her voice were subdued to their lowest pitch, harmonizing well with the bewildering charm of her fresh, fair face. Bending tenderly over the nursling in her lap, Wailéle crooned her lullaby over the sacred dog, with the pious fervor of one who loves her task.

But as blackest darkness is to living light, or storm is to calm, was the swift, vehement change that swept over her mobile face, when she discovered an armed warrior standing unannounced, with spear in hand, upon the veranda, and flaunting her own *tabú* flag defiantly before her.

Her dark eyes flashed with the aroused lightnings of the approaching storm as she confronted the intruder who had thus forced her hospitality and defied her tabued domain.

The six timid priest-girls sprang up from their couches each with a cry of alarm, as they dropped their yelping nurslings and gathered quickly about their mistress abashed and afraid. But not a feature of the haughty

Priestess' face showed a trace of alarm from this unseemly intrusion of a strange armed man.

But when she spoke in answer to the courteous greeting of the lordly stranger her voice grew strong and arrogant as she found he seemed unconscious of his iniquity. Still she sought by an effort of will to subdue her anger at this outrage upon her priestly seclusion.

"Aloha, Kahúna wahine!" exclaimed the smiling chief, amused at the chorus of alarm he caused among the pretty maidens, and the uproar among the nursling puppies.

"Aloha, Alii! but you anger me greatly by this rudeness. What brings you here?" responded the imperious Priestess, as she quietly draped her long trailing hair about the sacred nursling and over her shapely breast, patting the whining puppy gently to subdue his alarm.

"Business with the Priestess of Mukíni has brought me here," he replied, unabashed.

"Know you not that it is the *Kapu Mahealani* (full-moon tabu); a time consecrated above all others to the divine Pele? And yet you come in defiance of my *kapu e make*—death tabu—when but a word from me would slaughter *you* for the altar, instead of the *Ilio poli* which I have prepared, and leave you forgotten among the ranks of men."

The chief only drew himself up the more proudly as the indignant Kahúna grew more arrogant in manner and more threatening in tone. Yet he realized something of his danger, and the immediate necessity of making known his rank; as even now the secret man-slayers, belonging to all *heiáus*, might be gathering stealthily about him with their deadly lariats or poisoned spears.

And though the noble-looking stranger still replied to the Priestess with calm eye and a commanding tone, as he answered her threat of vengeance, yet as he spoke he took double measure for assuring his safety. He unloosed his *tapa* mantle from about his neck and freed his spear.

To the six trembling priest-girls this movement seemed an act of menace, intended to free his spear-arm for action. It was all the more emphasized when the chief tore off the *tabú* flag from his spear, and flung it contemptuously behind him. But to Wailéle, the sudden act of the Chief had another import. He thus displayed his royal *lei* of yellow feathers and its appendant *palaoa*.

"You say rightly, noble Kahúna, it is the *Kapu Mahealani*. But We are of the rank that make the *kapu e make*, and fear not that which we can promulgate for others at our pleasure."

As the secret sign made by the chief comported with the rare insignia which he wore, a new light came quickly into the face of the Priestess, as she replied with less arrogance in her tone.

"Sire! what do you here? Is not the Kahúna of Mukíni entitled to the poor homage of an official herald, ere she receives an *Alii Moi*—a sovereign chief?"

Then, without moving from her seat of state near the entrance to the *heiáu*, Wailéle held out her soft hand to the king, and graciously rubbed noses with the noble old monarch.*

Still wishing to remain incognito, the chief replied: "How know you that I am a king? I climbed down your terrible *páli* to make a secret visit to Mukíni, and the

---

* An embrace of noses was then their most affectionate mode of salutation.

first person I meet divulges my secret, and threatens to sacrifice me among her puppies." And the old chief was inclined to make merry of her fears and her anger.

"Sire, Pele long since admonished me that you were coming to Mukíni, and that you wished to consult the oracles about an heir to your throne."

"All that is no proof I am the king you looked for."

"*Alii Moi*, the very birds knew you as you waded up the river with a hope to surprise us. Did they not shriek your name from every bough of the algaroba trees? And do not your *lei* and your *niho palaoa* (ivory tooth) proclaim you a king?"

The Priestess well knew there were but few men in Hawáii who would dare for their lives to thus venture into the ancient sanctuary unannounced. One of these was Pepehi, her murderous half-brother, the *Kahúna maóle* of the mountain *heidu*, Puukeekee. And among the very few others who might intrude with impunity was this noble king who stood before her with a smile on his face.

"*Kahúna wahine*, if I am the king you take me to be, give me, in the *Ka ke* words, the password of the insignia I wear."*

"*Kulia i ka Nuu!*" and she accompanied the ancient password of the kings with the appropriate sign. To this the king replied, but with no further attempt to dissemble his rank; only demanding that his name should never be divulged to mortal ears.

"*Auwe!* and have I intruded upon your sacred duties, noble Kahúna?"

"Sire, you have; and my duty to Pele must be con-

---

* *Ka ke* is the secret dialect of the *Ahu Alii*, the "Council of Nobles," formed by Pááo.

sidered before that due to a king. My task must be completed before I can even offer the hospitalities of my *heidu* to your majesty. It becomes my sacred duty to make this choice offering to Pele against the coming full moon."

"But will the *tabú* moon prevent your attending to my mission?"

"No, sire, for the sacrifice will not take place until midnight, when the moon sits in the sky to watch our pious labor from above the mountain snows."

"And shall a king disclose his state secrets before these babbling tongues and gaping ears?"

"Not so, *Alii Moi* (sovereign chief). Neither would it be just to the adorable Pele for her priestess, while thus engaged in communion with the goddess, to utter prophetic words to mortal ears."

"And what is your wish?"

"Retire into the *heidu*, and seek the needed repose till I come."

"Priestess, the sun has climbed high enough to look down upon the western snow on the mountain, and I would seek the homeward path by the river before Mauna Kéa's shadows creep down over Waimánu Valley."

And the grave old monarch spoke almost severely, while a touch of kingly arrogance crept into his voice, and kindled upon his brow; to think that a sovereign was thus required to submit to the Priestess, though it were to the noblest *kahúna wahine* among the isles. But the Priestess was his match in matters of etiquette and church prerogative, being herself an hereditary *Mookahúna* (history-making priest), and versed in all the lore of church and state.

In answer Wailéle only bowed her queenly head in resolute silence, and waved her imperious hand for the king to pass into the temple as she had bid him. This to a powerful and passionate chief whose slightest word, or averted face,* when among his followers, brought death to whomsoever he wished! It bespoke a heart of courage in Wailéle more remarkable than the transcendant beauty of her face.

The despotic king obeyed without a word, recognizing the absolute power of the high-caste priests while in their own *heidus* or during religious ceremonies. He remembered the historical example where Hakau, the wicked king at Waipio, was slain by the priest Kaleihokuu, who placed his foster-son upon the vacant throne. He remembered, too, the display of priestly power where the priest of Kau killed the king by hurling a huge tree upon him from the high *páli* of Hilea.

Passing through the dwelling into the rear, and entering the massive wall of the grim old *heidu*, the scene of so many historical events and human sacrifices, the king mounted the middle terrace of stone, where stood a large cool bamboo temple, and a calabash of holy water, with which he sprinkled himself.†

Near the altar of ancient Hawáiian *heidus* stood a highly decorated calabash containing *wai Oha*, or holy water, with which the priest sprinkled all who were to officiate in religious rites. This corresponded to the lustral waters that stood in a vessel at the entrance of Greek temples; prepared in the same way as the *wai Oha*, and with which all must be sprinkled who entered the temple.

---

* "*Halo ke alo*"—face averted—means, "Let him die!"

† The Hawáiian priests prepared three grades of *Ke wai Oha*, or holy water.—"Polynesian Races," vol. I., p. 115.

The Inner Temple. 41

The Hawáiian *kahúna* prepared three especial grades of *Ke wai Oha ;* for purification, prayer, and sanctification ; severally called *wai-hui-Kala, wai-lupa-lupa,* and *wai-olena.* Holy water was also used for all public rites and private consolations, as well as to exorcise demons and disperse disease. Used at the baptismal font and as the sacrament for the mortally sick, it was thus a *vade mecum* for the living, and the *viaticum* for the dying.

On a large paved square in the centre of the temple stood the black stone altar, or *Lele,* and an octagonal wicker-work, the holy of holies. Around these, throughout the whole inner circuit of the temple, were piled luxurious *lauhála* mats, and pillows of the golden *pulu,* or silk of the fern. This arrangement was made ostensibly for the audience of high chiefs during times of religious observance. But the couches were oftener made use of by the *kahuna wahine* and her six priestly satellites, whereon to repose during the brief intervals of their pious duties.

These inviting divans were made with great care, with a view to obtaining springy, easy lounges for sitting or lying. The mats were piled upon each other twenty deep, and placed upon long rows of yielding bamboo poles reaching across the whole length and sides of the temple.

The king made choice of one of the couches a trifle more dainty than the rest, which, to judge by the rich feather *pau, lei,* and *kahili* made of golden O-o plumage, tokens of Wailéle's regal birth, showed evidence of being the Priestess' own place of repose. He was soon sleeping soundly, but not before Pemilani, one of the priest-girls, came in to use the feather *kahili,* assuming her hereditary office of *Paa-kahili,* "fly-brusher," for the king, as was her custom with her loved mistress when she slept.

This imported plague of flies, which added to the uses of the *kahili*, only dated back to the wreck of the last Spanish galleon.* Naturally they were looked upon with abhorrence; for though the natives endured lice, fleas, and grasshoppers, yet if a fly fell into a dish of *poi* the whole mess would be thrown away as defiled; while such a casualty, in the case of a naturalized brother insect, did not impair their appetite.

How long the tired king slept he knew not. He woke to find the six maidens singing about the *Lele*, or altar, chanting a soft prayer to Pele for the king. The pleading, supplicating tones of the charming priest-girls touched the old king's heart to tears. It was not wholly the pathetic words of the prayer, but more their tender appeals to the mother of gods, calling upon Pele as upon their own earthly mother.

Not until the holy chant was ended did the king become aware that Wailéle sat behind him waving her feather *kahili* over his head. As he turned to greet her, and sat up to look about him, he saw that the sacred dog had been killed and dressed and laid upon the altar. It was ready for sacrifice under the midnight moon.

About the *Ilio poli* floral decorations were tastily arranged. The heart, liver, and entrails had been cleansed and prepared especially for the worshippers during the midnight oblation; while the delicate meat of the *Ilio* itself was offered to Pele. In like manner the viscera of the far-famed Cook were devoured in later

---

* Mosquitoes, like flies, were also unknown in Hawáii before the advent of the pest-bringing whites. They are now very troublesome on the leeward side of the islands. But the first mosquitoes ever seen there came from an American ship as late as the year 1823.

years at Kaawaloa, while the flesh was stripped from the bones and burned in sacrifice to the gods.*

Wailéle clapped her hands for the girls to withdraw, and then confronted the monarch to expound in oracles the state secrets, or answer the personal prayers which had brought him to Mukíni.

The interchange of glances between this royal man and priestly woman were both earnest, deep, and as searching as if each had profound inquiries to make. If there were any touch of bewilderment in the gaze of either, it was expressed as when the questioning eyes of our first parents met by the Euphrates. For undoubtedly they were both more interested in each other at that moment than they knew or would confess to themselves.

"Priestess of Pele, answer the wishes of my heart," said the king, gazing steadily at Wailéle.

"*Alii Moi*, the Kahúna of Mukíni awaits your request. Her ear is open to the voice of Pele, whose spirit is now round about us. While yet you slept it came in swift answer to our united prayers."

"Greet the goddess for your guest, for he has fought many a battle prompted by her oracle."

"Pele receives your greeting, and smiles kindly upon the noble king."

"I have sought the Prophetess of Mukíni to learn of Pele what the warlike Kaméhanui of Maui is contemplating; and to ask of the divine goddess an heir for my kingdom."

"Kaméhanui goes to fight Oahu's king. The war canoes of Hawáii may rest in the sheltering valleys for many a day."

---

* Though his heart and liver were saved by the priests, to eat, some children devoured them in the night.

"Who shall be the mother of my heir? I have three queens, all comely women, and yet I am childless. Is it the will of Pele that my kingdom shall be battled for over my bundled bones?"*

Wailéle seemed for a moment wrapped in trance; then the answer came: "The wish of your heart shall be answered. The blood of a great king should descend to his people. Pele has heard your prayer, and long since whispered her bequest to the stars. She has willed you to be the father of the mightiest Hawáiian among all our kings."

"And whom, *kahúna wahine*, has the goddess indicated as the mother of my boy?"

"The decisions of Pele are ever crowned with wisdom. She leaves you to make choice of a queen as mother of your child."

"Is there wisdom in giving a despotic king that which is already his own?"

"Sire, would you appeal to other gods than Pele?"

"I have sought help from the united wisdom of the gods, and I am told: 'Go do as you please.'"

"Wise king! does it pass your understanding that your heir must be begotten by twin love, in the hallowed hour of the *Kulu* (full moon)? Does love go where love is sent, that you seek to have it sent to your palace door?"

"All who might love a monarch are not worthy to bear an heir. I ask for directions how to know the woman who is to bear my child."

"As the fierce sun was made companion for the timid day, and the gentle moon was mated to the blackest night; so the gods in the day of creation formed great

---

* A chief's bones are cleaned, bundled, and hidden in some secret tomb.

hearts in pairs, that their children should become mighty among men,—mighty as are the mountains to the lesser hills. There is but one noble heart equal to the grateful task you would put upon women. Seek, and you shall find her; and your progeny shall be blessed by the gods."

"Have I not already sought her for thirty years of vigorous life? I came to Mukini to seek wisdom, but I am answered in riddles."

"Do you not know the sun when you see him? And can you mistake the subtle influence of the *mahina* (moon) in her hour of fulling? The king will know the mother of his child when his great heart thrills at her coming; as the blue Pacific thrills at the coming of the maiden moon."

"It is well! Wonderful is the wisdom of Pele. If one should demand of her a star, he should have it for a footstool. And if an old king should find a young love, though the gods had hedged her about with the beauty of holiness, yet could Pele persuade her to become mother of a king. It is well. I will seek until I find her."

The half-satisfied monarch gave his hand to the Priestess with a gracious smile, in tender commendation of her wisdom, grateful for the mysterious behest of the gods, whatever it might prove to be. He said no more of hastening his return to Waipio. He seemed content to tarry and witness the sacrifice to Pele under the weird influence of the midnight moon.

Though matters of state called for the king's return, a yet stronger influence bade him remain. Already enthralled by the dark eyes of Wailéle, the monarch sought to give himself up to the yet deeper witchery of the hallowed place and the radiant night. The mystic influence was upon him, under which human hearts are charmed by Eros, when lovers awake to the divine impulse which prompts them to mate in bonds of wedlock with those whom they desire.

The hallowed hour when Flora unfolds her tender leaflets to *Mahina*, prompts her blossoms to exude their sweetest incense over the moonlit land, and hastens her tropic fruitage toward fructescence ; when even the finny tribes of the sea seek to climb the moonlit beaches ; while the leaping tides press landward, like human lovers, eager to embrace the moonbeam.

VI.

HOW TO WOO A PROUD WOMAN.

ONLY by the deepening tints of peach-bloom in her soft oval cheeks, and by the increasing languor in her large lustrous eyes, could a superficial observer guess how deeply Wailéle's tropical heart was stirred by her prophetic discourse with the king.

But to the keen eyes of the watchful monarch there were many other confirmatory intimations of how deeply a strong woman may feel, and yet not willingly betray her emotions. The wise old king had not failed to interpret the quivering lips and drooping lids, the instinctive lowering of her long lashes to hide her tell-tale eyes, lest they disclose the secrets of an ardent heart.

Clapping her hands in recall, one of the priest-girls came at the signal of her mistress, and soon after the whole cluster of maidens came and brought in a repast for the king: a feast consisting of baked dog, fish, and bread-fruit hot from the earth-oven without, together with *poi* and the choice fruits with which the valley abounds.

When the evening meal was spread before him, the maidens hastily withdrew because of the perpetual *tabú* against women eating with men. A still more oppressive phase of the *tabú* law forbade women to eat of the best fruits and foods. A penalty of death was inflicted for eating a cocoa-nut or banana; and pork, and many other delicacies, were *kapu e make* for the *wahines*.

When the king had finished his meal, he came out of the *heiàu* and sat upon the veranda with the *kahúna* girls, with whom he chatted pleasantly about their fright upon his arrival. Most of these *wahines* had previously seen and become acquainted with Keoúa, a handsome brother of the king of Hawáii, and of him and Kahekili they wished to inquire, expressing their admiration of the courtly manners of both the royal chiefs.

So an hour passed pleasantly, when the royal guest expressed a wish for a nearer view of the cataracts, the greatest wonder of the kind among the Pacific isles. Wailéle left the chiefesses to "tidy up" the temple and the abode without, and accompanied the king to the head of the valley, half a mile away.

As they walked through the green meadows along the river-bank a brilliant rainbow sprang across the deep vale, arching it over from *páli* to *páli;* as if in greeting to the royal guest.

Hundreds of joyous birds flew to greet them, fluttering their bright plumage and pouring out their liquid notes to attract the loved mistress as she passed, unawed by the presence of the stately man who walked gravely at her side.

But at times so tender were the glances of the noble king, so winning his royal smiles, that even the timid birds might well have been drawn to him, won by the magnetic attraction which served to charm their imperious mistress. Great indeed must have been the fascination of the old monarch thus to lead Wailéle to forget her dignity of priesthood, and suffer him to clasp her small patrician hand as they walked together, she half bewildered by the ardor that was glowing in his royal eyes.

Wooing a Priestess.   49

The valley narrowed quickly as they approached the falls, until at length they stood where the wind-blown spray from the cataracts fell cool and grateful upon their upturned faces. The younger face had become as flushed and radiant as the winged rainbows that floated off from the feathery margins of the falling waters.

Making choice of a grassy seat on the river-bank, Wailéle and the king sat down to watch the cataracts, and to let their glory and vastness touch the quivering fibres of their souls.

When in presence of such elements of grandeur, the mind shrinks from giving utterance to its sweetest raptures. Awe-stricken, and tremulous with delight, they listened to God's voice in the falling waters, as to the crash of ocean waves thundering on the rock-bound shore.

Was it not instinctive wisdom in the wise old king that led him to entice this proud, self-centred woman into the spiritual presence of a greater god than Pele?

The worship of idolatrous gods hardens the heart and belittles the soul. The love of Nature's God softens the heart, disarms pride, and engenders kindly feelings for all mankind. It is questionable if the king could have won a confession of love from the woman he sought for his queen had he not wooed her in the hallowed presence of Nature.

No pen can describe the conflicting elements of beauty and mystery in this secluded vale of Waimánu. Charms of ethereal witchery are here blended with grim mysteries that haunt the soul as when one stands before the unhallowed graves of murderers.

While the all-pervading beauty of the spot may fill the soul with enchantment and the ear with melody, yet on turning the eye from the glorious cataracts to the Plutonic precipice behind them, you see that it is caverned into catacombs for the graves of a thousand murdered victims. Then mark the palpitant heart-beat! the furtive eye searches about with the dreadful assurance of beholding some dismal spirit lurking among the yawning sepulchres. Foul intangible ghouls are said to be flitting through the gloom beneath these over-arching waters. They are victims from the black altar of yon heathen *heidu;* victims who were sacrificed for no crime known in the records of justice.

It is only by a strong effort that one can rid himself, in the upper valley of Waimánu, of these pervading horrors. And yet such scenic beauty cannot be found anywhere else in Hawáii. What a mighty growth of forest-trees is scattered about the cataract! what gigantic *koa*, bread-fruit, and *ohia* trees! Their luxuriance of foliage is owing to the constant humidity of the atmosphere, tempered by the noonday sun. Some of these giants grow near enough to reflect their emerald leafage in the three black basalt basins, channelled deep and wide to receive the five plunging water-falls.

Wailéle was a *Moo-kahúna* (history-keeping priest), as were most of the high-caste *kahúnas* who were descended from Pàáo. As they sat there discoursing of the early history of priesthood and the mighty power it had attained since the coming of her ancestor, two centuries before,—a subject upon which the gifted priestess was ever eloquent,—the watchful eyes of the adoring monarch were weighing every emotion that he saw welling up into the animated face before him.

Slight as were the blushes on Wailéle's cheeks while absorbed in her duties about the temple, yet now, while sitting there beneath the ardent gaze of the king, rosy and impassioned flushes suffused the translucent olive of her queenly face,—heart-felt blushes caught from the sunset hues of her native clime. The exalted emotions of an eloquent woman now played upon the sweet mysteries of her nature, deftly awakened by the manly king.

Yet with all this glowing tenderness that stole like a thief into the vestal heart of the maiden, it needed but one quick thought to recall the proud celibate to herself: the thought of her priesthood. Then she was aroused as by a tempest. A pallor whiter than the hue of Kéa's snows mantled over her cheeks. The roses fled from her compressed lips. The meek-eyed maiden of a moment since had vanished; and the arrogant Priestess withdrew the willing clasp of her hot hand now cold as the grave from that of the king. She sat stern and pitiless before the rebuked monarch, as if he enticed her to a crime, instead of love, for which all hearts languish.

In such moments of strong revulsion none but a thoughtless man would seek to intrude his love-plaint upon a Priestess of Pele, lest she stab him to the heart with his own dagger-blade—an act which Wailéle seemed half inclined to do.

Not until the roused lightning had gone out of her matchless eyes, and the pale lips were winning back their roses again, did the angry Priestess venture a word of rebuke to the author of her emotion—the loved intruder into her vestal sanctity. When she spoke, her lips were tremulous, and her eyes were filling with tears. For none knew better than Wailéle what was due to this noblest of men sitting there as her guest. It was his privilege to woo any woman in the land. No limit was put upon the number of queens for a Hawáiian king.

"O king! why have you of all men come to intrude upon my sacred duties to the gods of Mukíni? Noble man, is the great world above not large enough for your state-craft and conquests, that you must come seeking yet another woman as a bauble for your throne? Why need you swoop down into our peaceful valley, like an eagle frenzied for a mate?

"Go back into the upper world and leave Mukíni as you found it. Leave Wailéle to the peace and piety she loves. Leave her to the thankless task of regenerating a great nation. Go! and seek your conquests, whether of queens or of kingdoms, anywhere but in Waimánu."

As the grieved woman ceased speaking she reluctantly laid her hand in the proffered palm of the king. For one moment the humbled monarch was full of that noble sympathy that the vestal asked. But ah! how could he give her up? Did man ever rise to the nobleness of respecting a woman's piety when piety barred his path to love? And then, had not Wailéle made herself all the more beautiful in his eyes by this new charm in her character? The charm of refusing to be won is the strongest attraction in a woman's magnet of love.

The majestic man had looked calmly, almost coldly, upon the sudden bursting of her storm clouds, gravely feigning to be in doubt as to the cause of such an uncalled-for outburst. And well could he wait for a calm, knowing well that the more impassioned the woman the more strongly will she bind herself in the silken toils of love at last.

By the fathomless depth of her large dark eyes and the auroral splendor of her blushes, and by the passing away of her anger like a cloud, the king knew that Wailéle was already steeped in the first delicious emotions of love. Such emotions are irrevocable; such joy, once tasted, ripens into willing wedlock as surely as first fruit ripens upon the parent tree.

Though the dignity of her sacred mission remained, yet a new-born witchery now possessed her maidenly soul. The stern monitress of sacerdotal life had now found her master. Strain at her new shackles as she would, in moments of remembered duty, yet love, once harbored in a virgin heart, cannot be cast out; it grows like a deluge of sunbeams, until it floods the young being with glory.

The life-purpose of Wailéle was indeed the noblest inspiration in her barbaric sphere. As we have said, she was descended from a long line of *Kahúna maóli* (high-caste priests) dating back to the landing of the priest who built Mukíni in the dark ages of history,—the very "night time of Hawáii."

Born among the idolatrous delusions of priestcraft, but gifted to see its ills, she early formed the purpose to abjure the cruelty of its many heathen rites, and lessen its crimes of human sacrifice, lust, and rapacity. She entered the priesthood with the strong heart of a noble woman wholly devoted to the life of a vestal, and with the firm belief that a maiden's purity is the surest passport to the presence of deity. She sought to become the oracle of Pele, for the surer redemption of her superstitious and priestridden people.

So great had been her success, so truthful her marvellous oracles from the gods, and so prescient her own wise prophecies to the people—uttered in her dual office of *Kaula* (prophet) and *Kahúna*,—that at the opening of our theme the matchless beauty and devotion of Wailéle pervaded every household in the Eight Isles. Her influence was not unlike the ever-present vision of the Madonna in the pious homesteads of Christendom. Instead of human victims being now snatched from her native valley for sacrifices upon her altar; instead, even, of accepting as victims the deluded few who sometimes—when demented by grief for some dead love or lost friend—wished to immolate themselves to Pele,* Wailéle fed her altar during *Kápu-káne* (the time of human sacrifices) with tender *Ilio poli*, young dogs nursed as we have seen, and these she made acceptable to Pele instead of human victims, so repulsive to her own tender soul.

Up to this hour the young *Káhúna wahine* had stood solitary and alone in her reforms. More than this, she had kept herself pure and undefiled, subduing the frailty of her sex in Hawáii. She was as unapproachable as the snow-peaks of Kéa's mountain crown, although because of her exalted rank and marvellous beauty kings had sued at her feet.

Kahekili—the renowned "Thunderer,"—the greatest monarch and the bravest warrior among Maui's long line of fighting kings, was among her supplicants, coming to obtain a prophecy from the far-famed Priestess concerning his impending wars with Oahu. Though he was the husband of other lovely queens, the gallant king had received from the imperious beauty oracles for which he gladly left his great heart in payment.

Keoúa, the handsome courtier and brother of Hawáii's king, later the monarch of Kau, came on a secret mission from Kalaniopuu, was capsized in the frightful surf that guards the valley, and though just escaping with his life, gladly repeated his visit because of his love for

---

* Such a victim was offered at the death of Kaméhaméha in 1819.

Wailéle. Rumor tells not how well he performed the several missions for his sovereign; but it was recorded by every enamoured priestess of Mukíni that this captivating nobleman left his heart behind.

It was further said that the heart thus lost by Keoúa was shared by six claimants, and equally distributed among the priest-girls about the *heiáu*, so captivated were all but Wailéle with this handsomest of living men.

The romantic interpretation of Keoúa's name is "Rain Food," and for many a month after the courtier's memorable visit to Mukíni every sun-shower that blew in with the trade-wind was adored as much by the six ardent *wahines* as by the thirsty flowers. To this day the sun-showers of Waimánu are looked upon as the weeping ghost-spirit of the disconsolate Rain Food; and he has become the beau ideal of every maiden's heart—her best type of manly beauty and undying devotion.

How sad it is that the very temerity of a strong woman, like Wailéle, ever becomes her first source of danger in affairs of the heart! Because of her acquired strength and courage, already tested in the social arena with courtly men, and of the very integrity of her heart, woman wrongfully estimates her moral strength when she defies all comers. Such a woman may be gifted beyond all others in the subtle mysteries and divine methods of her life-mission, and yet, alas! most ignorant of the veiled arcana of her own lovely being.

The primal strength of a great heart lies rather in the vital than the intellectual sphere—the lower rather than the upper brain,—and whatever the strength of the strongest feminine citadel, there are ever spies within and foes without cunningly awaiting the dominant hour of human exaltation presided over by the planetary powers of the stellar world.

Thus, because Wailéle has tested her maiden shield against the subtle influence of Maui's gallant king and Hawáii's most captivating chief, without dimming her bright escutcheon, it was with the feminine vanity that belongs to the weakest of her sex that she now deemed herself unconquerable by any comer, even by this wily old king.

Well might such royal homage instil a just pride into the heart of a cloistered vestal and impart a yet more imperious look to the impassioned beauty. Even the haughtiest chiefs, when they came to crave her priestly intercession with the gods, quailed under the arrogance of her dark eyes.

Yet because of this sweet feminine weakness, woman's inherent love of conquest, Wailéle had increased her priestly assiduity at the altar. At times she properly reproached herself for that in which her maiden heart secretly delighted as the glory of her young existence. So sweet a sin it was to dote over in her pensive moods! Such a delicious titbit to deplore in pious moments of humility.

Thus, when the new-comer came so suddenly and unannounced into Wailéle's presence, he found the bolts and bars of her unconquered citadel all flung back, and every portal open in proud disdain of danger, come who would, and woo who might her self-poised heart.

But the best wooers among men put not their ultimate intent into words. Words are too material outriders to rudely approach such an ethereal combatant as love. It is not by the rattle of spurs and the clang of sabre that such an alert maiden as Wailéle can be won. Even supplicating words create antagonism with a proud and arrogant woman, and put her upon the defensive before an opportunity for the conquest can be gained.

The wise man has other methods than these. His persuasive approach, his courtly manners, fail not to create interest and awaken some degree of curiosity as to his full intent. His art is to compel his fair companion to do the manœuvring for the conquest which he himself came to win.

Here lies the strength of a wise man's strategy. If his attentions are repelled as intrusive, the defence of the wooer is to disclaim the construction put upon his acts; and if no ground is won in these first approaches, at least none is lost. If, on the contrary, his attentions are reciprocated, the clue of approach is found; and this, warily followed up, fails not to lead the cunning wooer into the inmost chambers of that most profound of labyrinths, the woman's heart that he seeks to make his own.

The proud old king, who came ostensibly to receive an oracle and consult the gods as to his future desires, made that object his cloak. He became more imperious in manner, more haughty in mien, than the glorious creature whose prophecy he sought and whose love he determined to win. He knew the experience of his brother chiefs, and meant not to be wrecked where lay the stranded hearts of others.

Not a word of love or admiration had passed the monarch's lips, and but for his dignity of manner and suavity of tone his imperious language and commanding air might have aroused Wailéle's antagonism, in fear that the priestly prerogative of her temple should be assailed.

The grand old man before her talked with his tongue, but expressed his real thoughts only with his telltale eyes. His words seemed gravely charged with the state business that brought him to the *heidu*. But his looks were full of unmistakable admiration of the woman before him.

Revelling in the exquisite beauty of her dark eyes, so unconsciously illuminated by his presence and by the topic of discussion, he watched with keenest observation the witching play of thoughts and feelings in her mobile face, and interpreted them before her tongue found words.

At the end of the first hour's discussion in the temple Wailéle found herself piqued and dissatisfied with the courtly gravity of her guest. The commanding monarch seemed to require homage without a thought of returning it. And yet his hostess was of blood as royal as his own, and her royal ancesters had not only reigned over Hawáii but had even dethroned a king and ruled triumphantly in his stead.*

A proud woman soon comes to doubt the power of her much-vaunted beauty when in the presence of a person who fails to laud her charms. At such times she finds herself ill at ease; she watches with nervous solicitude for some recognition of her charms, and puts forth renewed efforts to captivate the tardy delinquent. But, do and say what she would, not a responsive word of admiration passed the king's lips. Wailéle was thus forced to be content with the kindling affection that she saw in his piercing eyes.

When a proud woman seeks to exact the homage she deems her due, she will soon find herself endeavoring to compel admiration from all comers. A vain woman once fairly entered upon such a conquest will give up every thing rather than abandon the task.

In her cool, calm moments Wailéle was not a woman to lose herself in pursuit of a sentiment. But in the na-

---

* Hakau, the wicked king, was slain by order of *Kaoleioku*, the priest, whose foster-son came to the throne.

ture of all women there are extraneous influences that wield a weird and mysterious power over their too receptive hearts ; a power not only beyond their control, but often wholly out of the scope of their knowledge. From the thrall of this primordial power the strongest and purest may not always escape, unless forearmed by knowledge of the subtle source of the ambushed danger that awaits them beneath the lunar ray.

VII.

MYSTERIOUS SACRIFICE BY MOONLIGHT.

AS they walked homeward by the river the vast gray shadows of the early evening drew down over the valley, soothing the ruffled mood of the haughty priestess. She suffered the king to retain her hand, which was still cold and tremulous from her late angry mood. The warm magnetic clasp of the monarch's hand soon brought the hot current back again, soothing every wild pulsation throughout her being, as only the tender touch of a loving hand could do.

Wailéle was a superb specimen of womanly beauty as she walked with flushed cheeks and drooping eyelids beside the stalwart king; and her own generous physique and commanding presence made her all the more charming. Yet there were conflicting traits in this brilliant woman which amazed him. Subdued and abashed as she seemed at this moment, still there was always a half reverent, half imperious spirit of self-consciousness pervading her aspect, and it puzzled even the king to understand it.

The royal pair arrived at the house. The priest-girls and other *wahines* had been busy, during the absence of their mistress, preparing for the coming sacrifice in the temple, and wreathing their heads with *leis* of flowers and their necks with garlands of blossoming vines.

They were still mirthfully occupied among the delicate

tendrils of running ferns. Some were deftly weaving the tessellated flowers of the *ohia*, crimson as the red-bird's wing, into garlands with which to decorate the holy altar and festoon the shrine of prayer, where their haughty priestess confronted the gods to receive their mandates, and in turn appealed to them for yet greater pity in dealing with human sins.

Soon after, the king was left to his own reveries while Wailéle and her *wahines* went into the *heiáu* to dress the temple and to light the fragrant torches of *kúkúi* nuts strung upon the wire-like ribs of the cocoa-nut leaf.

The water-falls were still dimly seen through the deepening gloom from the veranda. The lofty crest of the mountain was yet rimmed about with clear amethyst and gold; for the sun, already set to all below, tarried there like a lover for a farewell kiss upon the snowy brow, where he lingered at his setting, and which first he greeted at the dawn.

Ere the last sunbeams had faded on the mountain top, the night swooped down over Waimánu with the haste of a famished eagle. Darkness clutched with hungry talons at every hollow; and Silence stalked into the vale, hooded like a monk, followed by ghostly spirits from out their caverns in the cliff. A hush fell upon the joyous bird-songs and the thousand choruses of the brief tropic day. Even the brave old king cowered at the unseemly haste of the gloom. The vast cataracts still leaped from out the starlit heavens, yet tempered their turbulent voices as they groped down into the gulf of inky blackness below. The solemn nocturne of their waters sounded like a multitudinous wail over the murdered dead.

No wonder that men's hearts grew sorrowful amid

such scenes in a strange valley, a valley so deep that every star shone out while yet the sun triumphed upon the last snows of Mauna Kéa. No wonder that a whisper of sadness stole timidly up from the once babbling river now bereft of its companion bird-songs.

Even the mighty ocean at the foot of the valley is mindful of the mandate sent forth by the usurping night, and softens his crash of thunders against the lava cliffs, subduing his unruly breakers where they flounder on the pebbly shore.

Pemilani, one of the prettiest of the priest-girls, now came to ask the king to come into the temple to rest after his walk. There he was met by Wailéle, who was perfecting her preparations for the midnight sacrifice.

Two beautiful *leis* (wreaths) of gardenia were lying on his couch, filling the whole temple with fragrance. One *lei* was evidently designed for the king, from the floral crown* of yellow flowers attached to the wreath; the other, for the priestess, was to be worn during the hour of sacrifice.

As the *kahúna wahines* were still occupied about the temple under the direction of their chiefess, the king lay on his couch to watch what occurred. Pemilani took her seat behind the *moi* to ply her *kahili*, and sang in order to woo the royal guest to slumber.

Before he slept, Wailéle and her maidens finished their labors of festooning the *lele* (altar) and the holy *anu* (holy of holies), and began chanting a religious melody.

A row of flickering candle-nut torchlights were placed about the *lele*, casting long moving shadows over the temple, while the six *alii wahines* (chief girls) paced solemnly around the altar, dressed only in their flimsy *pau* (skirt) and floral decorations.

---

* They imitated pictures of crowns worn by the Spanish kings.

Conspicuous above her pretty compeers towered the beautiful priestess, tall as the hugest chief of her native valley. Yet the ill effect of such unusual height in woman was fully redeemed by her majestic mien, and by the exquisite symmetry of her figure, as the lines of marine modelling find their best expression only in vessels of the largest class.

Pemilani tuned her lullaby to the weird chants sung by the chiefesses as they glided dimly about the altar. The last thing seen by the drowsy king, through eyes grown misty with sleep, was the priestess retiring into the holy of holies for a last communication with the gods before offering the *ilio poli* to Pele. Thus slept the royal chieftain in peaceful slumber, while the *wahines* sang and the Kahúna prayed in her shrine in behalf of her sovereign guest.

When the king awoke from his slumber, the moon was riding high over the valley; the altar fire was smouldering about the charred remains of the *ilio*, its smoke lazily gyrating up through the aperture in the top of the temple, dimming the lustre of the stars as it rose into the windless heavens. The sacrifice to Pele by the mystic light of *Hoku* was over.

The king was awakened by the singing priest-girls without the temple, crooning their melodious *meles* (songs) to Pele, as they gazed with supplicant faces upon the midnight moon. Soft and sweet was their prayerful chant. There was not a sibilant consonant in their bird-like notes, which caught their tearful key from the rippling river, the sighing air made drowsy with perfume, and the deep monotone of the mighty cataracts.

The maidens soon ceased their chant, and the king dropped into slumber again. But after a brief pause they again broke out into a sensuous rhapsody to the moon, which bathed their pretty faces in her beams. At length, as by some common impulse, they sang a *mele aloha*—a love song—of a king and a priestess of yore, when the Spanish galleon was wrecked on Pau Pele (Pele Point) in the long-gone centuries; when the *haole wahine* —the white maiden—knelt down on the shore at *Kulou*, "the place of prayer," and was taken as the fittest subject to bear kings for the great Isle of Hawáii.

And of such descent was their guest, the king. Fit match was he for the beautiful Priestess of Waimánu, she who was descended from the white priest Pááo, the noblest Spaniard of them all. As the song died away, and only the silence and the moonlight filled the temple, the half-awakened monarch heard a sigh in the gloom behind him. Turning, he saw Wailéle sitting in the darkness, her figure outlined against the moonlight, silently waving her *kahili* over him.

The king spoke to the priestess and bade her come to his side. The sigh of a lonely maiden, when winged with a moonbeam, sinks like a plummet into the heart of man. Taking her hand in his they talked of the sacrifice, which the king was purposely exempted from seeing; for the pure-hearted Kahúna had then wrestled with the gods as never before.

The dread oracle of fate which the gods had promulgated was not to her liking, and Wailéle was made sad. A lone heart beneath the moonlight is made doubly sorrowful because of its loneliness, its want of companionship, its tender yearning for love. None but a stern-hearted vestal, in such an hour, could refuse the love of a king.

The priest-girls had gone away to their couches. The

singing lizards were now piping their loudest chorus to the blended voices of the night. The gentle land-winds came cool from the mountain snows, made heavy with aroma snatched from the wayside flowers. The stars shone softly in the cloudless sky, but dimmed by the strong lustre of the full-orbed moon.

Since the sudden moon-burst over the south *páli* drowsy nature had seemed less solicitous to hush her teeming voices. The river was again rippling vocally over its crystal bed of sand. And after hours of almost perfect stillness, the joyful sea was now becoming restless. The land-winds had rudely awakened the blossoms soft folded in sleep, as they romped merrily down the valley to the sea. The orange * buds and *ohia* flowers burst into bloom, in half belief it was day, exhaling their fragrance to the breeze, all blending in delicious dalliance beneath the gaze of the moon.

Most glad of all things in the valley were the water-falls arched above the sepulchres. The moon looked over the *páli* and fringed their white curves rosy with lunar rainbows. A thousand hovering mist-spirits floated hither and thither, born of the falling waters and the witching moonbeam.   *   *   *

---

* Oranges and coffee were among the exotics brought by Spaniards long prior to Cook's time.

VIII.

MOON-SPIRITS IN THE VALLEY.

HIGH upon the mountain side overlooking Waimánu, rose clear and distinct against the forest belt the black-walled *heiáu* of Puukeekee. There took place the most cruel human sacrifices that were known among all the temples of Pele. Pepehi was the High-Priest, the murderous half-brother of the beautiful Priestess of Mukíni, the most feared of all the *kahúna maoli* on Hawáii.

Greater disparity of character among close kindred than this the world has not known. One, a truthful and pious spirit, full of the noblest sensibilities of humanity; supplying her heathen altar with brute beasts only, made acceptable to the deity of her temple by the tender nature of women; the other, a man who seized upon every occasion, whether grave or trifling, to slaughter his brother man, piling his foul altars with bleeding human victims, sacrificed with accessory acts of inhuman cruelty, in the dread name of Pele.

During the afternoon, while Wailéle and the king were sauntering up the river, the greenish-blue smoke of a human sacrifice was seen rising above the mountain *heiáu*. Pepehi had piled his stone altar with dead Kanákas, and sat eating of their cooked livers and prepared entrails while his inferior *kahúnas* roasted the slaughtered victims.

That hour of dread immolation at Puukeekee was the genial hour of love at Mukíni. The brutal priest turned his dull eyes down upon Waimánu, the loved valley of his birth, and beheld with surprise the brilliant rainbow arching lovingly over his boyhood's home. Gloated as he was with human flesh, his fierce red eyes shone with a malignant light as he watched the beautiful sign in the heavens.

What could be its import? Pepehi asked, as he sat on the high terrace of stone beside his smoking altar. He had believed himself the most favored among the priesthood because of his love for the inhuman duty assigned to the *kahúnas* of Pele. But here was a token of her approbation of another which the jealous priest could not fathom.

With a look of hatred gleaming in his deep-sunken eyes, Pepehi watched the radiant sun-bow fade slowly away in the evening sky. Sated as he was with his human feast, and drunk with *awa*, he fell asleep and slept till the midnight moon hung over the valley of Waimánu, casting its heavenly benediction down wherever human hearts met in holy impulse of love.

And lo! when the priest awoke, with a drunken leer in his eye, from too much *awa*, there slowly dawned upon his bewildered vision another fairy emblem of beauty yet more evanescent and mystic than the rainbow of the afternoon. A radiant lunar bow now spanned the dark valley from *páli* to *páli*, arched above the temple of Mukíni.

Here was a double mystery to be explained by the crafty old Kahúna of Puukeekee. It implied a double and yet more delicate sanction of some act of accepted devotion of the vestal Priestess of the valley. In what manner, he asked, could the worship of his priestly father's daughter be made more acceptable to Pele than his own energetic *kápu káne*—human sacrifice? Could it be that Wailéle's *ilio poli* were more acceptable in the Goddess' eyes than his own hecatomb of human flesh?

Pepehi grew enraged as he watched the beauteous lunar-bow. He saw its soft prismatic colors deepening, its clean-cut arch spanning the vine-covered walls of Mukíni, like a heavenly benediction of *Ke Akua maole* (the real God) which an aged prophet had recently discovered in the sky.*

What could it mean? Was a *kahúna wahine*—a priest-girl—becoming of more importance in Hawáii *nei* than an all-powerful *kahúna maole*, or high-caste priest?

As Pepehi continued gazing in this vengeful mood, a timid flickering glow came forth from the altar-fire of Mukíni, casting its thin rift of modest light up through the aperture in the temple roof. It was as the glow of a farthing candle to the lurid gleam of Pepehi's holocaust on the mountain. Yet the visible sign and blessing of the gods hung like a halo over the lesser altar-fire of the valley, to the shameful exclusion of his dreadful fire of human flesh, which now cast its fitful glare even upon Mauna Kéa's crest of snow.

Gazing with a yet clearer vision, Pepehi could later distinguish figures of aërial light gathering in countless numbers on the luminous arch of the lunar-bow, and flitting above the temple, around the dying glow of the altar-fire of Wailéle. A busy convocation of winged

---

* In the days of which we write a good old priest and prophet, Kalaikuahulu by name, much given to sagacious predictions, prophesied: "There is certainly another God than Pele;—*Ke Akua maole*, living in the sky. He will yet come to us; and after this there shall be no more *tabú*."

spirits at length pervaded the whole dark valley. Some of these airy beings appeared as timid as lovers' dreams, and as soft in radiance as St. Elmo's tribes. Others of greater dimensions were yet more visibly luminous; they pulsated with a soft lustrous light, and their eyes answered tenderly to other loving eyes in the sacred temple below.

Hours passed, and yet time was as nought to the spellbound priest of the mountain *heidu*. The bow of promise hung over Waimánu until the morning. Long past its usual hour the carolling land-wind ventured softly down the mountain side, freshening gently as it approached the shore, but stealing tender-footed as it blew, so solicitous was the breeze not to disturb the communion of Invisibles in the sacred vale, where every flower cried "Hush!" in softest undertone.

Never did mountain streams sing so sweetly as in that hour; toning down their jubilant voices to listen, curious as maiden ears to catch the faintest sounds of love in the valley below. Even the loud-mouthed sea forgot its bluster in this hallowed hour, floundering less noisily than usual far down on the rock-bound shore. The resounding dirges of ocean were now softened into the tenderest bassoon known to a lover's ears.

Beside the countless throng of fairy folk which then peopled the mystic valley, only heathen gods and holy angels were suffered to witness the hallowed act of sacrifice to Pele on that eventful night. And only these nocturnal Invisibles could sanction the immolation that was made in the holy temple in obedience to the divine will of Pele, prompted by the blended influences of the mystic hour of midnight and the lunar orb.

IX.

LAST INTERVIEW OF THE LOVERS.

WHEN the awakened king came out upon the veranda at dawn the whole household were up and away at their morning tasks. The sun was just tinting the higher snow peaks with a crown of glory. They shimmered and shone in the strong Eastern beam; springing into such gigantic eminence from out the dark green girdle of intervening forest that it seemed but an hour's ride to the summits high above the cumlous clouds.

Looking about the grounds the king discovered Wailéle in the distance, fresh from her bath in the river, and all aglow with the exercise. She was feeding her pet birds as they flocked about her in hundreds from the adjacent trees. Some of the affectionate creatures were alight upon their mistress' head and shoulders, and others, crimson as the *ohia* flowers, were pecking daintily at food in her extended hand.

Everywhere about the grounds the orange trees were at once in early blossom and ripest fruit, and mingled their grateful fragrance with delicious perfumes from the white flowers of the wild coffee trees. In strongest contrast to these colorless blossoms grew the red hibiscus here and there among the fruit-bearing trees, their boughs peopled with scarlet birds beautiful as the blossoms, but as songless as the crimson flowers.

As the chieftain walked across the enclosure to greet his hostess, he saw evidence that she was an early riser, for her long black hair was already wreathed with a fresh *lei* of gardenia, and her graceful neck was garlanded with fresh-culled flowers.

As they came back toward the house with lingering footsteps and frequent pauses, a keen eye could readily discern a look of exultation in the face of the king, while in the deep eyes of Wailéle there shown a lustrous, nameless light, which has as yet found no description in all the legends of song.

While breakfast was being prepared the king strode to the river for his morning bath. There he met three of the priest-girls, with numerous other *wahines* from about Mukíni, all wading merrily up the river from out the dark vista of the forest. Each maiden was deftly balancing on her garlanded head a green-leaved package of tribute *poi*, or pig, baked or squealing, together with nursling puppies to be tabued and fattened into sacred *ilio poli* and consecrated to Pele.*

The whole laughter-loving crowd of happy girls had brought their burdens from the Tribute Rock in the river, below the tabued line in the forest. Nude as the flowers, with their long hair trailing on the water like raven wings as they breasted the stream, they seemed more like wood nymphs or naiads than song-loving maidens of Mukíni.

---

* Pigs (or puppies) were made sacred by taking them before the great idol of the *heiáu*, pinching the ear or twisting the tail to elicit a squeal, while the Kahúna addressed the god in the name of the devotee and made known the giver. A hole was then made in the ear, into which was inserted a braid of cocoa-nut fibre; and thenceforward the animal was *tabú* to the gods, and none dare molest him. (Ellis' "Hawáii," p. 59.)

When the king returned from his ablutions breakfast was spread for him in the temple where only a tabued chief could be permitted to partake of food. And though the chiefesses of the *heidu*—being also *alii kapu*—could eat there during the sacrifices, yet even they dare not now break the death *tabú* by eating with the king, or even by remaining in the temple while any man was eating there. Thus the king's meals were both lonely and hurried for lack of companionship. When he again came out on the veranda Wailéle was alone and waiting his coming. She had previously allotted to each attendant her duties for the day, as the king was to leave for Waipio in a few hours' time.

As the early morning view of the falls was the most enjoyed, Wailéle invited her royal guest to a walk up the valley. Together they sauntered along the flowering river bank; and soon the priestess found herself alone with nature and the grand old king upon the same spot where, but a day before, a tigerish gleam of defiance had flashed from her eyes upon one who had tempted a vestal *kahúna* with love, the delicious weakness of her sex.

Could this be she whose angry glances had been turned upon her kingly lover because he had won her heart to such a lapse of human frailty as that of love?

Never could he forget the withering look of those magnificent eyes. They were so sinister and savage that even he, a brave old warrior, could not but mentally put himself upon the defensive when confronting such a dangerous mood in a woman of her physical strength and superhuman courage.

And yet this priestly despot now sits pensive and passive at his feet, revelling in the delicious dalliance of his glances and the manly resonance of his voice—a voice that had rung its bugle notes in the thick of many a battle, but had never till now led a charge so perilous as his late assault of love upon this priestly vestal's heart. But now, as the regal lover reaches out to take Wailéle's shapely hand, it is with a lover's delicious assurance that what he asks for will not be refused. Their eyes meet as the king possesses himself of her hand, and Wailéle's grateful glances become as tender as moonlight on the sea. Her full proud lips arch like Cupid's bow; as roseate in color as the young *ohia* leaves seen across the stream.

Above their heads, from bough to bough, clambers the blue convolvulus, whose azure tints seem caught from the blue of the summer sky. Around the tree-trunks near them twine the sylph-like running ferns, with purple star-like blossoms—the *gleichenia*,—their delicate tendrils drooping in soft clusters above them, leaning with almost human instinct above the lovers' heads as if eager to catch the cooing words of two enamoured souls.

Glinting down over the south *páli's* edge the ardent sun was just dipping his yellow plumage into the foaming cataracts. Darting his golden lance-beams everywhere among the cool shadows below, he illuminated the gray rocks of the north *páli* as with a flambeau of fire.

With the sunlight shining so directly into the valley, the charms of the place outnumber its gloom. But whatever the time or place from which one views the wonders of Waimánu, there is always inconceivable novelty in the situation. Wherever the eye may wander, the solemn boom of the falls ever assails the ear. Every foot of floating mist about the cataracts was now transfigured into winged bits of rainbow, while the edges of the plunging waters were all aglow with the rarest colors of sunset.

But the king was bent upon leaving the valley while the land-winds blew, and before the trades should arouse the surf at the river mouth and prevent his egress. A canoe was already in waiting to take him down the river from the *heidu*, and another, strong enough for sea service, had been ordered. In this the *wahines* in the employ of the Priestess would take the royal *incognito* to the uninhabited valley next to Waimánu, and thence he could easily reach his own place, from which he had come two days before. A *tabú* had already been put upon the lower valley for the day, which would ensure perfect secrecy in the passage down the river.

As they returned hand in hand along the margin of the river, sensuous nature seemed everywhere pattering for them numerous tasks of love. The ardent sun kissed the water-falls, and laid his hot cheek with delicious languor upon the rippling stream. The very trees upon the river bank leaned tenderly over the limpid water, coquetting with reflected cloud and sunshine alike as the three met in dalliance in the laughing stream. The mating birds sat on the low boughs gossiping about the sweet ways of human love, and twittering their matin pæans as the lovers passed along. The cool wind from the mountain snows, all unseen by the watchful king, kissed the hot flush from the Priestess' cheek.

X.

WOOED AND WON, AND PARTED FOREVER.

AT length the sense of their approaching parting impressed the lovers as they neared the *heidu*, and flung a shadow over them until their heart-beats met in fond confession in their clasping hands.

There is a touch of sadness in even brief partings from those whom we love. These lovers were about to part with no hope of meeting again this side the grave. Ah! who can tell the pang of tenderness that crept over their exalted souls?

They had met and lived a lifetime of emotions in a day; they had proved their strength of heart in their loving, and they now showed their strength of soul in parting. Part they must, because a great life-work had been allotted to each, and each was too noble to wish to entice the other from its duties.

The king was not willing to abdicate his kingdom and become the High-Priest of Mukíni. Its loved mistress, Wailéle, was strongly wedded to the hope of redeeming some of the inhuman savagery of her *tabú* creed. And yet this vestal Priestess had found in the noble old monarch the nearest approach to a kindred soul that she had ever known. But strong as the affections of such great hearts may be, they are also capable of an unselfish purpose in life which shall immolate love, and labor for toilsome years to accomplish some needed good for their kind.

No wonder that such emotional hearts as these lean more tenderly toward each other, as the proffered gift of human love dawns upon them in the hour of parting, like the vision of some holy Shechinah in the sky! No wonder that a yet sweeter cadence steals into their voice as hand clasps hand with poignant emotion, and eyes search other eyes with but one crystal window between two souls.

What a change had come over these two since morning! When they wended their way up the river but a few hours since, one lover was jubilant of his conquest of a proud woman's heart. The other proud soul, though she had been invoked by the gods and importuned by the noblest of men, was saddened with a boding fear of her too willing captivity. Yet there is a maidenly apprehension in all young hearts after their first confession; as budding flowers grow tremulous and deep-eyed on their day of blossoming.

Who has not learned the never-ceasing lesson of life, that our best joys are but half cherished until we are about to lose them? Wailéle had reluctantly given a brief glimpse of her heart to her lover when first he came, and then had snatched it away in petulant mood, as too precious a gift for even a king. Now that she is about to lose him, her poor heart seems but a bauble unworthy of his royal acceptance. For love had now exalted the loved one; and when won, he seemed the noblest and best of his kind.

They approached the *heidu* and saw the canoe made ready to carry the king down the river. Both stopped as by one consent, wishing to part without witnesses, as became the exalted rank of each. The calmness of the king was but the quiet of the cataract on the brink it must part from forever. The last moment had come, and glowing hearts blended in loving emotions through every sense, as the sun mingles his fiery beams with the palpitant waters of the river.

"Wailéle," said the king, his sad eyes feasting upon the beautiful face before him, its charms enhanced by the flush of emotion, " I came to Waimánu knowing little of the true nobility of womanhood. I came to demand a personal oracle and to propound a weighty question of state. I go, leaving my heart with the loved Kahúna of Mukíni, though she refuses to go forth as my queen."

"Dear king, you will not love me less for my refusal, for my decision is wise."

"Dear *Wahine!* you are as wise as you are beautiful. Your lover will leave you his war-spear—a sovereign's token,—implying that his warriors shall maintain Wailéle as *Kahúna nui* over the temple of Mukíni. He leaves you his *lei*, and *niho palaoa* (whale's tooth), as a memento of love, the most priceless insignia in his kingdom. None but an *alii kapu*—tabu chief—and member of the *Ahu Alii* must wear it, for the *tabú* is death."*

"*Alii moi maikai!*—Good sovereign chief"—said Wailéle, bursting into sobs and tears, while the king continued:

"And whoever brings this royal spear to your king with the password 'Wailéle' shall return to your defence with an army before the sun goes down. But to him who brings the precious *niho*, with the password 'Umi,' shall be given the best gift in my giving, though he demand the half of my kingdom. Conceal these things from all eyes. Keep them as a souvenir of a king's love for his darling."

---

* Members of the Council of Nobles (*Ahu Alii*) are entitled to certain insignia, tabued to all others of less rank.

"Kingly man, your love shines into Wailéle's heart. My memory will treasure the passwords sacredly. Whosoever comes from Wailéle shall bear the sweet name of 'Umi'—the ivory souvenir of the king,—and the tokens you leave at Mukíni shall be embalmed with my love and guarded with my life. The hiding place of the tooth shall be under the sacred *anu*, where your *kahúna wahine* invokes the gods she adores, and prays for the king she loves."

"Aloha! Pele, guard the life of my darling. Aloha, Wailéle! thou art grand as the mountain above thee, and gentle as the river by our side. To have known you, dear Wailéle, will make me more brave in the hour of battle, and more humane to my people through all my life."

And the chieftain gave into the hands of the Priestess his richly-carved spear, and his ivory necklace, the rarest decoration in the kingdom over which he ruled. Holding her throbbing hands, he eagerly awaited the last message from his darling, which she could not yet find voice to impart. Her lips moved as for speech, but her tongue was dumb. Emotions stirred her soul as with a tempest. At length she found voice, but hoarsely, as if speaking from her tomb.

"Farewell, dear king—we have met not wholly in vain. You have taught Wailéle that the love of a noble man for woman is the crowning glory of her life. You have wooed me for your queen; do not hate me because I refuse to wed. Know, *Alii moi*, that your loving Kahúna is wedded to a greater than mortal—her holy shrine. Believe that woman's adoration for the deity that prompts her to prayer is a greater bridal for a pure heart than wedded love, even with a king."

And together the royal pair walked hand in hand down the river to the canoe, in which the old king seated himself, while the priest-girls seized their paddles, awaiting the signal to go.

"Aloha, queen of my heart!"

"Aloha, dearest and best of men! Farewell to the only mortal Wailéle has learned to love. Aloha, forever and forever!"

And the weeping Priestess flung the king's hand from her strong grasp, as if doubting her power to give him up, and rudely pushed the canoe into the stream, waiting with compressed lips and clenched hands to see the loved one depart, though her young heart should be rent by the separation.

The king refused to give the order to go; the eyes of the proud chief were as full of tears as were his darling's. With a cry of bitter anguish he appealed to her to come and be his queen.

The proud woman waved her hand for him to go. Yet again and again he called to her to come, but called in vain. Then in soft tones of appeal, such as only a breaking heart could utter, he pleaded for her to go with him as far as the *tabú* line. It was with a lingering hope that she could not find courage to leave him there.

How strong is the power of one noble heart over another; how resistless the sweet influence of man over the woman he loves! Wailéle, the proud and arrogant Priestess, softened to the appeals of love, as the cold mist of the morning leaps at the touch of the sun.

Springing into the river with outstretched arms she swam to the waiting canoe, her long black hair streaming behind like the pinions of some black demon who had lent her his wings to fly away from her heathen shrine.

She reached the canoe, drawn by an impulse stronger than the cable-tow of a frigate. Stretching her hand out of the stream to the grasp of the king, she bade the *wahines* paddle swiftly down the river. But she resolutely refused to enter the boat.

The agile *wahines* plied their paddles vigorously, and the canoe soon entered the deep arcade of the forest. Wailéle swam easily beside the canoe, and neither king nor Priestess spoke as they sped down the river toward the Tribute Rock.

Tender were the appealing glances in the old king's eyes, as he watched every movement of the strong and beautiful swimmer. Wailéle gazed into those dear persuasive eyes, and her heart confessed those sweet emotions that transcend all other joys in life.

What passed in Wailéle's mind during that half hour in the river, she never told; so we can never know. But at times, as she swam there beside the canoe, her answering glances became irresolute and yielding, as if she were charmed to the very verge of willing captivity. It was the stage of sweet abandonment that all women love to indulge toward one noble heart.

The canoe neared Tribute Rock. The monarch's hand clasped hers more firmly, and his fond eye dwelt upon her with a delicious hope of detaining her. Wailéle's mobile face grew strong and resolute again. But the eyes lost their tenderness, and a touch of the old imperiousness came into them at the thought that the king might possibly attempt coercion. But that passed in an instant. Perhaps it was but the shadow of a cloud passing across the sun, for the next emotion depicted on the maiden's face, as they drew still nearer to the rock, was a look of supplication that this dear man's love should not wholly forsake her.

There comes a touching look into the eyes of woman when thus aroused by the strong agony of grief or love, an eloquence before which the tongue of man grows dumb. It was an expression so agonizing, an attitude of such unspeakable sorrow, that the chieftain half relaxed his grasp of her hand, while an appealing wish welled into his eyes, that spoke his desire to clasp the dear one to his bosom, ere they should part so cruelly.

Brief and beautiful was the moment's response which lit up the glowing face of Wailéle as she interpreted the king's wish. Then a deathly pallor usurped the color on lips and cheeks and brow, and the tender love-look in her eyes was displaced by an expression in which culminated all the agonies that the heart can bear.

Suddenly, and with a strength almost superhuman, Wailéle tore her hand from the grasp of her lover and plunged beneath the surface, that she might not hear his appeals. Then, with long, strong strokes, she swam up the river under water.

She turned a little tree-clad point on the north shore of the stream before coming to the surface. Then Wailéle rose and turned to look back down the river. The canoe was out of sight! Then indeed she realized that her separation was complete; that the king and his dearly-loved *Kahúna* were parted forever.

Climbing to the river-bank and seating herself in the kindred gloom of the forest, Wailéle gave way to the first great grief of her life. Only by articulate wails and a deluge of tears can a strong woman drain the depths of such a sorrow as this.

What the sun is to bud and blossom and the ripening of the fruit in the floral world, love is to woman. Without it she pines like a plant in the desert. Fill her soul—

if only for an hour—with its brightness, and she is crowned with beauty and glory as when a star is born in the sky. Rob her, when once it has been tasted, of this enchanted cup, and she quaffs instead the bitterest chalice in the whole domain of sorrow.

Burying his head in dejection, the sorrowing king bade the *wahines* speed on down the river. He sat in the stern of the canoe with his *tapa* covering drawn over his grief-stricken face, his massive hands clenched in the visible agony of a strong man who has lost his all.

Not a boat was seen on the usually busy river; not a human soul of all the ten thousand people living in the valley. The grassy banks and flowery nooks of the pleasant river were deserted. A *tabú* had been proclaimed from Mukíni for the day, by the display of the *tabú* flag from the highest tree in the forest, and it needed but a brief half hour to make the land a desert.

When the *kapu e make* was announced in the morning, while the king's canoe was made ready for his departure, the first native who saw the flag from the lower valley gave the alarm, crying lustily to all within his hearing: "*Kápu e make! kapu e make!*"

In an instant the sorrowing wail was taken up by a thousand voices, bearing the fearful knell over the whole valley in a few minutes' time. Whoever was laboring in his *taro* patch, or fishing or bathing in the river, hurried home to his thatched house, there to hide throughout the day; not knowing, nor likely ever to know, why the *tabú* had been promulgated.

Boys who had climbed a hundred feet up the swaying mast of the palm-tree, and who were twisting off cocoanuts for the coming meal, left their task half finished, slid down with precipitate haste to the ground, and fled homeward, full of wildest apprehension of the deadly *tabú* cry.

Girls swimming in flocks along the flowing river bank, sporting with one another in the crystal waters, or diving for objects among the fine dark sands of the bottom, heard the death-cry sweeping down the valley, and looked aghast into each other's faces. Darting through the water for the shore, they seized their *paus* from the bank, and ran to their homes undressed. Some ghostly monster, born of their own superstitious terrors and the *tabú* cry, pursues their lovely nude figures to their very doorways.

Fishermen out upon the sea, tanning their brown skins in the sun while they patiently watch their lines sound the tranquil waters below, caught the anguished *tabú* cry, or saw the dread flag fluttering in the land-wind from the cliff. Instantly they cut adrift from their much-prized lines, and paddled with desperation for the shore ; some, still more terror-stricken, paddled far out to sea, fearing that they were personally wanted by the Pepehi Kanáka to take part as corpses in the cruel sacrifices of the day.

What many of these sudden *tabús* are for, none but the few connected with the neighboring *heidú* ever know, or can ever guess, for the solemn behests of a priest are as well kept as the secrets of the grave.

Not even a dog or a stray hog was discovered while the king was being paddled three miles down the river. A funereal hush lay over the sequestered valley. Even the sun shrouded himself with unusual frequency behind the clouds that floated landward upon the soft trade-wind ; and the birds sang mournful strains from out their secret coverts, as if it were the sepulture of some mighty dead.

The river canoe was too frail to encounter the huge surf ever rolling upon the shore. But ample provision had been made for the occasion. A strong double canoe awaited the king's coming; it was secured to the river bank near the high intervening ridge of boulders above the beach.

In this stout **sea-going craft** the king took his seat, followed by the four priest-girls, who carefully avoided treading upon the monarch's shadow,—an offence which is death if he choose to make good the *tabú*. At a motion from the king the canoes were pushed out from the bank and down the river mouth, where they met the inrolling sea.

As they came into the spent waters of the gigantic breakers, here floundering noisily on the shore, the real peril of the attempt to pass out aroused the old monarch from his grief sufficiently for him to view the situation. He was familiar with surf from his boyhood. But through such a surf as this, thundering upon jagged rocks, he had never sought to pass before. The king seized upon a strong steering-paddle, and nerved himself to act as pilot during the dangerous passage to the sea.

By a few backward strokes of their paddles the four fearless *wahines* held the canoe in the harmless wash of the surf, and watched patiently until three of the largest successive breakers had rolled in with the shock of an earthquake, their angry roar echoing from cliff to cliff. Then, as the third breaker thundered on the beach, ere the stranded foam-bubbles had burst, the brave maidens bent to their task with a stern resolve mantling over their lovely faces, like those who appreciate the peril, but fear not the danger.

Steady and strong was the even dip of their four paddle blades. Such a triumph of quivering nerve and muscle could not but bring a smile of approval to the sad face of the king. He looked kindly upon the comely priest-girls; they were the last links between him and Wailéle.

Dashing up over the inrolling breakers with quick, strong paddle strokes, the canoe sometimes pointing to the sun, sometimes to the bottom of the sea, they weathered one after another of the great rollers. Increasing the strength of their strokes, now to port and now to starboard, as rocks barred their way, at length they gained the open sea, and headed south for a ravine five miles away.

The change from the deep cool valley to open water was marked and uncomfortable. There was a hot metallic glint on the calm surface of the sea, for though the land-breeze blew too lazily to invade the ocean far out from shore, yet the trade-wind had not yet asserted its daily power. At the end of a brief pull the king was landed in a neighboring valley, and after a brief exchange of kind farewells, the tired *wahines* put up their sail, and sped back to Waimánu without mishap.

XI.

UMI, THE GOD-BORN CHIEF.

NEARLY a year had passed since the mysterious visit of the royal chief to Mukíni. Ten happy months had sped over the devoted priestess and her pious household, ever busy with her religious duties at the altar of sacrifice, or within her shrine of prayer.

The day had been passed in observing the annual religious feast, that of the *Makahiki,* and the usual *tabú* rites of the new-year's day. The sun was now dropping down the west, and would soon be hidden behind the snow crest of Mauna Kéa. Most of the Waimánu people had already dispersed down the river in canoes, or waded in gossiping groups to their homes beyond the tabued forest, gladdened by the joyous events of the day at Mukíni.

A few privileged families of the great chiefs of the valley, those of sufficient rank to witness the final religious rites within the temple, had remained at the request of Wailéle, and were collected on the divans of mats about the altar.

The final sacrifice of the *kapu hua* was about to take place. It consisted of offerings of the first fruits and first flowers of the new-born year, which were now clustered tastefully upon the *lele* (altar), around which the six rosy priest-girls marched, themselves adorned with floral *leis* and garlands of vines. Circling about the *lele,* they sang

The God-Born Chief.

thanksgivings for the happy past and songs of greeting to the new year, ending with hopeful predictions for the future.

Wailéle, after giving her directions to the maidens, had retired into the *anu*, or shrine, there to plead with gentle Lono, the god of peace and plenty, fruit and flowers. Though in this enclosure of fine basket-work she was quite invisible, yet her supplications and her songs were distinctly heard by those without; her clear voice was in sweet accord with every melody sung by her maiden-satellites. Each one of them had been chosen, not only for her high rank, but for the rare melody of her voice.

But now, while the six *wahines* were singing the last vesper-melody of the day, chanting soft and low, as if the heart of each pious maiden were breathing her own requiem with that of the dead old year, suddenly a small new voice joined in the solemn chorus. To the astonishment of all, it came from within the shrine of prayer, making a novel discord with the sacred chant without.

It was the cry of an infant, new-born with the year! Still the voice of the priestess faltered not in a single note; she sang as if she were unaware of the precious gift bestowed upon her by the gods, the divine gift from Pele to the beautiful Priestess of Mukíni!

Surprise and astonishment mantled on the faces of the grim old chiefs and their dumpy dames. Wonder and fear seized upon the priest-girls, until every voice broke, wandered, and ceased entirely, as they stared at one another in apprehension and amazement. And the sudden, soft baby cry again piped up distinctly within the holy of holies.

It was as if a Peri from heaven had found its way to their temple, and now essayed to take part in their worship. So had some of the huge idols on the walls of the *heiau*, when prompted by the gods, opened their wooden mouths in vocal gesticulations, as if they too were appealing to the people.*

Rebuked by Wailéle's unfaltering continuation of her chant, and in fear of the displeasure of their haughty Priestess in any thing pertaining to their religious duties, one by one the six abashed young girls again dropped into song; but with wide open eyes, and ears alert for some possible evidence of Pele's supernatural apparition among them, as she had often come to their mistress in times of prayer.

When the songs and *tabú* rites were ended, one after another of the grim old chiefs and their dames rose from their seats and gathered about the central altar, each face full of pantomimic dismay. What meant the voice of the god-born child thus joining in the chorus of the altar songs?

But when their last note had died on the air, and every eye was turned upon the *anu* full of expectation of something supernatural, Wailéle flung wide the lattice door of her sacred shrine, and stepped proudly forth to confront the hundred questioning eyes.

The beautiful face of the vestal was lighted up with a glory only known to a young mother in the first hour of exultation over her new-born joy. Walking to the altar, bearing the child proudly in her arms, Wailéle placed her baby boy tenderly among the flowers. There all eyes could behold him, and become witness to his parentage on the mother's side, from which Hawáiian heredity acquires its strongest claim, whether in the

---

* It was a not uncommon trick of the priests to open and shut the mouths of idols while some apt ventriloquist did the talking.

inheritance of rank or of property. Solemnly uttering her *wandna* (prophecy), she sprinkled *wai oha* (holy water) on herself and her child, a baptismal rite.*

Dropping upon her knees in earnest prayer, the happy Priestess called aloud upon Pele with a young mother's full heart, in solemn thanksgiving and praise. While proffering her god-born boy as an *alii kapu*, she dedicated him to Pele, as one given her for the regeneration of his priest-ridden and war-worn country.

Completing this first religious rite by dedicating her child as a chief tabued to his country's shrine, Wailéle rose and took her rosy babe in arms and walked swiftly to the river, into which she plunged, joyous as a dolphin long deprived of its element. Tossing her new-born darling into the water for his first lesson in aquatics, the happy mother frolicked about her child, playful as a mother fish among her brood.

The stoical indifference of a Hawáiian infant to its customary birth-bath—though the aqueous element chance to be the briny sea—is no more wonderful than the merry mood and painless maternity of the Polynesian mother during the parturient hour.

Following the example of the glorified Priestess, after the usual custom of the country, a hundred other sportive swimmers were soon seen disporting in the river. Fat chiefs and rosy chiefesses, together with young men and maidens belonging to the great families, dipped and dove and swam about the juvenile centre of attraction.

All were eager to witness the preternatural feats of the

---

* During these pious rites the Hindu laves with sacred waters from the Ganges. The Hebraic laver was the holy water of India,—compounded of we know not what. The Hawáiian *wai oha* or holy water was simply consecrated sea-water (or salt and sulphur mixed with fresh water), and sanctified by prayer.

god-born child, who, though left to squirm and sink down upon the soft dark sands of the bottom, as a falling leaf sways and dips and flutters to the ground, was yet fearless and alert to clutch the long black hair of his sportive mother, and pull himself up to the surface as she swam upwards in playing with her darling,—as a new-born babe is as much at home under water as in the air.*

To the pertinent questions of the feminine gossips as to who conferred this charming gift upon the virgin mother—for alas, even Kanáka *wahines* can scent a delicious morsel of scandal,—Wailéle's ready answer was merry and wise :

"Pele, the goddess whom we adore! She is both godmother and godfather to my child."

And from this response the diligent gossips derived their various cues. While the affectionate priest-girls were among the foremost to believe that Umi was a god-gift from Pele, having frequently heard the supplications of their loved young mistress, praying that a god-born chief might be given to her country, one having the goodness and power to give peace to Hawáii Nei in her hour of need, thus the *wahines* spoke as of their own knowledge.

As the sun's latest beams were now glinting upon the south *páli*, and pressing his farewell kiss on the upper arc of the cataracts, the chief people came to the river bank and rubbed noses with Wailéle, blessed her child, and took their canoes and sped homeward down the

---

* As long, that is to say, as the *foramen ovale* in the infant's heart remains unclosed,—the orifice through which the prenatal circulation passes without use of the lungs—a babe may dispense with pulmonary circulation for a time after birth.

river. And what a stirring message was that which they carried forth to the outer world! Umi, the baby chief,— a god-born child,—had been given to the beautiful *Kahúna* of Mukíni; and because he was god-born, he was entitled to go nude through life, thus outranking every *alii kapu* throughout the valley of Waimánu.

During the following days thousands of eager visitors came to pay homage to Umi. All among the ten thousand in the valley who were privileged to pass the tabued line in the river blessed the beautiful boy, and heaped the Tribute Rock with willing gifts for the mother of the new-born hero, of whom so much was expected in the coming years.

Not all born of woman in other lands have found even one tender bosom to nurture them in the helpless days of infancy, in these vicious days of artificial foods. But it was this infant's happy lot to have bounteous auxiliaries in the nursery. The six vestals loved the pretty nursling devotedly; and in the intervals of their duty toward the sacred young dogs, they vied with each other in caring for Umi, their future master. So the royal urchin was fed by the seven, played with the puppies, and daily swam with dogs and *wahines* in the river; and grew, in short, as never child had grown before in the kindly vale of Waimánu.

The fame of the chief-boy's birth went out over the land, and but for the remote seclusion of the valley, countless numbers would have brought tribute to Mukíni for the godson of Pele. Every priest in the islands made frequent reference to this wondrous event, this divine mystery, glorifying the dread goddess of Kilauea.

The birth of Umi is the only modern exemplification of Pele's power in the divine conception of god-men. In the long-gone days, sung of in the ancient *meles*, this had happened. One instance occurred when Kane and Kanaloa, two ancient deities, made the first man of hot lava. When the lava cooled it was but a stone-man. But Pele breathed her spirit into the stone, the stone became flesh, the flesh breathed, and a living man took possession of the earth.

This man was named Wakea. And because Wakea looked so godlike, and the human in him was so tempting, Papa, a beautiful goddess, sought him out to enjoy his human love. She became his wife, and helped to people Hawáii according to the commands of Pele.

At infrequent times during the early summer mornings in the coming years, ere the gray mists rose above the river, or the ghost-haunted shadows fled from the approach of day, the figure of a solitary man was sometimes seen on the verge of the *páli* above Mukíni. It needed but a glance to see that he was a noble chief, standing there reverently in the gray dawn; and always by the great pandanus tree, where he had once risked his life.

The chief carried a spear, on which he leaned as on the first morning we saw him. He looked like one meditating another perilous descent into Waimánu. But a danger so terrible never wholly quits the memory; once tried it begets a strength of wisdom that surmounts even the love of a beautiful woman, or a father's yearning affection for his unseen child.

The great heart of Wailéle beat wildly as she looked up from her morning prayers, and saw the loved figure of the royal chief, who had won her young heart by his manly bearing and his dear persuasive smiles.

No wonder that she sometimes prays to the pandanus, having included it among her gods, as it ever stands

there before her eyes during her morning orisons to
Pele.* That tree had felt *his* loved hand pressed upon
its gnarled side,—the kingly hand that had stroked her
own dark hair, and patted the rose on her cheek until it
flushed as it had never flushed before.

Yet, when all unexpectedly she catches a sudden half
glimpse of the dear form on the *páli*, growing clearer and
clearer with the morning light, ah, how leaps the warm
heart in her bosom! How yearns her soul for wings to
fly to him, that she may clasp him to her heart—woman's
one dear solace for a thousand ills!

What, then, to her were all the ambitions of priesthood
to one loving moment with yon man in the heavens
above? He stood there like a god, rimmed about by
the yellow dawn-light. How she would illumine his
whole being with her wild love, could she but hold him
to her heart now beating so wildly!

When Wailéle sees she has attracted the attention of
her lover, then she catches up her baby, Umi, and holds
him aloft to view. And only she can know who it is
that looks down so lovingly upon mother and child;
holding out his arms with a very frenzy of affection for
the noble woman and the darling boy. Waving his
great war-spear in farewell salutation, as day breaks in
the upper world, the chief makes the royal sign of "*Kulia
i Ka Nuu,*" as he turns sadly away,—the secret passwords known only to high-caste priests and to the reigning kings, members of the *Ahu Alii.* †

Even with her undying love for the noble monarch,
Wailéle does not chide him for not coming again to Mu-

---

* The Hawáiians made a god of any object which attracted them,—
bird, beast, or tree.

† The Council of Nobles created by Pàáo centuries before.

kíni, and disturbing her sacred duties of priesthood with his sweet human love. And yet none better than she knows the untold value of such an affection.

Dear soul! how little it matters what the daily task may be, if the one sweet avocation of love is denied her. Whether the vassalage of women is to holy church or intriguing state, debar her of love—the alchemic element of her existence—and the heart corrodes and the soul dwindles into insignificance, deprived of its power to soar in search of the immortal.

XII.

BOYHOOD DAYS OF KAMÉHAMÉHA.

WHEN attained to his fifth year, Umi had acquired the stature of a boy of ten ; and was strong enough to wrestle, paddle, and swim with his girl companions for competitors. But in his eighth year he lightly demanded companionship with the chief-boys of the lower valley ; and a few, of noble birth, brothers of the priest-girls, were occasionally permitted to come to Mukíni. Of these well-trained boys Umi learned his first feats with warlike weapons ; together with all the manly sports needed to develop his strength and mature his mind.

Not until the age of eight did Umi meet his uncle, the High-Priest of Puukeekee. This *kahúna* was called in at that time to preside over the *Mahele* of Umi, a religious rite similar to the Hebrew custom, but usually performed upon Polynesian youth of adolescent years. It was an occasion for feasting and all kinds of athletic games for the young chiefs, with dancing and singing for the chiefesses. The next event in boy-life was the tattooing ; and this was a more painful piece of surgery than the *Mahele*.*

Umi had heard terrible things of his cruel old uncle of

---

* Kahekili, King of Maui, sent requesting that the child should be tattooed over half his body, after his own example.

Puukeekee. He was a savage old *kahúna*, addicted to drinking *awa*, and gloating over frequent human sacrifices upon the most trivial occasions. Pepehi, "man-killer," was his dreadful name, and, as we have seen, he was the most murderous *tabú kahúna* in all the land.

Wailéle had schooled her boy about his uncle. She had taught Umi to show respect to him, whatever his dislike might be for the wicked man, for to offend him seriously would be followed by a dreadful vengeance which no human being could escape.

The old priest was a *kilo-kilo*, or sorcerer, as well as a *kahúna*, and would pray his enemies to death by fiendish devices of witchcraft too foul and terrible to be described. But oftener it was his policy to set his pepehi —man-killer—to waylay and assault or kidnap the offending person; and when brought to the mountain *heiau*, Pepehi would glut his ferocity by himself slaughtering the delinquent in the name of the gods of his temple.

So wholly unscrupulous was this savage old man, that the *kahúna* of Puukeekee was quoted by Hawáiian mothers to their rebellious children, as wolves and bears are threatened in other lands. Even the king and his great chiefs dare not confront Pepehi openly, lest he should pray to his great poison god, Kalaipahoa, when they would immediately sicken and die.

This poison god, a huge idol, three times as large as life, was made from a fatal upas tree called *Nioi*, that was once found on the island of Molokai, and nowhere else. It was so deadly that a little dust scraped from the idol and put in food or drink would kill instantly. The story of this dreadful idol is thus told by Pepehi:— "Failing to find out who had procured the sickness of several great chiefs by using the 'shaking waters' and the 'broiling fire,' I dreamed one night that an idol made from the poison tree of Molokai would always disclose the wicked person; and when he was found would serve to destroy him by means of a little of its dust put into his food.

"The god in the dream said: 'Go and find the tree on Molokai.' And when I did go, and found the tree, the tree spoke to me in a frightful voice, saying: 'Priest, bring offerings and worship me. Make a great idol of me, large as two giants. Place me in Puukeekee, within the holy place, and make offering of ten men to me; and let them be fat men; and each year offer me ten more fat men, and you shall have power to know all secrets, and may kill whomsoever you choose.'"

The wicked old Pepehi did as he was bid, and henceforth the poison god of Puukeekee was the most dreadful of all the heathen idols of the islands. Arrogant chiefs came to seek its aid against rival chiefs. Wicked people from every part of the group came, seeking to be rid of their enemies. Jealous women sought its aid against profligate husbands, and unruly men against their too faithful wives, in a land where wives of the lower classes were bartered like fish and *poi*.

The treasures of the land were brought to the mountain *heiau* in exchange for a tiny pinch of dust scraped from Pepehi's poison god. Thus it became even the beautiful sister of the old *kahúna* to beware of offending such a demon, and to teach her god-born child to show him a respect that he could not feel, lest the days of his youth should be early numbered.

From the feast-day of *Mahele* to the age of ten, Umi became a moody, reflective boy. Reared among the charming priest-girls, Umi seemed to join with his whole heart in the merry sports of the *wahines;* yet in his fits of musing the boy ever yearned for more stirring scenes in the great world above Mukíni.

Until his tenth year Umi's pastimes had been those of his *wahine* playmates : sporting in the river, swimming into the caves that extended beneath its precipitous banks, diving into the deep pools from their rocky heights ; fishing, bird-hunting, berrying ; climbing the forest trees for nuts and fruits, and gathering the rarest flowers from the high-running vines ; in all of which accomplishments the agile chief-maidens were as great adepts as their young master.

But now came a time when the strong youth could out-paddle his playmate girls, dart weightier bird-spears, and twang a stronger bow than any *wahine* about the temple.*
He was no longer content with the girls and the few chief-boys who occasionally came to Mukíni. He longed to enter the coveted world down the river, and attest his youthful powers and skill with his equals.

From that day Umi was permitted to pass the forest limits and join in the sports of the Waimánus boys, though at first always accompanied by his *kahu alii*—guardian chiefess—the wise and witty Pemilani, sent to report how the noble youth conducted himself among the sons of the haughty chiefs of the lower valley.

The need of such espionage soon proved uncalled for, as the old war-chiefs showed great respect for the royal boy, and a loving reverence for his mother, while the youth of either sex could never quite divest themselves of awe while in Umi's presence, because of the divine mys-

---

* The Hawáiians never used bow and arrows as weapons of war, but only to shoot rats, mice, and birds with in pastime.

tery of his birth, of which they were ever reminded by his going unclothed from his birth.*

Though the young chief had sometimes been haughty and overbearing with his girl-mates—looking upon all womankind but his imperious mother as inferior beings,—yet the tact and keen good-sense of the boy curbed his pride of birth during every proof of athletic skill with his mates in Waimánu.

Umi's superiority in all feats of strength over boys of nearly twice his own age was soon evident. It was taken as a thing to be expected in one of his exalted rank and divine birth. But his modesty was equally remarkable. It charmed his companions to loving him.

It thus happened that in a few years the courteous manner and judicious conduct of the young prince won him a strong following of chief-boys from among the noblest families of Waimánu. To these Umi told his ambitious day-dreams, instilling into their hot blood something of his own ambition for the strife of battle, and of his love of glory in noble deeds.

Thus passed the uneventful years of the youth. Among the mystic doings and religious rites of the pagan temple grew up this strange wise boy. From his reflective and retiring habit he received the title, now so famous, of KAMÉHAMÉHA,† or "The Lonely One."

His juvenile mind was ever alert to question the mysteries of Mukíni. He watched and wondered over the

---

* To go naked in public was deemed either a sign of madness or the mark of divine birth. Kings were sometimes attended by these nude men, sprung from the gods. The people said: "*He akua ia*," he is a god.—(See M. Remy's "Venerable Savage," p. 15.)

† Pronounced Kah-may' hah-may' ha, with the accent on the second and fourth syllables. Kahekili falsely claimed to have named the boy after his elder brother, King Kamehamehanui.

pious acts of the priestly mother he adored, and sometimes he questioned the lesser statellites who had been the nurse-girls of his childhood and the loved playmates of his youth. He grew fast beyond their companionship; yet as they had loved and nurtured the bright-eyed boy, so they now looked with pride, and almost with adoration, upon the manly chief, whose voice had become deep and resonant, and was now as musical as a bird-song to their ears.

So often had he heard that his mother had personal interviews, on momentous occasions, with Pele, that his desire to behold the dread goddess became the all-pervading thought of his life. This desire so grew upon him that it begot an ardent wish to join Wailéle in her daily worship at Pele's shrine. It also impelled him to acquire greater proficiency in the art of war, that he might attract Pele's attention by deeds of valor.

Often when "The Lonely One" sought the deep seclusion of the adjacent forest, and climbed to the topmost boughs of the great *ohia* trees, he climbed less to pluck the crimson apples than with intent to harmonize his young mind with the silence and the mystic bird-notes of his deep-foliaged retreat, ever hopeful that he might some time call down Pele from her mountain throne in the mighty crater of fire. Or, if this great revelation could not be, perhaps some of her lesser gods would answer the ambitious promptings of his heart. Fear of supernatural things, good or evil, was never an ingredient of Kaméhaméha's soul. His constitutional fearlessness was derived from his mother. Already it was needed, for many and startling were the revelations that now dawned upon him as he lay pondering in the tree-tops.

The Ghost-Loving Boy.

Ghostly apparitions sometimes peopled the Waimánu forest; whisperings like distant bird-songs vibrated upon the stillness, full of answers to his questionings.

When once the least vision of the hidden *arcanum* is made known to us, then its remotest mystery awaits our endeavors. It was so with Umi. When at length he propounded to the mystic powers about him solemn questions pertaining to his coming life-work, answers were vouchsafed by the Invisibles.

Thus with his mother's wise teachings in the gloom of the *heiáu*, and his own enquiries made in the ghost-haunted valley, Umi came to the knowledge of many mysteries. Such was his courage, and so eager was he to know the supernatural, that he now nightly sought the basins where the resounding cataracts fell, where grim, shadowy apparitions of long-gone *kahúnas* swim in the black pools and ride down the falls from the rocky fastnesses above.* But the long-coveted vision of Pele still continued to elude the keenest scrutiny of his ear and eye.

Failing in his persistent purpose of an interview with the gods, which had now become the strongest motive of his life, Umi finally contemplated a pilgrimage to the volcano of Kilauea, the dread habitation of the supreme Goddess of Hawáii.

When the boy's courageous design was unfolded to his mother, the proud woman's heart showed its delight in her eyes. Holding out her beautiful brown arms, Wai-léle caught the manly boy to her bosom, forgetting the austere manners of a *kahúna* of Pele. The mother's love overmastered the dignity of priesthood for the mo-

---

* The *Au Makua*, ghost spirits of dead ancestors which the Hawáiians think remain on earth.

ment; she wept tears of joy over the ambitious daring of her Umi. For none but stern priests and the bravest of men dared venture upon such a pilgrimage alone, least of all when bent upon a midnight interview with the Goddess of the Volcano.

On that auspicious day the brave boy of twelve was officially made an *alii kapu*, or tabu chief, with solemn rites; three other chief-boys were also confirmed. A strict *tabú* was promulgated throughout the valley on the occasion, and a few of the great chief-families were called in to take part in the ceremony. Proper oblation was made to Pele, and a large *puaa hea* (sacred hog) was offered in sacrifice upon the altar.

As the company knelt about the sacred *lele* where the offering was being roasted, and the grateful odor of the sandal-wood fire filled the dome-shaped temple, the Priestess and her six *wahines* marched round the altar singing anthems to the Goddess. Within the charmed circle knelt the four handsome chief-boys, joining in the hymn, while the audience from the lower valley knelt in an outer circle round about them all.

The heart of Umi in that exultant hour burst the bonds of boyhood; henceforth his was a boy's heart no more. To treat a youth with wise consideration above his years, is to exalt him into the proud domain of manhood. Umi was confirmed as tabu-chief; as Kaméhaméha, "The Lonely One," because by that newly acquired name the unseen spirits had always addressed him. This was thought to be ominous of good.* The names of the three other *alii kapu* were Kameeimoku,†

---

* The family name of his mother, Kakuiapoiwa, was added to his own to constitute his full title.

† This chief was the noble ancestor of King Kalakaua, and one of

Kamanawa, and Miomio. They all in after-years became most efficient warriors under the reign of their young master.

After the ceremony about the *lele* had been completed, the Priestess immured herself in the *wahi kapu*, or sacred place, to hold personal communion with Pele, and to transmit the oracles, whether signs or sayings, to the kneeling audience without.

It was hours before the Goddess deigned to answer the supplications of her loved Kahúna. But at length the divine message came from the far-away crater, *Halemau-mau*, and with joyful heart was interpreted to Kaméhaméha and his boy-companions:

"Aloha! love and greeting to Wailéle of Mukíni! Pele discovers a new worshipper at her shrine in the deep vale of Waimánu. It was good to make the godborn youth an *alii kapu*; for he is not a stranger to the gods about Kilauea. A great destiny is recorded for Kaméhaméha on my tablets of fire. Witness whoever hath eyes! Because of this event yet another peak shall be added to the six snow crests of Mauna Kéa; an eternal token that 'The Lonely One' is loved of the gods, and shall rule among men.

"Aloha! my *kahúna*. Aloha! my *keike alii*" (king's son).

As long waiting brought no further response for the other boy chiefs, Wailéle came out from the sacred place, and after embracing her son, led the way without the *heiáu* to see if Pele's word was fulfilled.

All eyes were instantly turned to the majestic mountain top, towering three miles into the air above the

---

Kaméhaméha's most formidable warriors. He captured the "Fair American," whose cannon won several battles during the conquest.

valley, and with a shout of joy it was announced by every voice: "'T is there! 't is there!"

And there indeed was a *seventh snow-crowned peak*,* pointing with icy finger to the blue heavens; the eternal sanction of the gods to the forthcoming greatness of Kaméhaméha, the god-born son of Wailéle Kakuiapoiwa.

From that hour till the day of his death Kaméhaméha lived in closest bonds of brotherhood with those three knight-companions. The first of the number became the noble ancestor of a new dynasty of kings who came to the throne a century later.†

---

* On the truncated top of Mauna Kéa, within a circumference of six miles, there are seven snow-capped peaks, from 800 to 1,000 feet high; the central and westernmost peaks being the highest.

† Kameeimoku and Kamanawa were the tabued twins of Kekaulike, of Maui, and were thus half-brothers of Kahekili, the reigning king; who, when he heard the wonderful promise of Kaméhaméha, sent these two royal *aliis* to become his life-long *kahus*, or guardian companions. This is evidence that Kahekili greatly loved Wailéle, and perhaps really believed that her ardent love had inspired her to invoke the deities for a god-born hero.—("Polynesian Races," p. 261.)

XIII.

HUMAN SACRIFICE IN THE TEMPLE.

KAMÉHAMÉHA'S second interview with his savage old uncle was at the ripening age of ten. Their first introduction had been two years before, during the religious rite of *Mahele*, when the grim old Kahúna performed the right of circumcision for his nephew.

Pepehi now came to the valley on business with the great war chiefs, demanding more tribute from their rich vale for the *heidu* of Puukeekee. Coming to Mukíni to visit his sister—the only being of whom he was proud,—the keen-eyed old monster started with surprise to see what a promising lad Kaméhaméha had become. He at once suggested that the boy should return with him to his mountain *heidu*.

Wailéle blanched to an ashy paleness at the thought of parting with her boy, trembling to think of consigning him to such murderous hands. For there were now indications of a temper developing in her boy that she feared to think of. He had fits of passion upon small provocation when the rights of others were encroached upon, though he was rarely aroused by any intrusion upon his own rights. The passionate boy would often burst into tears at the suffering of others; but he bore pain like a Stoic himself.

How could a mother trust such a boy with Pepehi,— one so sensitive to the suffering of others, so ferocious in righting others' wrongs? Yet the intuitive tact of the wise woman came to her aid, and she remembered the yet greater danger of arousing the venomous dislike of the old Kahúna, which would become a more certain peril to her darling.

At their previous interview the hideous old priest had failed to inspire the boy either with respect for his holy office, or fear of his man-killing propensities. Such want of reverence, if shown by any other youth, would have aroused the deadly hatred of the old Kahúna. But at that time the crusty priest seemed to enjoy the imperious spirit of his loved sister's child, and instead of the boy's doings awakening vindictiveness, they rather quickened Pepehi's interest in the precocious youth, and awakened something almost akin to love for the fearless boy.

If the arrogant old man chid the child for disobedience to some savage command, the dark eyes of the chief-boy flashed with fierceness equal to his own. And not until the corrugated face of the priest softened into a smile of approbation at the boy's fearlessness, would Umi do the thing he had been bidden.

Sometimes the mystified old priest would snatch the boy to his arms and fondle him with almost paternal tenderness.

At such times Umi, always won by affection, would suffer his uncle to stroke his dark hair with his long lank fingers, stained with the blood of a thousand victims, and grown talon-like by strangling men with tigerish delight to see them die.

How strange it seems that even the most cruel soul will sometimes disclose a beam of affection—coming like a sun burst from a storm-cloud—when thus confronted with the spontaneous witchery of a noble child. It is the one reminder which takes him back to the prattling days at the mother's knee.

Never in the knowledge of man was this crusty old Kahúna known to love any one but his beautiful sister and her fearless child. But the kindly impulse was ever brief, and produced a terrible reaction. The monster always selected some innocent victim for sacrifice on his way back to Puukeekee, as the peculiarly colored smoke of his altar fire made known immediately after his return.

The priest's fondness for the boy resulted in giving him not a little information about the upper world with which he so longed to mingle in the great events of life. Pepehi taught him, among other things, the origin and history of the ancient *tabú*. His first lesson, imparted at the *Mahele* as part of the religious rite, was as follows:—

"The tenets of the original *tabú*," said the Priest, "are these:"

"1. Certain rights are *tabú* to the king, and certain other rights to the queen. So with all men and their wives.

"2. Woman shall not eat with man, else she die.

"3. The first fish, fruit, and flesh is consecrated to the gods, and it is death for woman to eat thereof.

"4. Build *heiaus* to Ku, Lono, Kane, Kaneloa, and Pele, and worship the 40,000 idols. Temples are *tabú* to women except they are born of an *alii kapu*, and dedicate their lives to priesthood.

"5. Pork, bananas, cocoa-nuts, turtle, and all rare kinds of fish are *tabú* to women, and instant death shall overtake her if she eat thereof.

"6. There shall be four regular *tabús* in the month, which must be strictly kept lest the gods rend our island with their wrath:

"a. *Kapu-Ku*, the set or fixed *tabú*, at *Hilo* or the new moon, and for two nights after.

"b. *Kapu-Hua*, the fruit *tabú*, at *Mohalu*, or the first gibbous moon, and one night after.

"c. *Kapu-Kaola*, the cooking *tabú*, for the two nights from *Olepau*, or the second gibbous moon, coming after the full.

"d. *Kapu-Kane*, the man *tabú*; for the three nights from *Kane* to *Mauli*, when a man must be sacrificed in every *heiáu* of Pele."

This first lesson from Pepehi was kept fresh in Kaméhaméha's memory by the priest-girls, as even a boy is held responsible for breaking a *tabú* after his *Mahele*.

Though the noble chief-boy could be overbearing to one of dictatorial manners, or unjust assumption, like the priest, yet he possessed an innate courtesy and an intuitive dignity of speech when in the presence of people noble by birth or made eminent by heroic achievements. This ingenious perception of character by children is of unfailing accuracy. In the young chief it was derived from his high-born mother.

It will be seen that there was abundant cause for Wailélc's anxiety in trusting such a sensitive boy in the hands of one so inconsiderate as her hard-hearted old brother. Nevertheless, as the least of present evils, it was thought best to consent to the lad's going with his uncle. And with a proud mother's appeal for watchful care and safe return, Kaméhaméha was permitted to go with the priest.

Parting from his mother and the weeping priest-girls at the river side,—with last words of warning from all in the ears of the boy,—the craft sped down the river to the sea-shore, where stout men with a stout sea-going canoe awaited the Kahúna. Though born in the valley, it was the first time that Kaméhaméha had ever been to the river mouth. It was all a new world to him. And he was soon to climb the mountain which he had worshipped as a shrine from out his valley home.

Their perilous dash through the surf and quick movements to avoid the rocks, which shówed in the trough of the seas like monsters lurking for prey, was a severe test to the boy's courage. The eyes of the old Kahúna were upon him, curious to watch this first trial of his mettle in the presence of a new danger. But to this god-born youth the moving grandeur of the breakers, and the turbulent fret and whirl of the foam as it towered above them, rolling shoreward with power sufficient to jar the cliffs, was an inspiring scene. The flash of his eye and the curl of his lip showed something of the wild exultation which possessed him.

Landing at the next valley southward from Waimánu, from which egress was found leading up the mountain side, the gnarled old Kahúna and the strong, active boy climbed their toilsome way up to Puukeekee. The priest expressed surprise at the endurance of the lad, who lent a strong hand to assist the waddling steps of his uncle.

As they sat down to rest after the tussle up the steepest places, the Kahúna took occasion to sound the thoughts of his bright-eyed nephew. Gratified by what he said, and perhaps by the comfort of having such a helpful hand in time of need—for there is too often a modicum of selfishness in the benefactions of a loving uncle,—the cunning old wretch hinted at the probability of making a high-priest of the boy, if he should prove respectful and obedient. Some one, clearly, would have to take the Kahúna's place in the near future; for though he was still strong and lusty, his years were many.

But Kaméhaméha had taken his lesson from his mother. He regarded the situation as one suitable for his first attempt at diplomacy, though the odds of Pepehi's age and long experience were much against the boy. Without rudely rejecting the proposal, he left the wily old Kahúna to believe that he would favorably consider the matter, and defer his decision until he should be old enough to choose for himself. This was a mistaken, even a dangerous, step to take in dealing with a man in power. Difficulties in life are easiest strangled in their infancy. The danger may be destroyed by a word fitly spoken at the time; but difficulties grow with delay, and often become matter for contending armies.

Within his wise young head the chief-boy despised the cruel old priest, and hated the brutal manner in which he perpetrated his butcheries for sacrifice. And perhaps it would have amazed the Kahúna to know that the boy had already mapped out a larger and loftier field of action than priesthood for his young ambition. Little did he dream that "The Lonely One" aspired to become, not the head of a heathen *heiáu*, but "The Lord of the Four Seas," as the broad channels between the Hawáiian Islands are called, and monarch of the entire group.

As quiet reigned at the *heiáu* for several days after the young Alii's arrival, Pepehi took the trouble to initiate his prospective heir into the deeper mysteries of the *tabú*. He was surprised to find how readily the youth comprehended its crafty policy as applied to governing the church and strengthening the state. To make thorough work the aged priest began at the creation of the world.

"Boy, if you are to become the *Kahúna maole* of Puukeekee, you must know all things from the beginning. For a Kahúna must also be a *mo-o-le-lo*—historian—as Pepehi has been the Moo-Kahúna of Hawáii in his day.

"In the beginning, the first thing was *Poeleele*, or Night. It was so dark that when the volcano was not burning the earth was black everywhere about.

"Wakea was our first parent, the Adam of the world. He was made by the gods from hot lava, to which Pele gave life of her life, and she saw her work was good. As man was not made to see in the darkness, when Loa was not burning, Pele sent to Tahiti for *La*,*—the sun. When Kana first brought the bright thing home to Hawáii, it was hung aloft in the sky, as you see it now. Papa, a goddess of great beauty, saw Wakea and loved him, and the man took the divine creature for his wife, and she bore him many children.

"The *tabú* was originated by Satan and Wakea, the king. The *tabú* was made to cover the great original sin of our first parent. After a hundred years of happy wedded life, Papa bore her last daughter, a child of remarkable beauty. Hoohuku-kalani was as beautiful as your mother; so attractive was the girl that when she grew up, Wakea, her own father, came to look on her with unnatural affection, and told the queen he should marry her.

"The jealous Papa became justly indignant, and forbade the incestuous act; and threatened terrible vengeance from the gods with whom she was connected. But the wicked Kahiko, king of *Milu*, the lower world, appeared to Wakea and tempted him on to evil.

"Wakea demanded of the archfiend a religious creed which should permit man to put away his wife and marry

---

* This word is probably identical with the Sanskrit *Ra*.

whom he liked. Kahiko devised the *kapu* for the benefit of the king and the coming priests (for there were no priests until after that time), and he succeeded so well that Wakea made him High-Priest of Hawáii, because of satanic services.

"Hence arose the *tabú* system, which made the priest vicegerent of the gods, and compelled man to sacrifice his fellows as the wages of sin. It imparts power to inflict death on whomsoever evades the oracles of the gods as transmitted through the priests. The *tabú* grants polygamy to men and polytheism to women. It prohibits women eating with their husbands, and forbids her many of the best kinds of food. This I taught you at the Mahele.

"*Tabú* sanctions separation of husband and wife at the pleasure of the man. It permits the union of father and daughter, brother and sister, and the marriage of one man to many sisters,* all of which unnatural bonds are now held in great esteem among the high chiefs in all the islands.

"As may be seen, priest-power has sometimes become strong enough to overshadow and overthrow the secular power, making use of some divine mandate imparted by the gods. Hence, to elevate kings above the malice and cunning intrusion of priest-craft in affairs of state, monarchs now assume the sacred title of *Alii Kapu*—tabu chief—and take upon themselves the headship of church as well as state.

"For appearance' sake the *kahúna-nui* (high-priest)

---

* Which unholy tenet Kaméhaméha subsequently made good use of by marrying three sisters from one royal family, Kaahumanu being the first. And great was her indignation when Kalakua was brought home as a second bride; soon followed by Namahana, the third sister, all daughters of Keeaumoku.

Human Sacrifice. 113

is always suffered to occupy the *anu* (holy of holies) during religious ceremonies, while the king and great chiefs sit without to interpret the oracle—and perhaps recast the god-given message for the people which the petty chiefs are to distribute to the heralds outside of the *heiáu*.

"I will now make known the *tabú* rules of sacrifice at the death of a king or great chief. Before the corpse is removed from the death-bed, one man is sufficient for sacrifice. If taken from the house where he died, four Kanákas are required to satisfy the gods. If sacrifice is delayed until the grave is prepared, then ten men are called for. But if the corpse is already deposited in the sepulchre, then fifteen Kanákas must be immolated to appease the growing anger of the gods; and if the delay is made for one day after the priest has promulgated a general *tabú* over the land, then forty men must die, or the island will be rended in twain with earthquakes, and the volcanoes will devastate the land with their rivers of fire."

Just here the tipsy old Kahúna fell asleep, for he had been constantly sipping *awa* and eating sugar-cane, while he was instructing his nephew.

These days of quiet were soon followed by sudden activity, caused by news of the death of a great chief at Waipio, the residence of the king. The herald who brought the news was soon followed by natives from Waipio, bringing baked hogs, dogs, and *poi*, sent as tributes to the priest and to his people about the *heiáu*.

But Pepehi's man-killers had chanced to be at Waipio when the death occurred; and a few hours afterward they came to Puukeekee, each one of them dragging a Kanáka by a lasso, ready for the coming sacrifice. The faithful servants had not waited orders from their master to select their victims for the coming obsequies.

When a lean fellow was brought in, the priest muttered a frightful malediction on the head of the executioner who brought him. But the next being fat and young—a toothsome subject—the murderous old Kahúna rubbed his shrivelled hands with the utmost satisfaction. Eagerly seizing a *laau palau*, or war-club, he beat out the brains of his victim with the ferocious eagerness of a shark who tears his prey.

One young Kanáka, who had been entrapped at some distance up the mountain, was brought in dead, having become exhausted from fear and rough usage. This handsome young fellow was from Waimánu. It was his business to gather *pulu* (fern wool) from the fern trees on the mountain, and he had been caught while descending with his load of the golden fibre, which is used for stuffing pillows and cushions.

Kako was a brother of one of the priest-girls, and had been a friend of our hero. Kaméhaméha questioned the inebriated priest why so good a man should perish because of the death of a stranger chief at Waipio? The exigency of the state was the only reason, said the priest. And having given this explanation, he added in a surly voice: " Remember, boy, you were born a chief. Never forget to uphold the privileges of your class without a question."

The live prisoners who were not wanted for immediate use were bolted into a strong stone cell in one of the great rock-built pyramids. There the poor wretches awaited their turn to be disembowelled and roasted on the altar. Once entrapped, none are ever reprieved except by order of the king or some powerful chief.

The dead were prepared for sacrifice as sheep for the shambles, piled one beside another on the altar with the pigs and dogs to insure the quick passage of the departed soul to the realms of *Akua*. This part of a priest's duties was usually well performed; for he dreaded the dual ghost-soul which otherwise might remain on earth to strangle the enemy of the dead.

Altogether this was too sickening a scene for the young chief to look upon, and as the priest was too busy gloating over the victims to watch him, Kaméhaméha passed quietly out of the *heidu* and kept secluded in the mountain until the dreadful sacrificial scene was over.

Not quite daring to go home to Waimánu without permission from the old Kahúna, Kaméhaméha returned to the *heidu* for his uncle's leave. To all appearance he had not been missed by the blood-stained wretches, every one of whom had gorged himself with human flesh, roasted to the turn that suited the experienced palate of each.

At the chief's request for permission to depart, the surly old Kahúna bid him begone, muttering that the dog-fed cub was too pampered to relish human flesh. But the priest so far aroused himself as to think of the boy's safety, for his mother's sake, and ordered one of the least drunk of his executioners to accompany the lad, lest some other of his man-killers should entrap the youth, deeming him a good subject for a roast at Puukeeke.

From the *pepehi* who escorted him down the mountain, Kaméhaméha learned that thirteen victims had been caught, or killed and left where they were slain; five out of the number having been disembowelled and sacrificed. The brutal man-killer inadvertently admitted that the choice of subjects for immolation was always made with a view to obtaining a tender morsel for the priest's palate.

XIV.

MIDNIGHT INCANTATIONS AMONG THE GHOSTS.

GLAD indeed was the anxious priest-mother to see her boy again after his visit to Puukeekee. She knew by the smoke that a human sacrifice was taking place at the *heidu*, and well she understood what her boy must look upon ere his return. The priestess remembered her own childhood, and the sickening horrors that she had seen, though her father, the venerable Kahúna of Mukíni, had never permitted unnecessary brutality with his victims during *kapu kane*. Pepehi's love of cruelty, even in boyhood, had led his father to send him to his uncle at Puukeekee, whose place the young priest took when the uncle died; while Wailéle had been trained for the priesthood of Mukíni before the death of her father.

Sad were the mother's reflections when told of the savage demeanor of Pepehi to her boy, the effect of intoxicating *awa*. When Kaméhaméha told of the sacrifice of the Waimánu native, a piteous wail filled the temple for the dead, for he was a near relative of one of the priest-girls, and they knew him well. The grief-stricken girl was permitted to go down the river in a canoe to acquaint his parents and friends with the dead boy's cruel end.

Pepehi's design of making Kaméhaméha the high-priest of the *heidu* was not approved by Wailéle, and his exasperation when refused would involve a deadly peril which must be provided for at any risks. Wailéle could only repeat that he must be gently dealt with, put off from time to time, until—until——

Why his mother should so frequently end her wise injunction so abruptly, and why her lovely face should flush at what was left untold, the dutiful boy could not conjecture. In answer to his questioning glance she would always fold him in her arms and whisper: "Some time my noble boy shall know all. It is enough now to know that you are very dear to your mother."

Kaméhaméha was urged to give daily attention to acquiring the utmost proficiency in the arts of warfare, that whatever the occasion and whoever his foe might be, he should be found equal to the emergency. Little need was there of prompting her lusty chief-boy, who was already the champion of the valley, and who soon after his return from Puukeekee acquired the new name of *Puhikapa*—"Strangler of sea-snakes."

This cognomen arose from the boy's attacking a snake-like monster which came into the river and drove everybody out in dismay. He grappled with the frightful creature and killed him. It was one of many instances of the boy's remarkable strength. In after years he could crush a man's skull or break his leg by the mere grip of his gigantic hands.

Waimánu Valley had a high reputation for skilled warriors, and the lad could find no better teachers than in his native valley. And that the god-born chief of Mukíni gave such attention to learning the use of war weapons imparted a new impulse to athletic and martial exercises.

A recent disastrous battle with the king of Maui made

it probable that a new accession of young warriors would soon be called for, and all were eager to go. Kaméhaméha's remarkable proficiency stimulated new valor in every chief-boy in the valley.

So the next coming years passed, and the chief-boy of Mukíni grew to be a young giant; not only herculean in strength and stature, but fearless of every known form of danger. His dexterous power in the use of arms amazed the grim old war-chiefs of the valley. He was so cool and unflinching in the presence of danger, so agile and flexible in his movements that a dozen sharp spears could be hurled furiously at his naked breast without touching him. This game of spears became a daily pastime for the heroic boy. It was an exercise requiring strong nerves, steady eye, and a marvellous motility. To duck, dodge, swerve, or to stand immovable when a well-directed spear was to be parried or caught in the hand instead of being avoided,—these were the accomplishments which decided for life or death in the combats of the Hawáiian warriors.*

Kaméhaméha had now become so popular that he already had a following of more than a hundred young chiefs from among those of highest rank in Waimánu. Though he became the champion athlete of them all, he still remained modest enough to seek out the famed old war chiefs and practise to catch their special quality of fence or thrust, or to learn their management of the massive war clubs, by which they had won many a battle.

Yet with all the boy's love of warlike exercise and knowledge of state-craft, the fierce, strong lad liked well

---

* A dozen or more spears would be cast at a chief, which he could nimbly avoid or catch and hurl back upon the foe.—("Jarves' History," page 66.)

to be with his mother on all special occasions of worship. He questioned Pele and the other gods, with the aim of learning so to comport himself that he might be blessed with a vision of the supreme deity of Hawáii. All this was as practically thought out as his art of war ; for, if he were to be a leader in the land, he wished access to divine wisdom ; he needed that every act of his life might be directed by the gods ; for nothing short of supreme power would satisfy his ambition for fame.

Even at this age the young *Alii* was wise enough to know that he must first become a priest-chief, or a chief warrior, in order to attain the supreme power that he sought. Which should it be ? This was a question that he wished the gods to decide for him.

With such grave problems ever in his mind, no wonder "The lonely One" frequented the old *heidu* at hours when all others were asleep. Kneeling by torchlight successively to every gigantic idol in the temple, the fearless chief nightly sought to conjure up some dark spirit, good or evil, from whom he could elicit some guiding precept.

Sometimes he would leave his bed to steal into the lonely *heidu* and uncover its most secret sepulchres, caverned beneath the stone niches where stood the great idols in the thirty-foot wall. Exhuming the long-buried bones of some famous war-chief,* he placed them upon one of the three altars, and invoked the war-ghost of him who had owned them, seeking to conjure up that one of the dual souls which lingered about the dead remains. How his heart beat and his eyes gleamed, as he watched

---

* The long bones of great chiefs were tied up in bundles, wrapped in black *tapa* cloth and decorated with red or yellow feathers according to their rank.

in the darkness for dread spirits to confront him in answer to his summons! What incentive he gained from these incantations in the *heiáu*, the forest haunts, or among the dreadful catacombs behind the water-falls, we may never know. But these midnight visits to the several ghoul-haunted places were the severest tests of human courage; and they served well to prepare the fearless chief for the more fearful experiences that awaited him.

The time had now come when Kaméhaméha could no longer be restrained from seeking Pele in her dread palace of fire. To a Hawáiian the *Hale-mau-mau*— "house of everlasting fire"—is a place too dreadful for any but a *kahúna* to think of approaching, unless to lay their dead friends by the crater and hasten away with fear. To intrude upon this sacred habitation of Pele for an interview was a thing unheard of. But the fear of personal danger from the gods was far from his thoughts. He was a *tabú* chief, and from his knowledge of the *tabú* creed was far above the low superstitions of his playmates. By his mother's advice his pilgrimage should be made alone. She taught him that the gods never show themselves to the multitude.

Pele had promised the pious priest-mother to receive her boy, if he should be found worthy; but by what tests he was to be tried in her fiery realm not even the priestess could tell. Provided with a heavy *tapa* to shield him against the night cold on the mountain, a pair of sharkskin sandals, and a single baked *kalo* root slung to his spear for provision in a place where no food but wild berries could be found, the brave boy parted with the household and sprang into his canoe. Only his much-loved Pemilani accompanied him to bring back the *waa* (canoe) from the shore.

At the river mouth a thousand friendly people were gathered to see their god-born chief depart on his pilgrimage to Pele. Some of the more timid chief-boys begged their loved leader not to go, relating well-founded stories of many who had never come back. Other bolder chiefs among the youthful heroes wrung his hand with affection; rubbing noses with high admiration of his courage, and offering appreciative sympathy.

Sheltered in boat-houses belonging to the Mukíni there were always strong double canoes, with crews attached to each. But when Kaméhaméha had made his choice, and the paddlers had launched the canoe in the river, a hundred of the noblest chief-boys begged him to choose his crew from among them, and to let them paddle him wherever he wished to go. Fearing to offend the many by such a choice the sagacious chief named one leader, and bade him select a crew of twenty paddlers. This done he made a brief address to all; then leapt into his canoe and ordered his young nobles to dip paddles and away.

Passing through the surf without accident, the canoe skirted the shore to the west, seeking the most available place to land on the rock-bound coast. Laupahoehoe offered a passable landing, and the canoe was shot into the small creek. Bidding good-bye to his companions and receiving an affectionate *aloha* from all, Kaméhaméha watched them pass safely back through the surf, and then took his way upward toward the mountain valley of Waimea, across which lay his path to the crater of Kilauea.

At length the tired boy climbed to the northern foothills of Mauna Kéa, and sat down on the green slope of the mountain in ardent contemplation of the marvellous new world spread out at his feet. To the eastward lay the Eden lands of Waipio and Wiamánu, ever fresh and fruitful, three thousand feet below him, in strongest contrast to the barren desolation about Kawaihae Bay on the rainless western coast. To the southward lay the green rolling valley of Waimea—a high plateau,—bounded on the east, south, and west by gigantic mountains. The lofty dome of Mauna Loa rose heavenward thirty miles away in the south, its two gigantic volcanoes now slumbering in brief quiescence. Still farther away appeared the blue heights of Hualala, while towering above his head, higher than both, was reared the sun-gilded snow crest of Mauna Kéa, the loftiest monarch of them all.

What rapture filled the young chief's heart as he drank in the scene before him! The mountains and the boundless blue ocean begirting his island home! It was probably the grandest panoramic view in all the world. There is an unrivalled grandeur, an almost human semblance of conscious pride, visible in Hawáii's lofty mountains,—an aspect of eternal peace and majestic repose, a sublimity only vouchsafed to the mountains of the gods. Seen against the enchanting blue of the upper air, thus crowned with the snows of ages, the venerable mountains look grandly down over the green land and the blue Pacific, gold-fringed with sunset clouds, until they impress the beholder with a sense of their spiritual kinship with man.

What wonder that the enthusiastic boy's young soul was filled with beauty, as when the golden portals open to admit the blessed!

Just before sunset the brilliant arch of the vast rainbow spanned the evening sky. Bisecting the sun-tinted snow crown of Mauna Kéa, its northern foot rested on the tree-clad mountain top of Kohala, while far in the south it touched the plain of Waimea at the foot of Mauna Loa.*

Time passed swiftly as the Waimánu boy pondered over the picture. At length the gorgeous spirits of a tropic night gathered in the west to bid farewell to the departing sun. It was the first true sunset Kaméhaméha had ever beheld, for from the deep valley where he was reared the mountain shut out the sun in mid-afternoon. And now for the first time he saw the whole west arrayed in its glory. Robed in chameleon colors of purple, crimson, and gold, the scene was so beautiful that he knelt down and clasped his hands in fervent prayer to the Deity—to some great unknown God of whom he had never been taught. A flush of awe crept over him as he witnessed the final parting of the sun. It seemed as if he were spying down on a sacred meeting of spirits, and saw them change their festal robes to funeral vestments, as the dying dolphin doffs his gaudy hues and dons the purple raiment of death.

The fires of sunset were hardly dimmed in the west before the full moon rose resplendent over Kohala Point, gilding the calm waters of Kawaihae Bay until it glimmered like a mirror. So clear was the twilight air, so cloudless the purple hue of the evening sky, that the snow-capped mountains shone like silver thrones over the tranquil land. Peaceful were the thoughts awakened by the ennobling scene in the reverent chief-boy. His ambitious schemes of future greatness took on the hue of the tranquil night and the hallowed hour.

---

* Various travellers have seen this remarkable rainbow spanning Kéa at sunset, a reflection cast up from the glassy waters of Kawaihae Bay.

How long the young *Alii* mused he knew not. Suddenly the low rumble of an earthquake was heard reverberating in the distance. The whole island rocked until trees swayed and fell, cliffs loosened and rolled valley-ward with a sullen thunder. A strange illumination now burst upon the night and flung its angry glare athwart the sky. Preluded by the earthquake, Loa had rent his rocky mountain top, and was now hurling his red fountain a thousand feet above the snowy dome.

Flickering and flaring against the shimmering gloom of moonlight, the red lava glare shone far out over the ocean, two hundred miles toward every point of the compass, and lighting the quivering landscape as by a sudden sunburst. And soon the fountain stream of lava could be seen rushing headlong across the white snow line and down the rocky declivity in the direction of Hilo, fast broadening into a wide river of fire which engulfed every thing beneath it. Awakened by the earthquake, ten thousand people came forth from the villages of Kohala to gaze upon the eruption ; the dismal wail of their voices came creeping up the mountain like the roar of breakers from an angry sea.

Before the eruption had disturbed his quiet reflections, Kaméhaméha had watched the rising moon glinting softly down the Upolu Sea, driving the shadows away from the western shore, and turning the spirit-peopled night into a softer day. Absorbed in the tranquil scene before him, his young heart was prompted to seek greatness only through humanity to his fellow-man.

But alas! what a change now came over the boy; as he watched the furious flash of Pele's red scimitar in the evening sky ! He saw the gory stroke of the volcanic fire gash through the placid waters of Kawaihae Bay, and smite the night gloom far out over the ocean, and it roused a new-born lion in the chief-boy's heart,—a ruthless demon which evermore possessed his soul. In an instant the vaunting ambition of the young hero overleaped all barriers to a throne. The calm, ennobling influence of the tropic night was gone ; gone were his pensive musings on human greatness won through human goodness. Forever gone were all the schemes of the hour before, when the moon and the star-flecked sky imbued his young soul with peace and good-will.

Never again from that terrible moment did Kaméhaméha's fierce ambition cease to lure him on to achieve the utmost greatness in the compass of his island world. In that hour of Loa's volcanic fury, the fearless boy conceived his first idea of approaching Pele in her loftiest abode of fiery splendor, the summit crater of *Moku-a-weo-weo*,[*] an abyss over which the foot of mortal had never stood, scorning the dreadful legend : "Whoever approaches the summit craters shall be turned to stone!"

He was thus prompted to give up his intended visit to Kilauea, Pele's usual abode, by the current belief that the goddess could only be found where the volcanic action was the most furious. There he would climb to confront her, that she might either prompt or condemn his schemes of greatness.

From that weird hour, for Kaméhaméha to conceive a plan of action, was but brief prelude to some bold act of accomplishment. Without even waiting for daylight, the chief-boy now sought the wild trail across Waimea that led toward Mauna Loa. He vowed to abide there until he could win full recognition from Pele in exchange for a lifetime of fealty to her shrine.

---

[*] "A red gash in the mountain."

XV.

KAMÉHAMÉHA'S PILGRIMAGE TO THE GODS.

GUIDED by the strong light from the pillar of fire, and by the shimmer from the blood-red stream which glowed against the sky, the tireless boy pressed forward through the long night hours, his young heart aglow with the unearthly scene and with the daring purpose that had aroused his soul. The footpath he followed led southward toward the district of Kau, winding along among rank grass and occasional clusters of *ohia* trees, from which he quenched his thirst with the juicy apples as he tramped along.

Kaméhaméha approached the river of fire toward dawn. While yet miles away, he heard thunder-peals like the discharge of artillery, and furious explosions that shook the earth. These detonations increased as he neared the scene of action, until at length he came to the borders of the swift-rushing lava flow. Climbing to a rocky hillock two hundred yards away, as near as the terrific heat would permit him to approach, Kaméhaméha sat dazed with wonder and awe as he watched the seething river rush down the mountain, melting every thing before it as it swept over the old lava beds. Sometimes a lateral stream of molten lava followed an underground fissure until it struck some obstruction, when a singular phenomenon would take place. The pent-up current slowly lifted the earth-crust above, until at length the imprisoned lava and

Appalling Scenes.   127

gases would explode with loud detonations, tearing the ground to pieces with the throes of an earthquake as the red current burst forth.

Just in front of the boy the lava had come to a high mass of rocks and trees, around which it divided and ran on either hand, joining again below the mound of trees. As he watched the grass, shrubs, and trees take fire, he saw the rocky border begin slowly to melt and sink, until the flame-encompassed island, its rocky foundations completely fused, suddenly gave way and floated down the crimson river, tossing like a light-ship on a stormy sea.

But a greater surprise was in store for him. The ledge of lava rock on which he sat continued to tremble and quiver with the vibration of the roaring flood. Suddenly he felt a motion beneath him ; but spurning the thought of danger he kept his seat. Presently the rocks moved more perceptibly under his feet, groaning and grating as if disturbed in their beds. He stood up, and found himself reeling and rocking as if in a canoe. The trees swayed and bowed as if about to fall. Then he leaped down the declivity and ran to another position near at hand, still half ashamed of his retreat. A moment after the rocky hillock rose, swelled, and swayed ; then, with a roar, a jet of lava burst out from its top. It gave vent to the caverned mass below, melting the rocks and setting the trees afire ; and soon the whole ledge fell in and the grove of flaming trees floated away to join the main stream of raging lava.*

Alert to avoid a danger like this the lad again plodded upward. The track leading to Kau now diverged to the west, and compelled Kaméhaméha to leave it and to take

---

* See descriptions of similar scenes in " Life in Hawáii," by the Rev. Titus Coan, pp. 76, 283.

his course into a completely unknown wilderness. He followed the cooled beds of ancient lava flows, and wherever the nature of the ground permitted, walking on the edges of the streams. The jagged lava tore his shark-skin sandals. In the belt of ancient forest through which he passed charred stumps of *koa* trees rose everywhere about him, the record of ancient eruptions. Many large trees had been burnt to ashes, leaving deep circular pits in the lava, traps from which one never could emerge if he should fall into them. Great caution was needed to avoid this danger.

Much of the old lava flow which had burnt through the forest of *koa, ohia,* and sandalwood trees was *pahoehoe,* or " satin " lava, over which Kaméhaméha found passable walking. At times he came upon great masses of scoria and clinkers, too jagged and sharp to walk upon, the so-called *a-a*, or broken-glass lava. This he had to flank at whatever cost of travel. At times deep fissures, many yards wide, drove him a half mile or more out of his way. After passing the timber belt at 7,000 feet, only stunted *koa* and diminutive *ohia* trees were found. Straggling tufts of coarse grass and gray lichens were found up to a height of 10,000 feet. Here the real toil of the ascent began.

Here morning dawned. Before the tired climber rose the vast volcanic dome of Loa, sharp and clear against the crimson sky. How long he had watched that plutonic mass as he climbed, rising two miles above him into the heavens! The whole vast mountain side now opened upon him, a wild waste of volcanic rocks, where every species of lava was to be found, from the hard, sharp clinker-stone to the frothy pumice that crumbles beneath the feet.

For miles about him ancient lava streams had cooled into hills, hummocks, terraces, and long, undulating waves. These were only passable by avoiding the abrupt hillocks and bottomless fissures. In places the previous flows had been obstructed or spent their force, cooling at the front of the flow, and piling up into vast terraces that could not be scaled.

The observant boy soon learned that the path to choose was where some swift incandescent flow had levelled its way through the congealed mass of older lava. The caverns and crevasses are thus filled up, "evened off," and made passable if the material be *pahoehoe* or "satin" lava; while if it be *a-a* or scoria, neither man nor beast can pass over it. But even the smoothest flows of the most favorable kinds of lava are often made impassable by countless earthquake rents, mile-long fissures, out of which deathly sulphurous fumes well up from the seething lava deep in the mountain.

After a few hours' rest, taken, because of the intense cold, in dangerous proximity to the lava flow, the half-nude chief toiled upward and onward again. His face became flushed with fever, and his pulse leaped wildly from the violent exertion and from the rarefaction of the air at the height he had attained. Nothing but the sulphur fumes and the clear morning breeze prevented his now being exhausted by the usual mountain sickness experienced by all travellers.

When he came to the snow line, at 12,000 feet, he sat down upon it to ponder over the marvellous substance. All his life long he had lived in sight of snow on Kéa's crest; but he had never touched it, for few dared to bring down the god-born element. Tasting it cautiously, he soon found that its singular coldness tempered his fever and allayed his thirst. He pressed his hot forehead upon it; then, growing cold from lying upon the new-fallen snow, he approached near to the lava stream. To his surprise he found that the frozen substance was melting into water, and flowed spluttering and steaming into the fiery river. He was delighted to learn that snow was frozen water.

After quenching his thirst he set himself to his task again. The cold increased so fast that but for the warmth of the flowing lava he must have frozen upon the mountain side. Yet on he climbed with a hero's determination to attain his end—unless he should be congealed to stone as the legend had warned him. The legend was now solved. It was the cold that made the stone image, but he had discovered that fire was stronger than cold, for he had seen it melt both rocks and snow. The keen-witted boy rejoiced in his growing wisdom.

As he struggled up into still higher altitudes, new emotions suddenly awakened in his soul. The panoramic view of the great world widened as he climbed. How thrilling were his sensations as he looked proudly down upon the broadening sweep below! Is it not this sense of expanding vision which delights the half-freed souls of the dying, when they reach back the farewell handclasp to their weeping ones, while expressions of rapturous anticipation glow in their faces, as if they were looking back to us from a heavenly mountain?

Approaching at last the summit crater, the source of the lava stream, Kaméhaméha beheld a scene which appalled him to look upon. A hundred yawning fissures had been rent in the rocky mountain side, where now the vast fountain of *gold-tinted* lava* hurled itself a

---

* The color of the eruptions, when they first break from the higher mountain, is golden, not red.

thousand feet into the air. The jet came principally from one monstrous fissure a mile in extent, and from one to five hundred feet wide. Rocky hills had been split asunder and rent into a thousand tattered fragments. Fifty acres of old lava crust had been blown off and flung thousands of feet away. Such an exhibition of titanic force filled the young mind with horror. If such were the terrific force and fury of upheaving fusion at the very top of a mountain three miles above the sea, and whose base could not be less than three miles below its level, who could imagine the terrible dynamics of the subterranean laboratory six miles down beneath the mountain top?

At length the heroic chief-boy stood on the snow-clad summit of Loa. Human foot had never before trodden this solitude. Before him stretched a lava plain of sixty miles in area. Looking back in the direction from which he had come, he was surprised to see that dense fleecy clouds had gathered a mile below, shutting out every visible thing except the kindred snow peaks of Mauna Kéa in the north. The red lava stream ran down the declivity, disappearing under the cloud, which glowed above the fire river with the blood-red hues of a stormy sunset.

Though the ancient crater which he sought could not be far away, yet he could not see a vestige of steam or smoke to mark its position. Only a roaring as of distant breakers and the low rumble of muffled thunder could guide him to the abode of Pele. But that abode must be found, for his mission was solely with the goddess he adored.

Resting his weary limbs for an hour before quitting the life-giving warmth of the lava-flow, the resolute boy hurried on in the direction of the crater. It was indicated by the furious detonations that now shook the mountain, as if the hour of final destruction had come. The sun, at this elevation, bereft of both warmth and brightness, now hung a lurid red ball just above the rim of the mountain plain, casting a human look upon the lonely boy. He thought it lingered until he should have time to find the crater.

Following hastily along a wide fissure, filled to the brim with frozen snow, Kaméhaméha suddenly came to the brink of the abyss of *Moku-a-weo-weo*, a gulf sunk a thousand feet below the plateau of the mountain summit. Falling upon his knees with a sense of utmost humility, the reverent boy called aloud upon Pele as a child calls for his devoted parent in times of peril. His young soul was filled with horror at the scene he beheld.

As the boy pleaded for the goddess to come forth at his call, the darkening sky above the crater brightened as if it were on fire. Fifty volcanic flames and crimson lava jets burst forth from as many huge vent cones of the fiery lake in the crater below. Night was rapidly approaching. The crater was visible stretching miles away toward the south, and disappearing among sulphurous vapors. There was but little ebullition in the burning lake, except an occasional lava jet of from one to three hundred feet high, which caused much rocking and rumbling. The general level of the crater fires remained equal, a constantly sufficient supply for the fountain below.

The friendly face of the sun was gone. The young chief was alone in a frightful solitude; he felt a measure of loneliness which has no name. The glare of the two volcano fires bade defiance to night and made a brighter radiance than the sun-lit day. Patches of snow and ice were everywhere about him, piled in the lava fissures, or lying in isolated drifts over all the black lava plain; but the heat from the crater before him and the lava jet behind imparted all-sufficient warmth for the nude boy, who otherwise would have frozen to death in a few hours.

Not a moment's sleep came to him throughout that terrible night. He lay in a lava crevasse, with only the moon for a companion; half deafened by the rumble and roar and sharp detonations surging up from the crater, the thundering crash of the lava behind him, and the vibrating effect of the falling masses as of a thousand gigantic water-falls. Aside from the supernatural terrors of the place, this pandemonium of noises was enough to craze an older brain.

Sometimes hideous black objects rose up in groups on the incandescent surface of the lake. By their groans and shrieks, and by other dismal noises, the observant boy believed that monsters from the fiery depths were sent to frighten him away from the rocky battlement. But though he called to them aloud that his mission was to the goddess, or to whomsoever she would send, whether demon or fire-god, from the crater, no voice came back in reply. Only mocking leers and demoniacal laughter assailed his ear.*

Having eaten his last mouthful of *kalo*, and failing to

---

* Science disputes the supernatural visions of the days of which we write. Other visitors, in later years, see these same black demons appear on the lake surface during the night, disappearing and coming again and again. They tell us that the cooled lava crust congeals in small patches for a moment, melting again with the next influx of hot lava which comes with dismal noises. Let those who wish take this version of the case; the scenes we describe are truthful.

call up Pele or any spirit of the desolate place, it became necessary for him to hasten his return down the mountain while yet strength remained to him. As he walked gloomily back to the lateral crater on the mountain side, the friendly moon appeared from the clouds. Yellow as the goldent tint of sunset rose the vast lava jet as he approached it ; wholly unlike the blood-red color of the river of fire seen far down in the valley below. Higher and higher leaped the fountain of molten gold, as if it were the melted bullion of the whole financial world displaying its incandescent beauty to the mountain gods, and careless of being seen by watchful human eyes.

Next to the blinding glory awaiting us about the judgment-seat of God, such terrific outbursts from the fiery laboratory of earth must ever remain the most beautiful and awe-inspiring scenes known to mortal. Solitude and desolation are dismal companions ; but one who can master his fears among such elements of grandeur and beauty may become so utterly oblivious of all else, so unconscious of his own existence in the flesh, that it may seem to him at length as if all the world had been destroyed by fire, and that he, alone of all created things, is left to see the charred remains and tread upon the embers of earth's destruction.

Something of this thought filled the chief's mind as he reached the edge of the summit on the side of the lava flow opposite to that by which he had come on the previous day. The white clouds had dispersed from the valley, and the whole fire-lighted land lay clearly visible below him. The flow had struck the foot-hills of Mauna Kéa, and branched to the right and left; one stream running toward Hilo, the other flowing across Waimea Valley to the west.

Looking in the direction of Puna, Kaméhaméha could distinguish the red gleam of Kilauea to the southeast, sixteen miles away. Rejoiced to see the course he must take to reach Pele's usual place of abode, a yet more important question arose. Would the increasing cold permit of his descending the mountain by any other route than that of the lava flow? He must await the dawn to decide.

Morning dawned cold and clear upon the lonely boy,— too cold for him to venture far away from the warmth of the lava into an unknown wilderness. Without food or raiment, excepting a light *tapa* mantle, to be long detained upon the mountain would be to die of hunger and cold. Thus his downward course must be determined by the lava flow.

Following along the south bank of the rushing stream of liquid fire, where it coursed its rapid way down the steep declivity, Kaméhaméha passed the snow region easily in an hour. Beyond the limit of snow the pathless way was rough and toilsome down to the upper belt of forest, where the cold became less intense, and the stunted trees and hardy grasses once more gladdened his eyes. Plucking some of the coarse grass from the thin soil, Kaméhaméha devoured the bitter roots, hoping to allay the gnawings and sickening sensations of hunger.

While thus employed his ear was suddenly invaded by the furious crash of approaching thunder. Though he was yet at an altitude of two miles, a dense dark cloud was settling down over Waimea Valley and rolling on up the mountain above him. The pent-up clouds crept along the ground about him, heavy with blackness, and gleaming with electric fire. The full-charged mists crept up the mountain, ablaze with lightning. Hundreds of great forest trees were cut down, and others burned like torchlights for miles about the wondering chief. He had seen many a thunder-storm above his native valley; but here was one which left the heavens and played upon the ground. The lava rocks were ploughed up, and the crash of falling trees was appalling to his ear. The rain fell in torrents for an hour.*

As he sat there in a clump of *ohia* shrubs, within reach of the friendly warmth of the hot lava, which hissed past in the rain, suddenly an outburst took place in a cluster of stunted trees close at hand. A graceful lava fountain rose twenty feet above the tree tops, falling about on every side of the scanty foliage of the hardy trees. Not a drop of lava flowed away; but cooling where it fell, it slowly built up a wall of red lava about the trees, without burning a leaf or a twig on the mountain shrubs.

Watching with interest to see the molten fluid thus build up a lava tower, Kaméhaméha's superstitions were not fairly aroused until he noticed that the *ohia* trees were not burnt either by the yellow lava rising from among them, or by the red-hot wall that girdled them about. Still the fountain played, and the red lava walls rose into the air and covered the trees, closing gradually in about the fountain top, until the golden lava jet could barely be seen above the crimson tower.

Just then the figure of a fair woman rose up on the crest of the fountain, and looked down with soft blue eyes on the wondering boy below. Hair of the yellowest gold fell gracefully about her white arms and alabaster shoulders, a color so blended with the orange hue of the fountain that one was lost in the other. It was Pele!

---

* See the Rev. Titus Coan's "Life in Hawáii" (p. 272) for a description of a similar thunder-storm, at an elevation of 8,000 feet.

She spoke to the astonished chief-boy. He fell upon his knees and laid bare his heart to the beautiful goddess who had thus come to acknowledge his adoring love.

And she suffered this strange boy to gaze upon her celestial beauty at his will without blinding his vision by her glory. She bent with tender solicitude above the god-born chief; her beneficent smile warmed the very rocks about him. Kaméhaméha soon grew calm and collected as the greatness of the occasion dawned fully upon him. Yet his fluent tongue grew dumb when he became assured that this was indeed the august deity whom he had come to invoke.

But there is ever an aggressive quality in man's ambition which fails not to exalt him to the pinnacle of godhead. Thus when Pele repeated her question:

"Why comes my young hero in quest of his god?"— he reverently replied:

"Is the son of Wailéle known to the gods?"

"It is recorded in tablets of fire that my *Kahúna* of Mukíni is mother of the mightiest of men."

"If one worship Pele for life, will it not prosper his ambitious schemes for greatness?"

"Whoever makes much sacrifice to Pele shall win in battle, though he worship in fear and trembling. But whoso immolates offerings upon my altar because of great love for Pele, he shall not die by the hand of man."

"Is the wisdom of Wailéle inspired by the gods?"

"Wailéle is the wisest and best of my worshippers. Only for one hour in her priesthood has the noble *wahine* been won to desert my shrine for another. Caught in the mystic arms of Luna at midnight, her oblations were once forgotten, and the fires burnt low on her altar in the time of sacrifice. But as the mountain stream is purified by the attrition of rocks and water-falls, so the worship of deity grows stronger in the heart of woman by the vehemence of her love for a mortal."

Not comprehending the figurative meaning of Pele's oracular reply, Kaméhaméha continued:

"Beautiful deity! Is your god-son designed for priest of Mukíni, or to rank among the rulers of his country, to which he aspires?"

"One New Year's Day, when the people gathered to worship at Mukíni, there came the wail of a baby-boy from the sacred *anu*. It was Pele who willed the birth of the hero in that hour; and because of the holy birth of the *Alii* he is loved of the gods, and was born to supreme rule over the destinies of men."

How long he would have importuned the Goddess we know not, had not his tongue been suddenly struck dumb, and his keen eyes blinded by the sudden brilliance before him. The wind waved the golden tresses of the deity, and the whole mountain side seemed ablaze as with vivid lightning. The fountain sprang higher and higher, until the red tower built itself up and closed over the divine form of the Goddess. The fountain disappeared. Then suddenly the tower of hot lava exploded with a tremendous crash and was seen no more.

When the blinding light had passed away, the clump of *ohias* where the tower had stood was green and beautiful again, untouched by the fiery lava; buds and blossoms and ripened fruit hung plentiful on the trees, inviting the starving chief to quench his thirst and allay his hunger.

Though the beautiful face of deity was gone, it still seemed present to the ardent boy, beaming down upon him from the fire-fountain as tenderly as a human mother. A delicious vision, one that could never be snatched from his gaze, had been vouchsafed him. It would live in his heart a whole life long. The musical voice of Pele still rang in his ear, lingering like a soft bewildering strain of music in his soul. He was like one who had dreamed of a choir of angels, and awakes amazed and bewildered with the miraculous vision that has passed away. And the words of the Goddess would serve as a rallying cry in many a dark hour of his tempestuous life; " Because of the holy birth of the *Alii* he is loved of the gods, and shall rule supreme over the destinies of men!"

It was hours before Kaméhaméha could bring himself to think of his situation, and the danger of remaining longer upon the mountain. Toiling down through miles of dead leaves, with painful foot travel, he came at length to the level plain, where the lava flow ran slowly and broadened out into a fiery lake. The surface lava cooled, bridging over the flood with a black shining crust, until it ran as through a vast tunnel constructed out of its own materials.

When this tunnelled lava flow struck the foot-hills of Mauna Kéa its progress was checked for some hours, during which time it dammed itself up thirty feet high along a front of fifteen miles. When at length the fiery fusion burst through the black crust it flowed to the south and west in two lateral streams; this compelled Kaméhaméha to double around the lava flow to the south of Mauna Kéa, and to take the homeward path along the east side of the mountain. Having seen Pele, there was now no necessity of going to Kilauea.

A few hours after he had left the slow-moving lava, he came to a hamlet of hospitable natives, who, learning that he was the god-born chief of Mukíni, pressed him to tarry a few days, and feast upon their plenty, and rest after his dreadful toil.

When he again renewed his journey homeward, refreshed and strong, it was with a feeling of just pride and joyous exultation that is rarely allotted to a young mortal. Knowing the exalted destiny which awaited him, there was henceforth not an hour in which his young mind was not planning for the future kingdom over which he was to rule.

XVI.

THE KING AND HIS COURT AT WAIPIO.

TIME passes rapidly in the lives of historic men. We have come to the twenty-second year of Kalaniopuu's reign, about 1774, when the exhaustive wars with the Leeward Islands had for a time given place to a precarious peace between the kings of Hawáii and Maui. This peace, as often happened in the lands of chivalry two centuries earlier, led to the interchange of civilities and friendly jousts among the arrogant kings and their courtiers. Nor need we think that these courtesies among recent enemies were extended wholly for the purpose of spying out their rivals' resources. They sprang more often from an honest curiosity and a real admiration of the recent antagonist, as well as from a wish to become better acquainted with those whom they had met in valiant combat, or against whom they had practised all their strategy.

On one of these balmy days during the mid-reign of Kalaniopuu, Kahekili, the warlike king of Maui, unexpectedly announced his wish to visit his royal cousin and brother-in-law of Hawáii. Though the request was made with all courtesy, yet the unlooked-for event caused a ripple of anxiety among the ruling minds; while the greatest delight was manifested by the irresponsible ones about the Hawáiian court.

Kiwalao, the young prince of sixteen, and his brother

Keoúa, were out on the high *páli* which fronts the windward sea to the north of Waipio, when they descried the sunlight flashing on the white *tapa* sail of a large canoe in the distant northwest toward Maui. But the boys continued to practise with their slings and bird-spears upon the clouds of sea-birds swarming up the cliff from the sea below, and entirely forgot the canoe, so absorbed were they in the enjoyment of their sport; when suddenly Keoúa exclaimed, with consternation upon his handsome young face : *

"*He waa palua nui!* A great double canoe!"

"*Auwe!* what can they want?" asked Kiwalao. And well might the lads express surprise at seeing the craft urged on by forty paddlers and a press of sail; for in those years a great war canoe was more likely to come with intent of mischief than with messages of peace. The royal boys were now alert with curiosity.

"Let us run down to Waipio and tell the news," said Keoúa, full of boyish trepidation.

"No! Go you to the king and report what we have seen," said Kiwalao, assuming his usual arrogant tone, the prerogative of an heir apparent in times of sudden danger. "I'll watch here, while you go and tell the *moi* that there are sixty Kanákas in the great *waa*. Run, *wiki, wiki!*—quick, quick!" And away went the fleet-footed lad to the valley side of the *páli*, where, selecting a steep grassy incline, he secured some large *ki* leaves, upon which he slid down into the valley with the speed of a snow-sled.

Kiwalao sat down upon the cliff and nervously watched the approaching canoe, talking aloud to himself in lan-

---

* One of Kalaniopuu's two sons of that name, by Queen Kanekapolei (wife No. 5). This Keoúa became renowned.

guage too characteristic not to be recorded. The prince was a tall slim youth of sixteen ; a nervous, restless, unprincipled boy, whose dissolute habits were a poor example for the chief-boys of Waipio Valley. Young as he was, he was old in evil, and had already been connected with several rebellious plots against his father, while the king was at war with Maui. And it was even believed that he had conspired against Kalaniopuu's life, because of some justly deserved chastisement that the king had ordered him.

"I hope it is another message proclaiming war with Maui, as there is not much chance of coming to my kingdom in times of peace. I wonder what Kahekili thinks of my plan of his joining me against my father. Perhaps this canoe brings me word from Maui. I long to be king! But who knows but Kahekili would help me to secure Hawáii, and then keep it for himself? He is really too treacherous a king for a boy like me to deal with, though he is my uncle." *

As the canoe came near to the cliff, after surveying its occupants keenly, Kiwalao suddenly sprang up with an excited exclamation : "That's Alapai, the king's half-brother ; Kahekili must be sending me a message in answer to my proposal for an alliance. I must away and meet Alapai when he lands. *Auwe!* who knows but that this Maui chief is coming to inform my father of my plot? I think Kalaniopuu would fling me from the *páli* if he knew what was in train."

Keoúa arrived at the palace in time to arouse a strong body of chiefs, who were quickly ready to receive the new-comers, whatever might be their purpose. Kiwalao

---

* The prince's mother, Kalola, Kalaniopuu's chief queen, was own sister of Kahekili, King of Maui.

remained behind long enough to feel sure there was no warlike intent, and then followed the example of his half-brother. He slid down the *páli*, and was on the beach in time to meet the strangers at the landing, where he assumed the honor of leading Alapai, the chief in command of the canoe, to his father.

Kalaniopuu, the much-loved king of the great island of Hawáii, lay reclining on a soft divan of mats, spread out under the shade of beautiful king-palms, clustered about the palace door. He had just come from his river bath, and was now enjoying the grateful *lomi-lomi*, and receiving his customary anointing with aromatic oils. But neither by look nor act did he show his curiosity about the new-comers. Keeaumoku, the leading war chief, had quietly ambushed a few hundred men about the palace and the beach-landing, in case of need, and now came back and stood by the king's side, with a half score of other noble *aliis*, anxiously awaiting the coming of the commander of the canoe party.

A chief of gallant bearing, closely followed by ten others of less rank, was seen approaching the palace under the guidance of Kiwalao. Both of the royal chiefs kept up a lively conversation, witty if not wise, to judge from the laughter and friendly gestures of the two and the echoes of gayety from those who followed. The party stopped respectfully before the reclining king, who bowed slightly to the leading chief with a smile of courtesy that softened the austerity of his face. Kiwalao stepped forward and introduced Alapai of Maui, half brother to Kahekili, the king.

Coming at once to the message of state which had brought him to Waipio, after the greetings and *alohas* were over, Alapai assumed the usual oratorical attitude of all chiefs who had matter of importance to disclose.

"Great is Kalaniopuu, the resistless warrior and wise king! For he rules over the mountain land of Hawáii, the land of Pele and her palace of fire; the land which climbs so high that its tops are white with the snow dust of the upper world. Every man who dares approach its dreadful summits is turned to stone,* standing there like an idol to the end of the world. Great is Kalaniopuu!"

The king waved his hand graciously in response, while a pleased expression came to his venerable face at the eloquent words of Alapai. Nodding to Naihe, the hereditary orator of Hawáii, the handsome young chief came forward to reply.

"My king has heard the pleasant voice of Alapai, the *alii wohi* (chief next the king) of Kahekili, who rules over the fruitful island across the sea; the land of *Ha-le-a-ka-la* ("House of the Sun"), whose dreadful crater is larger than all those upon Hawáii; where Pele once held her fiery court until the dreadful *Moa-alii* (the mighty sea-god) drowned out her fires by pouring the great ocean into *Ha-le-a-ka-la*." To which Alapai replied:

"Kahekili—the mighty Thunderer of Maui—sends greeting to his cousin of Hawáii, with whom he would rub noses and drink *awa*, if a visit would give pleasure to Kalaniopuu." This was said with a graceful bow to the king, who made an affirmative sign to Naihe."

"It is well. Request the warlike Kahekili to come to Waipio at his pleasure. The sun will shine brighter over all Hawáii because of the friendly meeting of the noble kings. Bid him come, for my king is impatient to greet him. He shall be feasted on *ilio poli*, fatted by our

---

* The mountains are said to be the abode of the gods, and tales are told of Kanákas being turned to stone, which prevented our guides going to the summit.—Ellis' "Hawáii," p. 383.

wahines, and abundant *puaa hea*—sacred hog—shall be baked for one hundred warriors." He cunningly put this fixed limit to the number lest there might be some treachery beneath the pleasantry of the royal chief.

This ended the formal greeting. Alapai was now invited forward to rub noses with the old king; and his followers proffered the same affectionate greeting to the crowd of chiefs. All gathered merrily about the monarch, whose oiling and hair-dressing having been completed, now sat half reclining upon his couch, with nothing but a gayly colored *tapa* lightly thrown over him.

After Alapai had partaken of *poi* and fish to his content, he again greeted the venerable old king and chiefs with *Aloha nui!* and departed on his homeward way, as the trades were now blowing up strong, and he had twenty miles of rough passage across the Upolu Sea, after leaving the surf-beaten coast of Hawáii.

As Kahekili was the dominant mind among all the Leeward kings who ruled over seven of the "Eight Isles," he was entitled to the best reception the monarch of Hawáii could give. Thus the garden-land of Waipio soon became a busy scene of preparation for the event.

The first thing of importance in these matters of state visits was to notify the priests and prophets of the *heiáu*, in order that the *kahúnas* may sacrifice to the gods and learn the secret motives of the visit, if such there be; and that the *kaulas* (prophets) should propound oracles sufficiently significant for the occasion.

With this motive in view Kanuha, the swiftest-footed courier on the islands,* was dispatched to acquaint several wise old *kahúnas* of the coming visit; and especially

---

* This venerable courier was living in 1853, then 116 years old, and could clearly remember Alapai's reign, preceding that of Kalaniopuu.

was he charged to impress Pepehi, the priest of Puukeekee, with the anxiety of Kalaniopuu to learn the real purpose of his guest. Peace, indeed, now prevailed ; yet the recent battles had been stubborn and bitter contests, and the known treachery and warlike ambition of Kahekili made it hard to believe readily that his coming to Hawáii was wholly for friendly purposes.

While the courier was hastening to the inland temples, a messenger was sent by sea to Waimánu on a special mission to Mukíni, as the prescience of Wailéle was held in the highest esteem on all such occasions. More than this, Kahekili had once paid his addresses to the beautifnl Priestess, and it was thought that she of all others could best interpret his designs.

In anticipation of the coming festivities, great joy was exhibited among the lesser nobility about the court. Not having the cares of state on their minds, they were wholly given to the pleasures of feasting, love, and fighting ; exercising themselves in mimic battles when they could not be indulged in the real combats that they loved.

But among the *kanáka wále*, or commoners, a shadow of fear was soon observed haunting every face. Not a poor fellow among them all but might already be the one secretly chosen for immolation on this momentous occasion. Few of the *wahines* could wholly hide their anxiety for the loved ones—husbands, fathers, lovers, sons—until after the man-killers from the *heiáus* had snatched away other victims.

This terrible state of things arose from the unlimited power of the *kahúna* in his office of *tabú* priest. A human sacrifice is demanded on some sudden exigency like the present, and the priest decides irrevocably who the next victims on his dreadful list must be. The office of priesthood was hereditary, and the power of a *kahúna*, or high-priest, was transmitted equally to sons or daughters. Priestesses were sometimes cruel and unrelenting as any priest. And not even the king could prevent the *kahúna* from making choice of his victim. Since Pàáo exalted the sacerdotal order, the high-caste priest was the peer of the haughtiest noble. He was assigned his portion of arable land in the estate of every chief in his district. And woe to the chief who withheld from the *kahúna* his rights! If the priest could not sacrifice the chief upon the altar, he could help himself to his favorite followers until the supply was exhausted.

The power of the *kapu alii* thus cast a gloom over every class of society. Woe to the careless or defiant person whose sun-cast shadow fell upon a *kahúna!* If the priest's victims were not plenty the offender must be sacrificed to Pele for breaking her *tabú*.

The day passed; and throughout the night many a wretch was dragged from his terror-stricken household. When morning again dawned over the upper world, and subsequently illuminated the deep valley, the peculiar bronze-colored smoke seen curling up from the three altar-fires of Puukeekee, and also rising from the several smaller *heidus* of Waipio, told all eyes that the victims had been slain and were being immolated to the gods. Several Waipio natives who had thought to escape the *kapu kane* by fleeing to the mountains, had been kidnapped by the dreadful *Pepehi Kanáka*, and their bodies were now dissipating in sickening smoke.

Thus the second day was a dark one to many a household. The second night gave opportunity for the concealed ones to come stealthily back to their sorrowing

Preparing for the Feast.

homes. The over-timid ones, and most of the *kanakas* lack courage, came back haggard and worn as by a year's suffering. They were quite unfitted for the joys anticipated by those whose rank exempted them from the *kapu kane*.

At an early hour on the third day the look-out on the *páli* sighted an approaching fleet of canoes. Word was quickly passed down to Waipio to prepare for the feast; and the discordant sounds which filled the next hour could be better referred to Pandemonium than to the beautiful valley of Waipio. Dogs barked, hogs squealed, and fowls cackled in their accustomed concert on a feast day. Tiny fishing canoes put out with noisy haste into the river and the private fish ponds.

The fires of the ground-ovens everywhere blazed brightly, heating the smooth stones for the baking. Great heaps of *ki* leaves were piled about the fires; these were to line the hollowed earth ovens after the hot stones had been duly packed within them. Breadfruit, sweet potatoes and *kalo* were then judiciously interspersed with parcels of fish, flesh, and fowl; altogether making the most delicious "field-bake" known in any land.

Such was the work of preparation amongst the male laborers; females, as we have seen, being tabued from touching or cooking men's food. But the women were also busy gathering flowers and vines with which to construct wreaths and garlands, not only for themselves, but for every notable man in the valley. Thus the *wahines* were as joyous and songful as the singing bird in the flowering *hau* tree. Some went to the woods in pairs or groups to gather the gay hibiscus blossoms for *leis*, and to pluck the red *ohia* apples for the guests, the *ohia* not being prohibited. But the delicious banana and the nectar-filled cocoa-nut were tabued to them; these the men had to gather and spread for the feast.

XVII.

THE FEAST OF THE KINGS.

ABOUT mid-day the royal canoes arrived from Maui,* bringing a company of kings and chiefs from the Leeward Islands. In the boat with Kahekili came his brother Keao, King of Kauai, and his younger half-brother Alapai, the *alii wohi* of the Maui court.

In the next canoe sat the young King of Molokai brother of the King of Oahu. Why Kunakoa came in the train of Kahekili, his natural enemy, none could tell, for it was rumored that the army of Maui was even then organizing to attack Oahu, and if such were the case Molokai must be already doomed.

In the next canoe followed Keliiaa of Lanai, a chief whose kingdom was subordinate to Maui. This made four royal visitors, together with Alapai and forty other high chiefs; while even the sixty paddlers were warriors of renown. The limit named by Naihe, in his invitation of the guests, had thus been exceeded by four. This was a trifle in itself; yet the discourtesy was just sufficient to show the arrogant and unruly temper of the dominant king among the guests.

One after another of the great war canoes dashed through the high rolling surf, paddling with exceeding

---

* A royal canoe is red, having a red sail and a red pennon flying at the peak.

swiftness up to the landing at the river mouth. There Kalaniopuu and a hundred of his choicest warriors were gathered to receive the guests.

Among the historical characters who were present with the Hawáiian king was Keeaumoku, the *kiaimoku* of the island,* and father of the princess Kaahumanu, who afterwards became the most noted woman of Polynesia. Keeaumoku was the most gigantic warrior among the islands, a chief of such prowess that few men could stand before him, in single combat, for a moment. It was this chief whose heroism won the battle of Keei; at the end of eight days' fighting, after every one of his own soldiers lay dead around him, he slew the opposing king. He was distinguished also by the deed of publicly assassinating King Keoúa, of Kau, and seven other chiefs in the same canoe, having been prompted to this base deed by revenge.

Keoúa, the brother of the Hawáiian king,† was conspicuous among the company. He was the handsomest chief in all this group of gigantic nobles. Kameeimoku, another young warrior, became notable as the chief who subsequently captured the "Fair American," killed Captain Metcalf and all but one of his crew, throwing them to the sharks, and beached the vessel on the Kona shore. But this piratical act was done in revenge for an unpardonable insult on the part of the whites.

King Kahekili was the most remarkable man of his party of kings and chiefs. A powerful, active, and fearless warrier, he was the most renowned general among the Leeward Isles. While by nature he was stern and

---

* The spy or police, to watch that the *tabú* is not broken.—Ellis' "Hawáii," p. 365.

† Uncle of Kaméhaméha.—Ellis' "Hawáii," p. 111.

cruel, yet he could be genial, social, and apparently good-hearted in his kindly moods. Resolute, tenacious, and persistent of purpose in whatever he undertook, he was naturally successful in every enterprise of his early reign; and not until after conquering Oahu, and he had clouded his mind by dissipation, did he meet with reverses. He presented the anomaly of a warrior who easily conquered the kingdom of another, but who could not maintain his own heritage.

Though ornamental tattooing had become unpopular in his age, yet Kahekili made himself hideously conspicuous by covering one half of his face and body with a black tattoo, unrelieved by any attempt at embellishment, leaving the other half of his person unmarred.*

Living in a polygamous state of society, when many wives were deemed indispensable to adorn a great chief's establishment, Kahekili contented himself with but two. He lived much by himself, and gave no entertainments at his court.

Born the younger son of a suspicious and cruel family, with neither prospect nor expectations of ever ascending a throne, this cunning, scheming man had the tact to live

---

* Black was, however, deemed the sacred color in Polynesia, as in many other ancient countries. Thus the chiefs—male and female—assumed the sole right of tattooing. There was a proverb: "*He weo ke Kanaka; He pauo ke Alii*"—meaning Red is the Kanaka; Dark is the Chief. The *puua hiwa* (black hog) was sacred to the gods, as the black bulls Apis and Mnevis were sacred to the gods in ancient Egypt. Black was the robe of the Kahúna, as with the priests of Egypt. The recent eruption which threatened to destroy Hilo was believed to have been stopped by the sacrifice of Mrs. ———'s "sacred black pig to Pele, after the Christian people had prayed to God in vain." Mrs. ——— was one of the group of Pele worshippers who went up to the crater and sacrificed her *puua hiwa* with the present king's sister and others.

as a private nobleman in retirement. During two preceding reigns, he had been a dutiful son and loyal brother. At the death of his brother, the king, in 1765, Kahekili, at the age of fifty, seized his brother's throne. There were young heirs and a rightful queen. But he had bided well his time, and now knew his power. None proved sufficiently strong to dethrone him, and he became a very fiend of deception and cruelty in his greed for power.

A physiognomist could detect the true character of this brilliant king in his small, restless, evasive eyes. However kindly they might seem to smile upon you for the time, they never failed to disclose the serpent cunning of this treacherous savage in times of war. It was this foxy-eyed monarch who subsequently, while promising our young king (whom he affectionately called his son) that he should be his heir, and have Maui at his death, at the same time sent a strong body of warriors to another king to assist in destroying the "son" to whom he had just promised his kingdom.

Yet Kahekili was greatly beloved by his warlike subjects, and greatly feared by his enemies. His friends accepted his cunning and treachery as strong auxiliaries in savage warfare; as being, indeed, the soundest principles of ethics when practised against an enemy. His foes naturally could not endure his methods of deception. These had often tricked them into death-traps after the king's own promise of safety had been solemnly given.

It was found to be the best policy for a newly conquered people to give prompt and zealous allegiance to Kahekili, lest his piercing eyes should detect a want of *aloha* in his newly acquired subjects. For such delinquency he had given the people of a whole town to midnight slaughter; as at Moanalua, after the conquest of Oahu. A house was subsequently built of the bleached bones of the victims.*

Every notable chief of either party had his enmities against others of the terrible warriors present, against whom he had battled from his youth. Yet the greetings of all these ferocious spirits were meant to be most cordial; for the Hawáiian nobility cultivated polished court language and elegant manners.

But abundant lack of sincerity was disclosed in many instances. Sinister looks and sarcastic remarks were often too thinly disguised to deceive even the person to whom they were addressed; as when the polished Kahekili met the sarcastic and fearless Keeaumoku. This happened at a moment when Kalaniopuu was absent with the other kings. The Háwaiian warrior was married to Namahana, Kahekili's half-sister, and had lived in Maui. But because of jealousy arising out of this very family connection, together with the treachery of his wife's three brothers, Keeaumoku had felt obliged to seek personal safety at the court of Hawáii, where he was welcomed as the descendant of a previous Hawáiian king of his name.

Namahana having been the queen of Kamehanui, her half-brother, a former king of Maui, her three remaining royal brothers were naturally suspicious of the widowed queen's motives when she abruptly married so formidable a warrior as Keeaumoku, fearing lest the marriage should

---

* This dreadful event received the name of *Kapoluku*—" the night of slaughter." The river Niuhelewai, to the west of Honolulu, was dammed up with the dead bodies of the slain.—(Dibble, p. 52.) At the Waipio " *kimopo* " (Waipio assassination) men, women, and children were murdered without mercy. The aristocracy of Oahu were nearly extirpated.—(" Polynesian Races," p. 226.)

cover some design upon the throne of her dead husband Thus beneath the courteous demeanor and veil of pleasantries between these four notables, now met at the feast of kings, there were visible gleams of ill disguised hatred. For had not this most valuable of all their subjects carried his allegiance across the sea to an enemy's court?

"Ah! Keeaumoku, I see that my sister's noble husband has not lost flesh since he so suddenly changed his place of residence to Hawáii," remarked Kahekili, as the royal chiefs met to make choice of fruit from the same sugar-banana tree. A covert sneer was implied in the stinging tone of the king's words. It made Keeaumoku forget the fruit he had plucked, for he tossed the rare edible into the river, and replied with ill-concealed bitterness:

"Your majesty is right. The observations of those small keen eyes are unerring. This is a tranquil court to live in. One need not always carry his *pahi* (dagger) about with him in this happy vale of Waipio, in fear of some court assassin stabbing him in the back."

This retort brought a venomous curl to the king's mobile lips, and a sudden increase of disquietude into his snakish eyes. But instead of abandoning his search for a banana, the crafty nature of the man was shown by his taking yet greater care in his selection of the fruit, while he responded with a sardonic laugh:

"Ha, ha, a *small* person like Keeaumoku ought to be able to defend himself without *pololu* or *pahi*—spear or dagger. But surely you did not consider our kingdom of Maui an unsafe place of residence for one of your mettle?" And the king actually attempted to eat his banana, but it choked in his throat.

"Sire, we all know that for any chief gifted with

greater prowess than the royal sons of Kekaulike,* Maui is the unsafest place to live in among the islands. And then it runs in the family of my royal brother-in-law to discover many aspirants for the throne. This unfortunate jealousy often brings one to taste Pepehi's poison god; as many a noble chief of the other line of kings could have testified just before he died."

"Fie, fie! noble Alii; there are too many gallant fighters in our family of kings that one should need to take such measures for the safety of his throne. Be rid of such notions, my gallant brother, and come across the sea and lead my new expedition against Oahu. And harkee! noble Keeaumoku. It is time you should aspire to a throne of your own. The blood of kings runs in your veins. Come to Maui, and when Oahu is mine, Molokai shall be yours."

"Thanks for the honor you propose. But to how many other *alii nui* have you already made the same tempting offer for like service? Henceforth Keeaumoku will lead his expeditions from Hawáii. But what has happened that you war against the kingdom of Kumahana of Oahu?"

"The arrogant king has said rude things about our family. Surely this will interest you. When Keao was paying court to Queen Kamakaheli, of Kauai, with a view to marriage, and becoming king of the isles, Kumahana interfered to break up the alliance and sent his own son, Kaneonco, to marry the Queen of Kauai."

"But he did not succeed, and Keao has become King of Kauai."

"True, but Kumahana showed a disposition to meddle with his superiors, and I will chastise him."

---

* Kekaulike was a former king of Maui, and father of the three last kings of that island.

"And what does the king of Molokai think of your fighting his brother? And how can you give away Molokai, an island which already has a king in dutiful allegiance to you?"

"Kumakoa must join my army, and fight against his brother of Oahu, or Molakai shall be added to my kingdom. While on the passage across to Hawáii I learned that he is not inclined to join my cause; and I have already sent back word for my army to sail at once and take possession of his kingdom, while I detain him and his prominent war chiefs in my train. Is not that a neat piece of strategy, my brother?"

"It is indeed a scheme worthy of the cunning of Kahekili."

Here Kalaniopuu came suddenly into the group, and changed the dangerous current of talk, for he had observed from a distance that Keeaumoku was handling his dagger nervously.

"What! noble Aliis, discussing warlike projects on this day of our festivities? Let us be content each one with his own kingdom, and let our neighbors live in peace."

"The *Alii Moi* of Hawáii may well be content with his," replied Kahekili. "He has a land broader than all our kingdoms together, and reaching upward to the snow-lands of *lani-loa*" (the high heaven).

"Our islands are enough for all. And let us remember that hardly three in a hundred of our kings die a natural death."

"Who asks to die like a *wahine*, sheltered in his house? I doubt if there is a chief present who would not rather die spear in hand, than live to be old, and be dosed to death by a *kahúna-lapaau*" (medicine-priest).

Just then Kiwalao came to tell his father that the earth

ovens had been opened, and the feast was ready to serve.

"Come, my guests, the feast awaits you. Kahekili, we shall treat you to the finest *ilio poli* ever nursed by *wahines*.* Our *ohelo* berries are fresh from the banks of Kilauea crater; they were gathered for this feast by the divine permission of Pele. Our geese and ducks were fatted on the strawberry fields of Waimea. Our raspberries grew above the forest belt of Mauna Kéa, and neither the red nor the white ones can be matched elsewhere in all the islands."

The hungry warriors seated themselves on the mats in the shade in two distinct groups according to their rank. Naihe called the merry *convives* to order; and while the chiefs were carving the hogs, dogs, and fowls with their keen bamboo knives, he made a pleasant speech charging the guests to give the king the pleasure of seeing that they relished the feast; and all fell to in earnest.

A monstrous breadfruit, baked in the earth oven, having been placed before Kahekili, he enquired where it grew. Being told that it came from Waimánu Valley, the royal gallant brightened up with a flash of real pleasure. Looking archly across the feast to where Keoúa sat he exclaimed in an undertone not meant to be offensive, his mouth still crammed with *poi* and dog-meat:

"Keoúa! most noble Alii, which of us two won the fair Priestess of Mukíni in years gone by?" And yet this query was a jest upon his own love affair as well as Keoúa's; for neither of them could win Wailéle.

"May it please your majesty, you made the last attack

---

* Though pigs baked in the earth ovens were relished by all, and *poi*-fed dogs were the delight of epicures, yet the *ilio poli* was considered the rarest delicacy known to the gastronomic art; a royal dainty, willingly nourished by women for the feasts of kings as well as for the oblations of the priests.

upon the noble maiden's heart, and by some defect of memory you have not thought to tell us of your own success," replied the handsome "Rain Food," his face reddening with all the blood it could carry as he endeavored to parry the exposure of his own failure.

"Most happily put, and I freely say to all present, that throughout the long years since my visit to Mukíni I have been without a heart. But with Kalaniopuu's permission I hope to visit Waimánu again, and there search for what I have lost." And he turned to the king for an answer to this request.

The large dark eyes of the Hawáiian monarch flashed, and his usually benignant face paled at these words. Only by the strongest restraint could he reply calmly to Kahekili's request. Yet not a soul among his chiefs knew why he was disturbed.

"King of Maui, I permit none of my guests to intrude upon the Valley of Waimánu. It is the one sanctuary of my kingdom; it is tabued to strangers."

"But I am an old friend of the pious Priestess; I respect her more than any other person living. Not the least of the objects of my visit is to see the beautiful Wailéle once more," persisted Kahekili.

"This company of kings and nobles will find the hospitality of Waipio sufficient to occupy their time during the three days they will remain with us."

Thus Kalaniopuu not only forbade the King of Maui to visit Waimánu, but limited the visit to his court to the three days for which the guests were bidden. The keen-eyed old monarch had already discovered that jealousies were aroused, which, under the excitement of too much *awa*,* would breed mischief among the warriors. More

---

* Chiefs were exceedingly intemperate in the use of *awa*, which often caused premature decay.—Jarves' "History," p. 492.

than this, he had been greatly perplexed by the ominous messages and threatening oracles he had received from the several *heiāus*, and could not quite determine how he should abridge the visit of his royal neighbors. But when his favorite Priestess of Mukíni was threatened with their riotous intrusion, then he found cause for limiting the stay of his dangerous visitors, even at the risk of offending the haughty chief at his side.

Both Pepehi and Wailéle had sent word that wonderful events were about to take place. It was surmised that some ancient god was coming to visit the islands; perhaps even Lono himself. The priests and prophets agreed that Kahekili's motives were to spy out the land, and that he would endeavor to win over some of the Hawáiian chiefs to fight in his cause against the Leeward Islands.

All this exciting news made the entertainment of his ancient enemies a serious task for Kalaniopuu, as he could only share his anxiety with Keoúa, Keeaumoku, and a few other trusty counsellors.

The feast over, dancing and games occupied the rest of the day; and the second day was spent in the same manner. The dignity and commanding presence of Kalaniopuu and his chiefs curbed the turbulent spirits of both parties, and nothing beyond wordy conflicts took place. But the most deadly enmities, engendered by long years of bitter warfare, rankled in the hearts of these fierce princes.

XVIII.

THE MAN-KILLERS ON THE CHIEF-BOY'S TRACK.

NOT until Kaméhaméha had passed the head of Waipio Valley, a thickly-peopled garden-land far down below his track, and had approached within full view of his own Waimánu home, did he think it best to visit his uncle. But as he approached the moss-covered walls of the ancient *heiáu*, in descending the mountain, he was impelled to tarry at Puukeekee for a day. Now that he knew his own mind, he felt that he ought to come to an understanding with Pepehi in regard to the future course of his life.

As he gazed down upon the grim walls and hideous idols of the murderous place, not without apprehension, to all appearances there was neither human sacrifice nor conviviality going on, so that the time seemed auspicious for his purpose.

Not a soul greeted him as he passed through the open archway in the thick wall of the *heiáu*, though Puukeekee was a place never willingly intruded upon by the outer world.

But as he climbed cautiously up to the central terrace, where stood the *lele* and the sacred temple of the priest, his ear was assailed by the furious barking and howling of a score of well-fed dogs. What these canine assailants were fatted upon need hardly be specified. In this sanctuary but one kind of meat diet was plentiful.

As the ferocious animals snapped at his heels, Kaméhaméha pricked some of the most violent ones with his spear-point, which sent them yelping into the adjacent domicile of their sleeping master, and served the good purpose of bringing out the angry old Kahúna to the rescue.

Pepehi came rushing out, dagger in hand, tumbling over the cowering dogs, and the human bones upon which they had been feeding, seen scattered about everywhere over the terrace pavement. Kicking the yelping brutes to the right and left as he ran, and grinding his few remaining teeth with rage, the blear-eyed old priest confronted his as yet unrecognized nephew with dreadful imprecations as he bellowed savagely at the intruder:

"What, what! who's this that dares intrude upon a sacred *heidu* of the gods? What ho! *pepehi kanáka*, where are you, lazy hounds? *Wiki wiki!* (quick!) and secure this fat victim for a *kápu káne*. Curses upon the vile slaves that leave their old Kahúna alone with dogs and intruders!"

Not a word was spoken by Kaméhaméha; not a muscle of his face moved to betray his identity. The matter became all the more perplexing to Pepehi. Drawing his dagger to the front, Kaméhaméha levelled his spear to defend himself from the maddened monster, now too nearly blinded with rage to see that it was his sister's son who had entered the *heidu* in the absence of its cut-throats. The spear in the hands of a lusty looking fellow who failed to show obsequious fear of a priest, looked more than a match for his dagger; and Pepehi discreetly came to a halt about two yards from its threatening point.

Glowering with rage which momentarily increased,

and panting for breath, the priest seated himself upon an altar to confront and question the intruder who had thus dared to let blood from his pet dogs. Half a dozen of the curs were lying snarling at his feet, lapping their bleeding spear-wounds while they eyed the offender.

Looking furtively at his visitor while recovering his breath, it was only after repeated surveys that Pepehi fairly recognized Kaméhaméha, quietly seated there upon a block of lava about a spear's length away. For a while an odd mixture of surprise and anger contended for the mastery on the shrivelled face of the *Kahúna*, before he could fairly conclude who it was thus calmly wiping the dog-blood from his spear. At last, with a long expulsive breath, like the steam puff before a volcanic explosion, Pepehi broke out:

"How is this? Is it possible you are Wailéle's boy grown to be a man since I saw you! Name of Pele! you are as big as a *koa* tree, and cool and cunning enough for a *kahúna*. What say you, Kaméhaméha? Have you come to live with me and become Priest of Puukeekee?"

"Not so. I came to tell you, uncle, that I will never be a priest. I would rather be a warrior, a man of the world."

Surprise had nearly obliterated every trace of rage in the old man's face before this speech was made, but this unsatisfactory reply to his pet scheme instantly brought back a new outburst of the most envenomed frenzy.

"Bah! a young *poolua* (bastard) must be something more than a man to make his way in a bustling world like this," answered the crafty old *Kahúna*.

Dark eyes never flashed more lurid fires than were hurtled back in reply to this affront. His glances were like lance-thrusts as Kaméhaméha leaped up from the lava rock with a tigerish spring, and drew his dagger with full intent to grapple with the murderous giant for thus having stained his priestly mother's name.

But with a mighty impulse of self-control, the thoughtful chief stayed his mad intent as he reached the altar over which the agile priest had deftly sprung. Standing there transfixed, with foot advanced and brawny arm thrown back in act to strike, Kaméhaméha posed like a gladiator intent upon a deed of death.

The young *alii* was the first to grow calm. Though yet too much enraged to answer the cruel words of the *Kahúna*, he still held him with an unquailing look of reproach and a dignity of mien which still further nettled the priest.

At the first forward move of the enraged young *alii*, Pepehi had sprung nimbly over the altar, and clutched his long-bladed dagger—once a Damascus sword-blade of Pàáo's—standing firmly on the defensive. His bloodshot eyes gleamed with joy at the thought of teaching this young bantling his unerring skill in striking home to the heart, even though the victim were his own loved sister's child.

Yet this blood-loving man was not wholly an unrelenting villain. Few such are born of women. This life-long assassin could not but appreciate the courage, dignity, and self-restraint that he had just seen in the noble chief-boy. A grim smile parted the thick lips of the *Kahúna*, as the two stood glaring at each other. A gleam of demoniacal pleasure lighted up his eyes,—lurid as a sunbeam on a crater's verge,—and the monster laughed aloud as he sheathed his blade with a lingering motion, as if yet half unwilling to lose such a toothsome victim for his altar fires. But with a surly effort to be civil he gruffly addressed the chief:

"Sit down, Kaméhaméha. Your mother has begotten a mettlesome warrior, I see. Whoever your father may be, he is a better man than I thought, to impart such manliness to you. Let this piece of fretfulness pass, my lad. Let it pass in your old uncle, who admires his nephew's willingness to fight."

"Why do you brand me with foul names. As you value your life taunt me no more." And the still defiant boy looked stern and unrelenting into the mocking eyes of his uncle. He went back to the rock for his spear, and refused to be seated.

"Let it pass, my boy. I for one am not sorry it happened, for you have won my respect as you otherwise could not have done. No fear but such a mettlesome lad will win his way in the world. Next to a ready hand in a land of daggers, the best of all things is your self-restraint; 't is a mighty power in time of danger; for had your eye wavered one instant, I should have stabbed you to the heart."

"But tempt me no more, uncle, be warned in time. My will was good enough to have killed you, but for the thought that you are my mother's brother."

"And I, too, would have slaughtered my troublesome nephew, and sacrificed his tender carcass as I would a dog's. Ah! it was a pleasant thing to see a youngster with such a lust for murder in his callow heart. It was the finest impulse of cut and slash my old eyes have seen. Pity it was spoiled by a puling sentiment! Pity that it checked your dagger-hand from stabbing your mother's brother! But whatever the impulse which restrained you, your courage to fight against odds of age and skill comes only of highly tempered metal, and I admire it."

"But why do you taunt me with *poolua?* Am I not a 'god-born' *alii?* None know better than you, a *mookahúna* (history-making priest), that honor and heredity come from the mother, not from the father."

"You are right, boy. There's truth in what you say. Who taught you this?"

"The blind bard and my noble mother. How many of King Keawe's hundred children, born on every isle, dare claim descent from that wandering rake, who took every pretty woman to wife without regard to rank? Only those born of noble mothers are deemed exalted; the plebeian children remain ignoble though begotten by a popular king."*

"So you are wise above your years, I see, and know the mother's superiority in this matter. True, the child of a noble chiefess needs not the prestige of a father; true, the brat of a *wahine wale* is not ennobled even by a monarch. But who is your sire, my mettlesome Alii?"

"I am taught that I was 'god-born,' as you well know, and I am led to believe that the divine Pele is my godmother."

"True, and with every priest in the land I, too, have taught that pretty creed, believing it, however, as little as most else that I preach for the good of priestcraft."

"The day is waning, uncle, and I must hasten to Waimánu."

"Nay, boy, tarry for some days with me. I cannot

---

* Kaméhaméha IV. and V. were noble only through their mother, Kinau. Chiefs descended from Keawe by common women feel dishonored, conceal their origin, and dislike to have their plebeian genealogy recalled.—Remy's "Venerable Savage," p, 31.

quite give up the thought of making you Priest of Puukeekee."

"No more of that. The thought of it makes the blood trickle to my spear-point. I must away. *Aloha!*"

And without mentioning a word of his recent expedition to Mauna Loa, or even waiting to partake of food, lest the dust of Pepehi's poison god should accidentally get mixed with his beverage of *poi*, he abruptly left the *heiáu*. He soon met a royal courier from Waipio as he passed out, who informed him that great events were about to occur at court, and asked where he could find Pepehi. Hastening down the mountain path on his lonely way to Waimánu, the fearless chief was not above the prudence of keeping to the most open trail to be found, lest some ambuscade of his affectionate uncle's assassins might be laid for him.

It had not escaped the observation of the keen-eyed boy, that immediately after he left the *heiáu*, Pepehi made vigorous *tabú* signals, meaning: Urgent need of victims. Kaméhaméha well knew, in spite of all the priest's professions of friendliness, that he could never again feel secure from his vengeance. Satanic craftiness was the strongest trait of the Kahúna; he would follow a trail of blood like a sleuth-hound until his revenge was sated. Most likely the murderous man-killers were prowling about Waipio. But as there was little communication with the inaccessible valley of Waimánu, the alert young Alii saw no cause for alarm. Striding rapidly along the south *páli* until he reached the great pandanus, he there made signal for a canoe, and was almost instantly answered by a dozen upraised hands at Mukíni.

A general uneasiness had been felt on account of his long absence, and one or more of the priest-girls were on the watch along the south *páli* for his coming. Wailéle had been impressed with some deadly peril awaiting him. Whether her maternal instinct had been aroused by what had already occurred at the *heiáu*, or the prophetic insight of the priestess had forecast coming events, it is not easy to say. This much is certain, the watchful eyes at Mukíni had already discovered two burly man-killers following on Kaméhaméha's trail, a moment after he left the pandanus, tracking swiftly along the *páli's* edge about half a mile behind the chief. The foremost *pepehi* had a lariat in his hand, ready looped to noose and strangle his victim, while the less powerful assassin carried a short sharp spear which had drunk the heart-blood of hundreds of innocents.

None understood better than the anxious priest-mother and *wahines* this dreadful portent. These inhuman creatures followed a trail as cunningly as serpents, and as noiselessly as ghosts, and they struck their fatal blows with the certainty of long experience. A second canoe was manned by some of the lusty slave men belonging to the *heiáu*, and dispatched with all haste to the river mouth. But the previous canoe had lost no time, and was already out through the breakers, and speeding swiftly for the adjacent valley, about two miles away. It was ardent friendship for Kaméhaméha, not fear of his safety, that impelled these swift paddles.

All unconscious of the danger on his track, Kaméhaméha arrived safely at the shore. The canoe from Waimánu awaited him, manned by twenty of his devoted chief-friends. They were full of joy to see their young leader again, and wild with impatience to learn the success of his mission to Pele.

Embarking after all had rubbed noses and embraced

him, Kaméhaméha was somewhat startled on looking back to see a glistening spear-point among the banana trees skirting the beach, and soon after, as the canoe receded swiftly from the shore, two beastly-looking faces were thrust cautiously out from among the bushes. One of them he remembered as Pepo, the gigantic *pepehi* who had once guided him down from Puukeekee.

The first impulse of the indignant chief was to return to the shore and give battle to the wretches, but on second thought he concluded that they must have been lurking there before he came, and were not sent to entrap him.

As the canoe sped along the shore Kaméhaméha could not resist the importunity of the chief-boys to relate his pilgrimage to the gods. When he told them of his climbing Mauna Loa by the light of the lava flow, and passing a night by the dreadful crater, and described the black demons in the lake of fire, every paddle was suspended, and every face displayed horror at the supernatural dangers from which he had escaped. Without betraying its special import, he briefly related his interview with Pele, which for ever sanctified him in the esteem of every chief of Waimánu. When they knew he was loved by the gods, and that his ambitious schemes were sanctioned, every arm that could wield a spear was ready to battle for him.

As they approached Waimánu River, their shouts collected hundreds of other chiefs, until the river bank was thronged. They changed canoes and paddled up to Tribute Rock, where other crowds had gathered to cry their glad *Aloha*. There hundreds of enthusiastic young souls were heard, vowing eternal allegiance to their young Alii.

This reception affected the noble boy to tears. Assuming the prerogative of a priest of Mukíni,—for he was ennobled by his interview with Pele,—he permitted the canoe which bore him and his twenty companions to pass the *tabú* line at Tribute Rock, and paddle on up to the garden entrance of Mukíni. There Wailéle and the whole family of priest-girls, with their yelping nurslings, were waiting to receive their young lord. Glad indeed was the meeting. One after another of the *wahines*, after the stately priest-mother had welcomed her boy with mingled pride and love, took their young Alii in their arms. The excited chief-boys had hastened to relate Kaméhaméha's adventures in brief epitome, ere the canoes touched the shore, and from that hour he was sanctified in their eyes.

A sumptuous supper was served for Kaméhaméha and his chiefs, after which all gathered with the *wahines* upon the veranda to listen to a more detailed account of the traveller's story. Great was the mother's pride in her boy as she listened to his wonderful adventures; his struggles in climbing the mountain, whose vast summit none other had ever approached; his courage in invading the tabued snow line, and approaching the forbidden crater in defiance of the howling demons of *Mokua-weo-weo*. And when he related his vision of the divine Pele, and the condescension of the deity to her child, the mother's heart burst forth in adoration of the gracious goddess for conferring such high honor upon her offspring.

When the chiefs had returned down the river, and the greetings of the household retainers were over, Kaméhaméha took his fond mother aside to unfold a less pleasant part of his experience. The story of the quarrel at Puukeekee he had purposely reserved. When he had related every thing which happened, and repeated every word that was spoken by the murder-loving priest, the transition of Wailéle's emotions from reverence to rage was dreadful. The beautiful face of the Priestess turned to a pallor that her boy had never seen before. Grief filled her flashing eyes with tears ; then came rage at the indignity Pepehi had put upon herself and her child. Woe to the old priest should he come within Wailéle's grasp in such an hour of resentment!

These emotions were followed by yet another one of greater import to her tender heart. Terrible as it was to contemplate the deadly peril from which her boy had escaped, the mother's anxiety for the future now surmounted all else. The old Kahúna was an experienced assassin ; seldom did he fail to avenge an offence by the death of his antagonist. And now the man-killers of Puukeekee had been already set upon his trail ; Wailéle well knew that nothing but divine interposition could save her child. But before she slept, unknown to Kaméhaméha, the Priestess set her most faithful slave soldiers to guard every approach to the *heidu* through the night, with orders to kill on the instant all who should fail to give the countersign. And lest her proud Alii should think that some of her emotions were due to the existence of just cause for the insulting epithet put upon his birth, the beautiful mother bid him know that he was not only legitimate, but of yet greater paternal rank than he knew, and that in proper time all the world should be informed who he was, and would gladly bend the knee to his power and rank.

XIX.

PEPEHI REBUKED BY THE GODDESS.

BEFORE noon on the following day the people of Mukíni were unpleasantly surprised by a visit from Pepehi. His coming was made the more suspicious and unwelcome because he was accompanied by his most savage *pepehi;* for bloodshed rarely failed to follow the presence of the gigantic Pepo.

Wailéle was struck dumb with consternation when she saw the murderous pair coming up the river path together. Before the priest could reach the *heidu* she found time to arm herself with a dagger, meaning to defend her boy with her life. Her first source of anxiety was for Kaméhaméha, who fortunately was absent at the cataracts, bathing in the lava basins in the dash of the water-fall. Pemilani was sent at once to hasten his return to the *heidu*, taking his spear, in addition to the dagger he constantly wore, and to bid him keep constantly upon his guard against Pepo, the *pepehi*. A few strong slave guards were ordered out to meet their young master as he returned, and to be guided by his wishes. Another *wahine* was sent hurriedly down the river to invite a half dozen of the old war chiefs to the rescue, with orders to come armed and to act on the instant in case of need.

The gigantic old priest was apparently in the best of humor; gracious to every one, most affectionate and smiling to the Priestess. But none were deceived by his manner. Pepehi's pleasantry was well known to be more ominous than his rage.

Wailéle received her half-brother with becoming dignity, bridling her rising anger until her guards should be collected and Kaméhaméha have time to return. Gladly humoring his affability, she attended to his polite demands for breakfast, in order to gain time and to delay the coming crisis until she could meet it with a stronger hand.

Having finished his deliberate meal, growling a little because of the insufficient amount of *awa* furnished him, he asked the Priestess into the *heidu* for a private interview. As Wailéle had received information that four of the high chiefs were in sight on the river, and would soon land, and as Pepehi continued his efforts to quiet her indignation, she led the way into the greater seclusion of the temple.

Avoiding all allusion to the quarrel with his nephew, the priest came at once to the secondary object of his visit—his primary object being murder if he could not carry his point,—urging with many arguments the necessity of Kaméhaméha's becoming the priest of Puukeekee. From this exalted position, he said, the young prince could best make his way in the world.

Listening with impatience to the end, the arrogant Priestess replied that this scheme did not accord with her wishes nor with the ambition of her boy, and after further decided protest, sternly averred that she would rather bury her son than consent to have him live at Puukeekee.

The sunken eyes of the old Kahúna gleamed with a lurid light as Wailéle let loose the pent volcano of her wrath upon his aged head. His tall, gaunt figure swayed and writhed with suppressed anger, as he listened to her savage rejection of his beastly companionship for her noble boy. Crouching lower and lower with a scarce restrained impulse to spring upon her, Pepehi clutched his dagger with nervous frenzy, contemplating the use of his one unfailing argument to end a debate. But recovering his self-control, he cast a withering look upon Wailéle and turned to leave the *heidu*. Kaméhaméha entered hurriedly at that moment, with an angry frown upon his face. Turning back to Wailéle with a malicious expression on his wrinkled visage, Pepehi cried:

"Here comes your proud *poolua!* If his precious life is spared make of him what you——"

Further insult was stopped by a powerful blow from Kaméhaméha. The gigantic priest tumbled headlong upon the stone pavement like a felled ox.

With the howl of a maniac, the ferocious Kahúna called aloud for Pepo, as he sprang up and drew his long dagger. The two combatants sprang at each other with fire-flashing eyes that meant a death grapple for both.

With the bound of a tigress alarmed for her young, Wailéle sprang between them at the risk of receiving both their blows. Grasping the uplifted dagger-hands of the two by the wrist, with the supernatural strength of a giant mother battling for her child, she shook the weapons from their strong grasp, as if they had been children; calling fiercely to Pepehi:

"Hold! villain, murderer! Would you strike a royal Alii—the god-born son of your king? Down on your knees and ask pardon of your future lord and master, or the woman's hand that disarms you shall crush you to the earth and trample you beneath her feet!"

While her arm was raised in act to strike the mad priest down, lo! a sudden whirr of invisible wings filled the temple, as it were of an angel hovering in their midst. A blinding radiance of divine glory burst forth and filled the place, admonishing them of the awful presence of a god.

It was Pele who stood before them! By the lightning flashes of her yellow hair; by her blue eyes, more beautiful than the stars; by the divine beauty of her person, softly wrapped about with a garment of lambent flame golden as her tresses, they knew that the supreme woman-goddess of Hawáii was there. Priest, Priestess, and royal Alii together fell upon their knees under the blinding light. A hush as of death filled the temple; then the dread goddess spoke to the awed supplicants at her feet:

"Peace! peace!" she cried, with a voice that vibrated through Kaméhaméha's soul like strains of music. "Behold! you are in the presence of your god! Hush your brawling passions, and hearken to my words. Let every voice proclaim this Alii as beloved of Pele,—'god-born' in answer to the prayers of noble monarch and pious priestess. Greet him henceforth as 'High Priest of Mukíni,' a priest outranking every living *kahúna* in the land!

"Hearken! that you may hear. Whom the gods love shall be exalted above all men in wisdom, and become foremost in war. From this hour, neither poisoned dagger of treacherous priest nor spear of honest foeman shall pierce his heart, because of this divine decree.

"Priestess of Mukíni, send forth the young Alii into the world. Events which will instruct him for his future mission are about to happen; events without name, full of unspeakable wonder. Men unknown to our land are approaching; people with strange white faces are coming in mighty ocean craft to land upon our shores. Great wars are also impending, in which Kaméhaméha must take part. He must become skilled above all warriors, against the happy end to come when all wars shall cease forever."

Then turning sternly to the old priest, who grovelled and trembled on the pavement, Pele expressed her disapprobation of himself and his doings:

"Pepehi of Puukeekee! You have lived a life useless to Hawáii and displeasing to the gods. Henceforth keep strictly to your mountain *heidu*, and come not here again, you nor your *pepehi*, into the sacred valley of Waimánu. In the moment when you defame these noble ones of Mukíni—either by word or deed,—in that moment you shall die, shrivelled instantly to a fiery cinder.

"And you, beloved mortals! *Aloha oe*, Wailéle! *Aloha oe*, loved young king!"

The beautiful vision of deity wavered and swayed like a strong expiring flame, and was gone. A floating perfume as of sandalwood incense only remained. Wailéle stood proudly by her young King and Priest, her eyes filled with proud tears of joy. A noble exultation glowed on Kaméhaméha's face at being thus sanctified by the supreme god of the land. The contrite old Kahúna, disarmed of his dagger, knelt at his feet. Extending his hands in supplication, he cried out:

"Praise to Pele! My old eyes behold a great future for Kaméhaméha, the warrior, the conqueror, the king. There rises before me a vision filled with the glory of his deeds. I behold great armies thundering into battle at his bidding. The mighty kings of the isles bend in supplication before him ; but the clemency of a conqueror must be tempered with daggers for the unconquerable. I behold a canoe full of royal chiefs lying dead on the boiling sands of Kawaihae.* A dead king lies among them, and it is the will of Pele ; for together the royal dead are piled on the altar of a new *heidu*, not yet built with hands.

"What vision is this? Stupendous battles come ; they are fought with weapons of fire and thunder, that scatter the fleets of combined kings as birds are scattered by a storm. How fast the island kingdoms fall! I behold but one kingdom and one king ; it is for the first time in a thousand years. The altars of the 'Eight Isles' cease to smoke as of old, and a hallowed peace pervades all the lands, such glory as dwells only among the stars.

"This is my vision. This is the prophecy which flames up before me, vivid as the night-fires on Mauna Loa. *Aloha !* I go to Puukeekee, never more to return to the valley of my birth. It is the will of Pele ; it is the command of the gods."

Ere the crushed and penitent old priest went from among them forever, Wailéle came generously forward to greet him, blessing him with tearful eyes for his prophecy. For none other in all the land could see with more prophetic vision than Pepehi in his moments of sober inspiration.

Kaméhaméha gave the Kahúna his hand in full forgiveness of his revengeful mission to Mukíni. The young Alii disclosed the newly awakened pride of his heart in his glad utterance to the aged prophet who still knelt before him.

---

* Sulphur water bubbles through the sand at high-water mark, near the *heidu* where Keoúa was slain. (Ellis, p. 376.)

"Aloha, Kahúna! You have made a man's heart beat in a boy's breast. Your words have but faintly described my own dreams of greatness. None but this darling mother knows how lofty are my plans for my country. I shall accomplish them all! The triumph of my valor in battle shall make a peaceful land, wherein old men shall lie down on the highways in safety."*

Fire flashed from the eyes of the stern old Kahúna as his own keen insight followed the vaulting ambition and the seer-like vision of the young chief. Pepehi rose up and departed, ashamed of his mission to Mukíni, and crushed by the rebuke from his god, yet kindling with a glow of pride in Pele's adoption of his nephew. As he came out upon the veranda, followed by Wailéle and Kaméhaméha, he meekly called for Pepo, and gathered his *tapa* about him to depart. Four of the grim old warriors of the valley were sitting quietly upon the veranda eating raw fish and *poi*. One of them delayed his repast long enough to point contemptuously down the path. There lay Pepo's body righteously transfixed by four huge spears. He had made a persistent attempt to rush into the *heidu* at Pepehi's call, and received his death.

For one instant the fierce old Kahúna forgot himself, and turning furiously upon the chiefs, savagely demanded:

"Who bid you do harm to my best *pepehi*?"

"Your master!" gruffly answered the four warriors in concert, pointing to Kaméhaméha, who bowed his head in full acknowledgment, and added:

"You sent Pepo and another *pepehi* upon my track yesterday. This one I have slain; the other I will attend to when we meet."

---

* See Jarves' History, pp. —

Without a word or even an angry gesture in reply, the old priest drew his poisoned dagger, and presenting its hilt to the young Alii, fell submissively upon his knees, and bared his shaggy breast that Kaméhaméha might kill him for his crime. But when he declined to take vengeance, Pepehi begged his young lord to accept the dagger as a gift, it being the rarest weapon among all the islands. He took it with pleasure, as the most valuable heirloom belonging to the descendants of Pàáo.

With bowed head and humble submission the old man rose to depart, first begging the war-chiefs to dispose of his dead friend and fellow-murderer, who had furnished Puukeekee with hundreds of victims. Seeking the river he paddled down the stream alone in the canoe which brought him, and disappeared from the upper valley, never to return.

The wise old seer's vision had included more than he chose to tell. He had seen that ere long a strong hand would restrain such murderous doings as his at Puukeekee, and that he must amend his ways in time. He saw that his hours of riotous wassail must henceforth be in secret, and his murders less open and defiant as his years rolled on.

XX.

KAMÉHAMÉHA SETS OUT TO CLAIM HIS BIRTHRIGHT.

THE disclosure of his royal parentage having been made known to him, it was now deemed best for Kaméhaméha to go at once to Waipio and present himself for recognition, as every thing yet depended upon the king's acknowledgment of his god-born boy. As Kalaniopuu had a son at court, a dissolute and rebellious youth a few years younger than Kaméhaméha, it remained to be seen how a sudden and new accession to the royal family would be received, not only by the king and his several queens, but by the heir-apparent himself, who had more than once been the nucleus of ill-assorted conspiracies against the king.

The day after Pepehi's departure was given to preparations for Kaméhaméha's trip to Waipio. The high chiefs were informed of all that had passed in the *heidu*, of Péle's startling disclosure about Lono's coming, and of the impending wars to follow. It was the advice of the chiefs that Kaméhaméha should take with him a company of fifty young chiefs of the highest rank in the valley, as a fit following for a royal *alii* when presented to the king; and they took it upon themselves to muster the young warriors and make choice of those best fitted to go.

Most of the coming night was spent by the Priestess and her son in maturing plans for the future. Great was the astonishment of the young chief to learn he was a royal *alii*, not only by his mother's side, but by his father's also. But his delight soon gave place to the sagacious desire to gain all the knowledge that would be needed in the deceptive world he was about to enter. Especially did he wish to acquire appropriate keys of conduct toward the ruling minds at court, according to the characteristics of each. Having unlimited confidence in the wisdom of his much-loved mother, endless were the questions that he asked about the king and his great warriors. This subtle method of dealing with men remained a leading trait in Kaméhaméha's character through life.

The "Feast of the Kings" was considered an auspicious time for Kaméhaméha's purposes, as now he could avail himself of the only probable opportunity of his life to meet the haughty rulers of the Leeward kingdoms. Kalaniopuu, too, had been informed of Pele's oracle of an immediately impending war ; and this made the present time still more fitting for the chief-boy's presentation to the king.

At the earliest approach of dawn the household of Mukini was called to worship in the *heidu*. An *ilio poli* was sacrificed to Pele on the occasion of their young high-priest's departure. Fervent was the worship and heart-felt the songs of praise around the altar and in the holy-of-holies on that eventful morning, for a more loving priesthood was not known throughout the Eight Isles.

At length the worship was ended, and Wailéle ordered the *heidu* to be cleared, that none should intrude upon her last instructions to her boy. Placing a double line of *tabu* flags at the entrance to the *heidu*, Wailéle brought forth from their hiding-place beneath the *anu* the king's spear and *palaoa*. Putting the royal insignia about the Alii's neck, and placing his father's richly carved spear in his hand, the beautiful priest-mother looked upon her prince with mingled tears of pride and joy—tears that were never forfeited by any act of his life. Kaméhaméha's subdued delight was exceeded by his sense of the momentous occasion ; for now he was adorned with the rarest insignia of rank in the nation.

The time was approaching for mother and son to separate, and perhaps to part forever. In such turbulent times there was no telling the fatal turn that events might take when a young man, almost unknown, should go forth to claim his birthright of a king. Though Kalaniopuu was believed to be the most noble of all the Hawáiian kings, yet so arbitrary and cruel were most of the rulers of the day, that if he should not be pleased with his new-found heir, it would require but a look askance to his guard, and a spear-thrust would instantly end the claim upon his paternity.

With such sad thoughts in her mind, Wailéle called her much-loved chief-boy into the holy-of-holies to impart her last prayerful instructions before they parted.

"Oh ! my child, this will indeed be an eventful day for us. Before the sun goes down you will either be the *alii wohi*—a chief next the king—of my great good king, whom your mother has loved better than her life for twenty years, or—alas! dear boy, must I tell you the dreadful alternative of kings ? If Kalaniopuu is not in the mood to receive you, death will be dealt to you on the instant. Watch every look of the king. It is a face never to be forgotten—lofty, noble, tender, and loving in his mood. But if that kingly face is turned coldly away when you greet him, then prepare to die manfully; there will be no appeal.

"Remember, above every other thought, that Wailéle will live happier to know that the chief that she bore can die as becomes his rank. Die not only courageously, but with a smile on your lips for the hand that inflicts the blow; a generous word even for the king who bids you die.

"But if you are accepted as the king's son, then an ordeal as hard as death awaits you. A thousand perils will hedge you about; treacherous hands lurk everywhere to kill the claimant to a throne. Counsel with your father how best to conduct yourself. Show only a becoming joy at your success; a modest pride best becomes the hero of Mukíni. Demean yourself pleasantly to all, and be not arrogant to those beneath you. Trust not the friendship of prince, brother, or any near relative of the king's, for you will be looked upon as an intruder, and plotted against with deadly jealousy.

"My son, listen now to my final instructions, for life or death depends wholly on how you fulfil them. Land from the river abreast of the palace, and bid your companions lie on their paddles not far from the shore and await your coming. Go straight to the palace without spying to the right or left. Speak to no one except to ask: 'Where is the king?'

"As you approach the palace from the river you will see the *puka pukaka*—a private door of the king—to the right of the main entrance.

"A numerous guard at the entrance of the enclosure will present their spears and demand your business. Answer: 'Where is the king?' and press steadily upon their spears with an unquailing eye; for armed men are like fierce dogs, only harming those who fear them.

"Across the path leading into the enclosure, a little distance before the *puka pukaka*, is extended the sacred cord of *Ahaula*. Whoever passes that *tabú* line, should the king extend his hand from the door, may live. If the king averts his face—he dies. Only royal *aliis* and the high-priest are privileged here.

"After passing the guard some will call to you: ' *Tabú! Tabú!* ' others will cry in their amazement to see you enter: ' 'T is death! 'T is death!' Heed them not, but pass the *tabú* line, lift the curtain, and enter the sacred door with a fearless, modest bearing.

"The king will be sitting on his couch, just awakened from slumber. Go straight to him with a calm, respectful bearing, meeting him unflinchingly eye to eye. To his question: 'Who are you?' point to your insignia and reply in the *Ka Ke* language: 'The name of this *palaoa* is Umi. That is the name you gave your child, when Wailéle of Mukíni and the king prayed to Pele for a son.' To his question: 'What is the password belonging to your *palaoa?*' say: '*Kulia i ka Nuu!*'

"Discourse with the king on these secret topics only in the *Ka Ke* (court language). If you live to accomplish this much, you will be accepted by the king, and a sure path to a kingdom is before you; this he promised for the time when the *palaoa* should be restored to him."

Her prophetic instructions over, the austerity of the Priestess gave way. The sorrowing mother clasped her noble boy with a frenzy of affection. Holding him at arm's length before her, she endeavored to trace the loved lineaments of the father in his manly face. The affectionate chief clung to the beautiful mother of whom he was so proud, and promised that every act of his life should be worthy of her love.

The Sad Parting. 185

"Dear, dear mother! you have given me a strong heart and an arm of power. You have filled my soul with great thoughts that lift me to the skies. You have made your boy wise above his years, and as good as poor human nature permits in this land of bloodshed and treachery.

"Watch me, darling mother, as I come to manhood! Every great act of my life will be prompted by you. In the hour of battle, listen to hear my swift blows fall; behold me battling for Wailéle and Hawáii. Never shall you blush for your future warrior, statesman, or king."

Leaving the *heiaú*, the two walked sadly down to the river together, followed by the six weeping priest-girls, two of whom, though double his own age, became Kaméhaméha's wives in after years. There they parted. A light canoe was in waiting for the young Alii, in which Kinau and his loved Pemilani took him down to Tribute Rock, where every noble chief-boy of the valley had been invited to meet him, having been notified by the old war chiefs of his final departure for Waipio. By their advice Kaméhaméha had concluded to take a company of expert warriors with him; this should have the effect of making his coming the more welcome to the king.

Joyous was the greeting of the chiefs, as the Alii came in view from the forest covert, swiftly paddled by the *wahines*. Landing at the grounds of the high chief of the valley, Alapai, of Waimánu, came forward to greet him, and presented to him fifty strong young chiefs, chosen from hundreds who wished to go with their royal leader and fight for the king. Several of these boys became great war chiefs and able counsellors for their future king.

Briefly addressing the multitude, Kaméhaméha told them something of his ambitious views for his country. He promised Alapai to lead his company of nobles where blows were thickest in the hour of battle. He charged the other young warriors to prepare for the wars of which Pele had forewarned them, as only by the skilled use of weapons could they hope to make themselves a name.

The water being too shoal for his large double canoe to come up the river, his party took small canoes and paddled down to the beach, followed by thousands of loving friends, running gayly along the river bank, cheering the chosen fifty as they ran.

At the shore he found the finest war canoe belonging to the valley, a present from one of the great chiefs to the royal Alii.

Thousands of people were gathered to see him embark. The canoe was pushed out into the river mouth, and the fifty paddlers shook their flashing paddle blades in the sunlight. From cliff to cliff the whole rang with the cry of "*Aloha! Aloha!*" Nor did the farewell shouts cease till the great canoe had passed out through the furious breakers into the bright blue sea beyond; then Kaméhaméha turned his prow southward toward Waipio.

XXI.

COMMOTION AT WAIPIO.

DURING the first two days of the "Feast of the Kings," the guests of Kalaniopuu had occupied themselves with various athletic games. Whether purposely or not, the dangerous exercise of spear-darting had so far been avoided, perhaps in fear of exciting the deadly jealousies that rankle between recent enemies. But all had passed so pleasantly thus far, that the third day, it was agreed, should be given up to spear practice, and to other skilled trials of warlike weapons. Great enjoyment was anticipated from witnessing the *hoo-palau*, or single combat, between some of the gigantic athletes present. Several of the chiefs were as formidable combatants as the world had seen. The Polynesians excelled all other races in physical strength*; and these were men of three hundred pounds' weight, yet graceful and agile, with iron muscles and strength to fling a spear clear through a man.

A number of exciting tests of skill between the giants had taken place, and the grounds were given up for a while to men of less note, while the great lordlings lay about in the shade of the fruit-trees watching the sport. During this interval Kalaniopuu went to take his accus-

---

* Compare Paul Topinard's "Anthropology" (Bartley's translation), and Jarves' History, p. 46. A stature upward of six feet six inches, and three hundred pounds' weight, were not uncommon.

tomed bath and to receive his *lomi-lomi*. It was perhaps an hour after the king had left the company that a sudden commotion took place at the mouth of the valley. A swarm of women and children, mounting the great sand-hills along the shore, lustily cheered some newcomers, who paddled their war canoe with amazing swiftness up the river. Abreast of the palace their leader leapt ashore, and the canoe lay off in the stream waiting his return.

At first this incident did not greatly disturb the sports of the combatants. But a ripple of greater interest soon pervaded the whole company, until kings, chiefs, and *kandkas* were alike alert with curiosity about the strange events that were taking place at the palace. Word was finally brought that a war canoe had arrived from Waimánu, bringing a company of noble chief-boys from nineteen to twenty years old,—young warriors come to offer their services to the king, and to enroll themselves among the war chiefs of the land.

But the mystery which had aroused especial curiosity was not that a body of young chiefs had come to Waipio to exhibit their war skill. This was not an uncommon occurrrence. But the young leader, it was believed, was now holding secret conclave with the king. This was the real cause of excitement.

The few who had seen the agile young Alii leap from his canoe, and, without *kokolo*,* walk unterrified and unannounced straight into the palace by the sacred *puka pukaka* (private door of the king), avowed that the god-born chief, recognized as such by his nakedness, was deterred neither by the spears of the guard, the warning

---

* *Kokolo*, the crawling posture required of inferiors when approaching a great chief or his residence.

cries of the priests, nor yet the sacred *tabú* line, over which no mortal but Kiwalao, Holoae the priest, and Keeaumoku the *alii wohi*, dare pass.

It was said that the arrogant motion of his hand alone sufficed to appall the guard, who uttered the cry: "*He akua ia! He akua ia!*" (he is a god!), and dropped their spear-points in dread from his naked breast, as they fell respectfully back to let him pass.

Even the sacred cord of *Ahaula*—the *tabú* line—was contemptuously trampled upon, and without an instant's hesitation the proud Alii strode into the presence of the sleeping king, where he was seen standing erect and undismayed before the astonished *kiaipoo* (guard during sleep), who failed to kill him as he ought. The astonished informer added: "I tell you, chiefs, he seemed like a god from the under world, come to receive homage from kings; not like one who would pay fealty to the proudest monarch of the " Eight Isles."

When the excited speaker left the palace grounds, the *paku*, or curtain, had been dropped before the door, and the stranger was still closeted with Kalaniopuu, the *kiaipoo* having been sent out to guard the private door, with orders to deny access to all comers. Even Holoae, the venerable high-priest, had been turned back.

The eloquent Naihe now made his appearance, and kings and chiefs eagerly gathered about him for the news. He had tried to glean information from the chiefs in the canoe. They had not landed, but lay out in the river, their prow turned seaward, awaiting their leader. They were not communicative, and would only say:

"We have come from Waimánu with our leader, Kaméhaméha, the god-born chief. His business is with the king, and ours to wait his orders to return or remain as he pleases." To this brief information Naihe added: "I saw the chief. A grand Alii, looking to be twenty; strong, graceful, and active, carrying his head like a monarch. He has an eye that pierces to the soul; it thrills the heart with admiration of his proud bearing or of his god-born origin. He is naked as a fish. He carries a spear carved fitly for a king. He wears a royal decoration about his neck, a large *palaoa*, attached to a costly *lei* of the royal yellow."

"He deserves to be flung from your highest *pali* where Kanaawa was slain for such an intrusion, a few years ago," said the scornful Kahekili.

"How dares he thus enter the presence of Kalaniopuu, if he is not a ruler in the land?" questioned Keao.

"It remains a mystery," said Naihe, "for he trod down the *tabu* line and entered the sacred precinct as if he were Pepehi himself."

"Whoever he is," remarked Keeaumoku, "he knows his right, whatever it may be, and Kalaniopuu has recognized him, or we should have seen him flung from yonder cliff before now."

"Here comes the prince. Perhaps he can solve the problem. Who is the new-comer, Kiwalao?" asked Naihe.

"We have just come from fishing in the upper valley. I only know there is a *malahini* (stranger) among us. The news run past us over the valley swift as a wail for the dead. I'll go and look up the matter."

The swaggering, dissolute youth sauntered down the river path toward the palace, intent upon solving the mystery.

XXII.

LIFE OR DEATH FOR THE KING'S SON.

WHEN Kaméhaméha landed he had no need to ask where the palace was, or if the king was within; for the strong array of guards seen in front of the enclosure was sufficient answer to his mental query. Briskly approaching the line of spears which barred the *puka pukaka*, the fearless young Alii remembered the prophetic words of his mother:

"Go straight to the king, looking neither to the right nor left. Show no fear of the loud warnings of priests, nor the threatening weapons of guards, for they harm only those who fear them."

His dark eyes were lighted by the fearless soul within, as he strode on exultant, in the hope of beholding his royal father. Almost to his surprise the twenty threatening spears parted and let him pass; the guards fell back with trembling and fear, exclaiming:

"*He akua ia! He akua ia!*" Made confident by this marvellous success, he dared even to put his proud foot upon the symbolic barrier, the dread *Ahaula*. Pressing the cord disdainfully to the ground, it broke with a twang, like the painful cry of a hidden spirit. The sound aroused strong superstitious fears. The croaking voices of many cried out:

"*Tabú! Tabú!* It is death to enter the *puka pukaka!*"

But Kaméhaméha was not one to heed these alarms. He put the *paku* (curtain) from before the sacred door and entered. He found himself in the presence of the sleeping king, while the gigantic *kiaipoo* sprang forward with a lowering brow, and pressed the point of his sharp spear against his breast, crying out loud enough to wake the king:

"*E imi oe kou make?*"—Do you seek your death?

Not a muscle of the chief-boy's face showed fear of the ferocious guard, or heed of the weapon that brought blood trickling from his breast. But admiration for the slumbering monarch kindled in him a strong outpouring of filial affection for the parent whom he now saw for the first time.

Kalaniopuu was aroused from sleep by the cry of the *kiaipoo*, and sat up on his couch of mats and *pulu* down, full of indignation and surprise at the scene. He saw a chief with inoffensive spear and dagger, adorned with the insignia of royalty. What could it mean? He could find no heart to give the word for his death.

Looking fixedly and sternly at the admiring chief before him, a glow of quick admiration crept over the benignant face of the king, as he saw the ardent look of love in the stranger youth, and his total unconsciousness of the savage guard or the spear-point in his bleeding chest. Holding up his hand for the guard to desist, the king exclaimed:

"Hold! *kiaipoo*. Noble Alii, *ua makapo oe?*" (are you blind?)

"No, *Alii Moi*, for I behold the noble king, my father!"

"*Owai oe?*—who are you?" exclaimed the king (in the *Ka Ke* tongue), his interest now fully awakened in the stranger.

Pointing to the ivory tooth suspended from his neck, Kaméhaméha replied:

"Sire, my royal father named me 'Umi' from the *niho palaoa* which I wear. My mother, Wailéle of Mukíni, bids me return this royal insignia to its rightful owner, the king." And he took off the priceless decoration and laid it reverently at the monarch's feet.

"*Malia!*—hush. This secret had best remain with ourselves." And turning to the faithful guard, he said: "*Kiaipoo*, we would be alone. Guard the *puka pukaka* with a sharp spear that lets neither prince nor *kahúna* pass. *E hele!*—begone!"

As the guard passed out and dropped the *paku* before the door, the face of the king lighted up with undisguised pleasure as he asked:

"And you are Kaméhaméha of Waimánu, spoken of as such a prodigy?"

"Yes, sire. Let me hope that I may prove worthy of my noble parentage."

"You are indeed a brave youth. Come here and salute me," and the king placed his thigh for Kaméhaméha to sit upon, and caught the manly boy joyfully in his arms, looking upon him with affection and pride.

"But you are older than my son should be."

"I am but nineteen this day."

"You are a noble fellow, and at this rate you will soon be larger than your father. Can it be twenty years since I prayed to Pele in the temple of Mukíni for an heir? You are indeed worthy of your noble mother, whom I won only by the promise that she should be forever left to rule over her loved Mukíni. Has she imparted her wise state-craft to my boy?"

"She has taught me to be brave in the face of danger, and faithful to my king and country."

"Noble Wailéle! What a worthy counsellor thou hast been! Is it true, my boy, that you ascended Mauna Loa, and climbed to the dreadful *Mokua-weo-weo?*"

"Yes, my father, I spent the night on the summit, sitting by the terrible crater, alone with the demon spirits."

"Did Pele come forth to greet you?"

"Not there, but at the upper edge of the forest belt the divine Goddess came to bless me with her presence, and entrusted to me a mission for my country."

At this moment a noisy tumult occurred without. The guard resisted the turbulent prince, who demanded to see his father. For an instant the old monarch's face assumed a severe expression, changing at length to a look of sorrow, for Kiwalao was a rebellious boy. Turning to Kaméhaméha, he said :

"My son, my noble boy, I cannot do by you now as I could wish. It would not be best to give you your full rights to-day. The world about us is full of treachery ; the court minions plot evil and foment jealousies. Therefore our precious secret had better be kept to ourselves, or shared with Keeaumoku only, whom I will appoint your *kahu alii* (guardian chief). Be watchful of your conduct, lest you make enemies at court. Let it suffice for the present that I acknowledge you as my son. Already I love you next to your darling mother.

"Keep your spear and *palaoa ;* learn to use the one and seek not to disgrace the other. As Keeaumoku is to be your guardian chief it would be well to give him your insignia, as he is somewhat vain of decorations. Such a piece of state-craft will repay you a hundred-fold. To wear these treasures would endanger your life in battle, and create untold jealousies at court.

"Remain at court as Kaméhaméha, son of Wailéle of

Mukíni. Don a *malo* and *kihei* (girdle and robe), and let the legend of the "god-born" become a tradition of the past. And now let us go forth among my guests, where I will present you to the kings, and place you in the hands of Keeaumoku for further instruction. It will need my hugest warrior to protect you from the hateful court intrigues, because of your fame, which has preceded your coming."

Throwing the *paku* from the door, Kalaniopuu and the young Alii passed out. The angry prince was at the door, still held in check by the sturdy guard. The king addressed his son in a gentle tone of rebuke:

"How is this, Kiwalao? Can't you keep the peace while your father receives a message of importance from Mukíni?"

"I did not believe you had ordered the guard to exclude your son, when the stranger chief was suffered to pass the sacred door without permission."

"My son, this is Kaméhaméha of Mukíni, son of Wailéle, the celebrated priestess of that famous *heidu*. Let me ask you to make it pleasant for him about the court, while he stays among us."

The two royal *aliis* greeted each other politely, for Kiwalao was a true courtier, and Kaméhaméha had acquired the polished manners natural to all high-born chiefs.

Seeing the canoe of the Waimánu chiefs in the river, the king asked who they were. He was gratified to learn that his newly-found son had been so wise as to surround himself with his own friends. Kiwalao was immediately sent to invite them ashore, to provide for them a good repast, and to lodge them as best he could until the other guests were gone, when permanent accommodations would be abundant.

Passing on up the river to where the court guests were still intent upon their games and spear-practice, Kalaniopuu presented Kaméhaméha to the kings, and then put him in charge of Keeaumoku, as his guardian chief. This warrior accepted the charge with apparent pleasure, greeting the young Alii with a degree of warmth which made them friends at once. This friendship was strong and true, and it lasted until death.

In the first glow of his admiration for Keeaumoku, Kaméhaméha took the occasion to present him his royal insignia. This touched his vanity as nothing else could have done. It was the first stroke of the young Alii's policy toward the furtherance of his deep-laid schemes.

It may here be noted that this same *palaoa*, at a later day, saved the life of Keeaumoku, caused the death of Kiwalao, and won for King Kaméhaméha his first hard-fought battle.*

---

* At the battle of Keei, after an eight-days' slaughter, the attacking force of Keeaumoku were killed almost to a man, and the great chief himself was stricken down and apparently mortally wounded. When supposed to be nearly dead, Kiwalao sprang forward to rob the dying *Alii* of his insignia, and lost his life and the battle by his greed for the bauble.—(See Ellis' "Hawáii," p. 115.)

XXIII.

COMBAT WITH SPEARS BETWEEN THE PRINCES.

IT was a most fortunate thing for the young *Alii* to meet these notable chiefs from the Leeward kingdoms; for such a gathering never took place again in the history of the islands. When presented to Kahekili and Keoúa, the two celebrities exchanged sharp inquiring glances, as if each was asking the other who was the favored parent of this young notable? As we have seen, both of these kings had been lovers of the beautiful Wailéle. And though unsuccessful lovers, history tells us that Kaméhaméha's fame and unrevealed paternity led each of these kings, from that hour, to claim his paternity for himself. So much for having been called a fatherless boy!

Kiwalao now joined the group, introducing some of the young chiefs from Waimánu, and wishing to show some of these untutored lads his own boasted skill with warlike weapons. Ere they took their stand for spear practice, Kiwalao discovered the ivory decoration upon Keeaumoku's neck, and with a sudden flush of temper turned to Kaméhaméha with a blunt request:

"I want that *palaoa*. You will not give it to Keeaumoku?"

"The gift has already been bestowed. You must confess it becomes the great chief finely."

"Why did n't you ask me if I wanted it before you

gave it away? A great monster like him does not need a decoration? Say, Keeaumoku, I want that *palaoa*. The *Alii* would have given it to me, if he had thought I wanted it."

"Be in at my death, my young *alii nui*, and you shall have it; but if good Pele permits me, I'll wear it with honor until then—and woe to the mortal who dares pluck it from my neck!"

The indignant prince dared not further provoke the giant; yet wishing some one to vent his rising spleen upon, he turned to Kaméhaméha:

"That's a nice spear of yours. Give it to me, will you?"

"Pardon me, Kiwalao, this is an heirloom in my family, and I can only part with it to one of my age who shall win it in single combat." A look of sly merriment gleamed in the dark eyes of Kaméhaméha, which both Kalaniopuu and Keeaumoku well understood.

"I'm your man for a *hoo palau* (spear game). I dare you try me at a test of skill? I don't suppose you Waimánu fellows practise spears very much."

"Yes, noble prince, I cannot find the heart to refuse you; if you will but have patience with us 'fellows from Waimánu.'"

"Oh, I'll be tender of you; especially since you are twice my size, and present two marks to my one. Remember, all of you, that I am to have Kaméhaméha's *pololu* if I win. What length of spear shall we take?"

"I will leave that to your greater experience to decide. We 'fellows from Waimánu' do not know very well."

Passing his own curiously carved spear to Miomio, one of his chief-boys, with a sly leer in his eye, Kaméhaméha selected one of Kiwalao's spears, and the two royal *aliis* took positions for a friendly contest. The prince showed his lack of fairness by assuming a position which would bring the sun in Kaméhaméha's face. The watchful Keeaumoku insisted upon a side-sun for them both, and the tricky prince had to yield.

Every notable in the company was gathered about the arena. Not that they cared for the skill of a petulant lad like Kiwalao; but Kaméhaméha's fame with the spear had reached every ear but Kiwalao's. At a signal given by Keeaumoku, the spears were let fly by the two combatants. Each acquitted himself well, catching the other's whistling weapon with ease and skill.

After a few such trials, Kiwalao invited three of the Waimánu chiefs to dart at him simultaneously. Catching the first spear, he fended off the other two. Then he tried four spearsmen; and with such success that he challenged Kaméhaméha to beat that if he could.

"Thanks, noble prince, for not setting me too hard a task. With such an example I 'll try to do my best."

The four Waimánu boys were now invited to fling their spears with their utmost force, and at the same instant. Thrown at a given signal, the four weapons hummed through the air almost side by side; but each and all were caught by Kaméhaméha and flung back to their several owners.

Folding his arms, he again bid the four spearsmen do their best to spear him. Dipping, ducking, dodging, he gracefully avoided the four weapons without moving from his footsteps. This elicited most hearty applause from the chiefs, and kind words from the watchful kings.

Warming with the active work, Kaméhaméha now requested the prince to join the four chiefs; and caught the five spears as easily as the four. Calling for yet another from his native valley, the young Alii caught the first, and with it parried the other five, amidst rousing cheers from all.

Elated with his warlike frolic, he now requested ten * spearsmen to take positions in line, three feet apart ; in which case the ten spears would be thrown from a radius of forty feet, all centring upon the heart of the fearless chief-boy. This was one of the most dangerous exhibitions of spear practice.

The whole multitude were now hushed into breathless watchfulness, and every eye was upon the noble Alii, as Keeaumoku kept them waiting for a small cloud to pass from off the sun. As the yellow beam again shone on the spear-points, the signal was given, and instantly the ten perilous barbs flashed in the air, Kiwalao's treacherous spear coming a length in advance ; all hurtled through the sunlit air at the naked breast of the chief-boy.

Catching the prince's spear, by an almost superhuman effort, he parried the rest, ending with flinging Kiwalao's ill-meant missile back to its envious owner ; but it was flung with such terrific force that it grazed the downy cheek of the sulky prince.

Wild indeed were the shouts that echoed from cliff to cliff, causing a great flock of birds to rise bewildered in the air. The four kings greeted Kaméhaméha with delight, while Keeaumoku hugged him like a lover. Even Kiwalao came forward manfully at length, and showed a generous spirit toward his antagonist.

This event lifted a weight from Kalaniopuu's heart, and swept a cloud from his anxious face. He no longer

---

* Some warriors could avoid a dozen spears when cast at once.— Jarvis' History, p. 66

feared that Kiwalao would continue to show indignation about the *palaoa*, or cherish a dangerous jealousy of the young victor's skill; and he was now well assured that his new-found son could defend himself quite as well as any warrior in Waipio. Still more, this exhibition of skill was an admirable warning to all court intriguers.

For himself, Kaméhaméha rejoiced in the pleasure that his success had given his father and his guardian chief; and he knew that his mother would almost forget her prayers when she heard of his success. Only the holy Priestess and her *alii kapú* knew that it was Pele who sustained him on that eventful day of his *début*.

Before the royal company left for Maui that afternoon, the cunning Kahekili found opportunity to flatter the young Alii for his remarkable skill, to inform him of the profound admiration he felt for his mother, and to invite him to accompany them to Maui with his band of young warriors. He even promised the ambitious youth to make him king of Molokai, if his warlike expedition against Oahu should succeed.

This was indeed a most flattering offer to a chief but one day launched upon his career. True to his allegiance to his king, he sought first to confer with his *kahu alii* before he could decide. Keeaumoku had watchfully observed what was going on, and fearing harm from the flattery of Kahekili, had quickly approached within hearing of the last part of the king's treacherous offer; an offer which that gracious monarch had previously made to three other royal chiefs, one of whom, as we saw, was Keeaumoku himself. When the blunt-spoken old warrior was told what was proposed to his ward, he came to the rescue in his characteristic way:

"It is my duty to inform your Majesty that I have been made *kahu alii* of the Waimánu chief, and I take pleasure in saying that we shall find a suitable field for his warlike skill before the world grows much older; therefore, under no consideration will he be permitted to fight under your Majesty's banner at present."

"Must you ever be intruding your personal aversions upon our family, my troublesome brother?" answered the enraged king, his eyes flashing at this unfortunate intrusion. He could not now hope to entrap Kaméhaméha and his gallant chiefs; but he dared not vent his rage upon the gigantic warrior before him.

"Sire, my personal interest always goes hand in hand with my duty, as your Majesty well knows. My present duty is not to my wife's brother, but to prevent this noble Alii from being inveigled into any treacherous scheme for the aggrandizement of base men."

"Keeaumoku, there will come a time when you shall repent casting your interest against our royal house. Mark me, the time is not far distant."

"Come when it will, Kahekili shall ever find Keeaumoku of Hawáii and this young hero fighting on the same battle-field. I, too, sire, have an eye to see that this young knight is the coming man whom priests and prophets have so long foretold."

"Keeaumoku, I hate you! May our next meeting be where spears fall thick and fast!"

"I second your wish; and I will further your prophecy. *Aloha*, treacherous king!"

XXIV.

THE COURT OF WAIPIO.

GREAT was the shouting of the multitude from the high sand-hills along the Waipio shore as men, women, and children gathered to see the departure of the kings, and to watch the swarthy warriors force their red war canoes out over the roaring breakers at the mouth of the valley.

The king had parted with his turbulent guests at the place of embarkation on the river. He stood with folded arms and furrowed brow among his great chiefs until the wild cheers of the multitudes announced that the kings had passed the surf in safety. With a sigh of relief he turned back to the palace, thankful that no serious outburst of passion had taken place to mar their visit, and to reflect upon his difficult task of hospitality.

What dangerous intrigues the visitors had started at court, or what treacherous schemes of assassination and poisoning the cunning sons of Kekaulike had accomplished, remained to be seen. Calling out a pleasant *Aloha!* to Kaméhaméha as he passed, the careworn monarch took the arm of Keeaumoku, and together they entered the royal house, intent upon matters of state.

Weary with the mental and physical strain of this eventful day, the young Alii sat down upon the river bank among his Waimánu chiefs to wait the return of Keeaumoku. Ten of Kaméhaméha's party had been allotted residences in Napopo, the thrifty village about the great chief's dwelling, while Kaméhaméha and his *aikane* (intimate companion) were to be taken directly into the family of Keeaumoku, as the ex-queen, Namahana, had once known Wailéle and the old priest, Wahupu, her father.

The palace grounds of Waipio and the numerous adjacent dwellings stood on a line of low green hills, half a mile up the valley, lying along the north bank of the River, which here skirts close along the lowest part of the south *páli*. Three quarters of a mile farther up-stream were the neat grass houses of Napopo, where Keeaumoku and other great chiefs lived. Every *hale* had its *kalo* field and garden plot of fruit-trees about it.

About the palace grounds were clustered fine groves of great king-palms and flowering *hau* (hibiscus), together with huge dark-green bread-fruit and tall *ohia* trees, crimsoned with ripened fruit. Graceful clusters of large-leaved bananas, with their red or yellow fruit, and guavas, orange, and coffee trees grew everywhere in abundance. Just across the river a dense grove of tall cocoa-nut palms almost hid the small *heidu*, over which Hewahewa presided, high-priest of Waipio, son of Holoae, the great high-priest of Hawáii, descendants of Pááo, and thus distant connections of Kaméhaméha.

Keeaumoku now made his appearance from the palace. He called to Kaahumanu ("Feather Mantle"), his pretty daughter of nine, and beckoned to Kaméhaméha and the chiefs who were to live at Napopo, the other chief-boys having been pleasantly domiciled wherever agreeable homes could be found.

Though Keeaumoku looked kindly upon our hero, as if prompted by some newly acquired interest, yet he was not communicative. He strode silently on before, with Kaahumanu clinging to his hand. Could he foresee that this lovely child would become the favorite queen of the chief-boy who followed them, and the most renowned stateswoman in all Polynesia ?

As to the young Alii, he always affirmed that he knew his fate was to be linked with those two, father and daughter, from that hour when he followed them thoughtfully along the river path. But he did not then know that the king had just taken Keeaumoku into his confidence, and told him the proud birthright of his new found son, for the story had been told under the closest ban of secrecy.

Although " Feather Mantle " was already betrothed to Kiwalao, the heir-apparent, and fully expected to become Queen of Hawáii, yet, like many other very young princesses, the air-castle of her girlhood had many coignes and turrets wherein to harbor another gallant admirer or doughty knight. The proud young beauty was not above flinging back a frequent bewitching smile of cheer, meant to encourage the timid advances of the young victor.

As usual at her giddy age, the insipidities and merry nothings of the gay young prince were far more to her liking than the sedate manners and wise discourse of the swarthy Alii. But there is also an equal fascination in receiving attention from the grand and noble whom others admire.

As the party wended its way beside the river, the earth ovens were everywhere ablaze preparatory to cooking the evening meal, as the royal guests had devoured all the available food before they left.

At length they reached the charming village of Napopo, and one by one the ten Waimánu chiefs were assigned their dwelling-places. Kaméhaméha and Miomio, his *aikane*, were taken home with Keeaumoku, and there the young Alii found a warm friend in the motherly Namahana, the noble descendant of the Maui kings. Little did she think that three of her lovely daughters would subsequently become queens to our hero, as veritable history fails not to relate.

How providential it seemed that Namahana should have once, when she was Queen of Maui, visited Mukíni; going with the king on business of state with the father of Wailéle, just before the death of the aged priest. The queen became warmly attached to the Priestess, then a girl of fifteen, and her remarkable beauty and winning hospitality had never been forgotten. And now there came a welcome opportunity for her to open her heart and home to the son of the loved friend of her youth.

The experience of the dethroned queen enabled her to put a more just estimate upon the qualities of the young Alii than her imperious daughter could do. The sagacious queen-mother was well pleased to discover the growing attraction that Kaahumanu's dark eyes had for the new-comer; for she expected neither truth nor stability in the intriguing Kiwalao, whose fickle character caused no little uneasiness among his friends at court. In later years Kaméhaméha used to tell many a pleasant reminiscence of that bright day, and none more interesting than the bewitching effect of "Feather Mantle's" dark eyes upon him, and how they had nerved him to do his utmost in the spear practice before the kings.

The proud and fearless beauty had been greatly petted by the visiting monarchs, and during the trial of skill between the prince, her affianced lover, and his unknown brother, "Feather Mantle" stood before her giant father, eagerly watching the contest, at first with only an interest for the prince, but ending with a paramount sympathy for Kaméhaméha. Thus, during the last desperate undertaking of the stranger chief, when even the hardened old warriors stood breathless, charmed with the danger of his situation, none could better appreciate the cool, calm bearing of the daring youth than this wise young princess of nine. Her small bare foot was proudly advanced, like that of the two contestants, and her dark eyes were alert, as if to guide her own girlish hand to catch the spears.

Never could the young Alii forget the inspiring look of the girl in that moment, when the ten keen spears were about to be flung at his naked breast. It was a picture never to be forgotten. Her parted lips, heaving bosom, and extended hands showed emotional feeling far beyond her years, as she threw every impulse of her impassioned soul into the perilous combat.

The scene exalted her into a wild ecstacy; she glorified the courage and skill of the young stranger, and no expression of doubt or fear of the result mantled her young cheeks as she looked upon the god-born boy.

More than all the magnetic charm of human beauty glowing in the girl's brave young face, that which most sustained the heroism of the youth in that hour of peril, was his conviction that she whom he looked upon was Pele in disguise. He felt assured that his divine godmother would be there in some human form to prompt and protect him. And surely this girl's supernal beauty must be divine; it so thrilled his soul, and prompted him to such unusual daring. It was but a brief glimpse of that divine instinct which in the heroic moment links all exalted souls with deity.

Yet how little could the inexperienced chief-boy understand the sudden reaction he subsequently witnessed! The over-excited maiden burst into tears when all was over, and sank trembling and sobbing at her father's feet, while all others were giving vent to their appreciation of the scene by deafening cheers. The young victor stood there silent, subdued by the very greatness of his triumph.

XXV.

QUEEN NAMAHANA'S TRAGIC STORY.

ON the second evening of Kaméhaméha's stay at Waipio there was a family gathering along the grassy river bank, met for social chat, and to sip in the perfume which follows along the cool-flowing river at the close of a sultry day.

It was a still, calm night; only the occasional glare of some weird fire-light broke upon the starlit gloom, the silence was made audible by the chirping crickets in the grass, and by the singing lizards in the *kúkúi* trees; there were no sounds but these, the low rumble of the surf on the distant shore, and the tuneful monotone of the far-away cataract in the upper valley.

Keeaumoku had just gone down to the palace at the urgent call of the king. Coming at such an hour, it was a message of mystery which broke rudely upon the companionship of the royal group; for rumor, since the departure of the Leeward kings, had filled the air with whispers of impending wars and dangerous intrigues.

Namahana with her daughters and sons sat grouped about Kaméhaméha and a few of his favorite chief-boys; and the queen was relating some of the tragic events in the family history.

The motherly queen affectionately held one of Kaméhaméha's hands between her two great palms—hands which had wielded many a war spear in the thick of battle; and the soft magnetic touch of "Feather Mantle" possessed the other hand. The chief-boys drank in the story of the dethroned queen; thrilling with horror at the dangers of dagger, spear, and poison from which the heroic chiefess had escaped in the treacherous land of Maui.

Namahana was the well-loved daughter of Kekaulike, the most renowned king of Maui's long line of warriors. She was queen to her brother, Kaméhaméha (the first of the name), and half-sister to the treacherous Kahekili, to Keao, and to Alapai. The reign of her Kaméhaméha was the most peaceful in the annals of Maui, though the brief wars of her king against Hawáii were unsuccessful, for East Maui was lost.*

But alas! when her noble king was taken sick, then her ambitious brothers hedged their sister about with poisoned dagger and envenomed spear, hungry for their brother's throne before the finger of death had beckoned him away. Chiefs and armies were loyal to maintain their queen against all comers. But the cunning of Kahekili was equal to the emergency. He smiled on his royal sister with affection, while the priest was bribed to poison her food with venom from Pepehi's idol, and assassins watched to slay her.

Keeaumoku had been the lover of Namahana before she was compelled, after the hateful custom of the land, to marry her brother. To him she now turned for succor against her unnatural assailants.† He was absent with the army of invasion on Molokai, and Namahana sent a messenger for Keeaumoku to meet her. He came

---

* Kalaniopuu claimed East Maui as the patrimony of his queen Kalola, and took it in the year 1759, and held it throughout his reign.

† Keeaumoku had previously quarrelled with Kalaniopuu, and was then living at the court of Maui.

to Maui, and the lovers were married ; but her new husband well knew that the Maui army, then on Molokai, had already been won over to Kahekili, and would soon sweep unopposed over Namahana's kingdom.

When the army of Kahekili landed on Maui, a few months after, Keeaumoku and the queen fled to Hana, the remotest end of her kingdom of Maui. There Kaahumanu was born on the famous hill of Kauwiki, the scene of Kahekili's cannibal feast, where his whole army was fed upon a garrison of brave Hawáiians.*

The assassins of her brother still hedged about the royal mother and her babe, and not until several of the men-slayers had been killed by Keeaumoku was it deemed best to leave Maui forever, and seek protection under the noble Kalaniopuu, who bid them welcome.

Twice "Feather Mantle" had narrowly escaped being drowned. Their home in Hana having been besieged by soldiers on the land side, the queen took canoe at night, and crossed the Upolu Sea for Hawáii. As they approached Kaawaloa, running before the wind under a press of sail, in the darkness, the baby princess lay asleep on the *polu* (platform) of the double canoe, rolled up in a wrap of white *tapa*.

Suddenly the babe was missing. A quick lurch of the canoe had tossed her into the sea, unseen by any one. Sail was shortened hurriedly, and the strong paddlers forced the canoe back against wind and waves into the black gloom of the foaming waters.

Terrible was the anguish of the queen-mother for her lost child. Some said they had seen a white *tapa* tossing on the wave crests long before, but thought nothing of it.

---

* See Dibble's "History," p. 53, for a full account of this cannibal feast.

She was mourned as lost, for a monstrous shark had been following the canoe before the accident.

But Providence watches over the lives of future queens. The paddlers, when hope was spent, caught sight of the white *tapa* in the distance; then it disappeared in the trough of the sea. The great shark, just before them, was thrashing the sea into phosphorescence with his tail, as sharks do when devouring their prey. The paddles bent in strong hands, and the canoe plunged into the gloom ahead. An instant more, and the white *tapa* was snatched up, and the unconscious princess found still asleep and unharmed. The shark was devouring a roast dog which had been wrapped in *ti* leaves and left on the platform beside the child, Kaahumanu. She was saved to do the great work, in the future, of breaking the *tabú* of the idol-worshippers. Snatched with a divine purpose from the midnight waves and the hungry maw of the shark, as baby Moses was rescued from the rushes of the Nile by Pharaoh's daughter, both children became the saviors of their people.

After waiting long for Keeaumoku's return, the party broke up and were seeking their mats for repose, when he appeared; and with great deference for Kaméhaméha, detained him a moment to impart his messages from the king.

One of the court spies had brought word from Pepehi that Kiwalao contemplated poisoning some new-comer about the court, as he had sent for several doses of the old Kahúna's poison-god. That person the king believed was his new-found son. He ordered every precaution to be used. If his boy's life should be attempted by force, the king wished it fully understood that Kaméhaméha was to slay his assailant without the least question of who he might be.

At once Kaméhaméha suggested that he should seek to win the good-will of Kiwalao in the friendly emulation of spear practice. In this and other athletic games, he said, he could impart to the prince some of the skill he had acquired by arduous application, and perhaps win his friendship.

This plan met the approbation of his guardian. He had himself suggested it to the king, who feared that the prince might use poisoned spears. So they parted for the night, the chief ordering the night watch to strike home, if need should be, without questioning too closely who were his foes, and to guard the Waimánu chief as one of the family.

Here was a detestable condition of society! Its contrast to the perfect security of Kaméhaméha's own Waimánu home hardened his heart against state crimes and criminals, and made his resolution sterner to crush them out when he should come to the throne.

It pleased the young Alii to find himself in such accord with Keeaumoku. The cool, fearless, far-seeing chief was by far the ablest counsellor of the king. His experience of life and his knowledge of men were greater than those of any one whom Kaméhaméha had known.

From Pepehi, Kaméhaméha had learned the wiles of the Hawáiian state-craft, and had been taught to believe that there was no moral quality in man sufficient either to guide him in the right or to engender a hate of wrongdoing.

By his mother he had been taught a beautiful wisdom. Nowhere but at Mukíni was it held that every noble man had a god within himself; nowhere else was it taught that the rights of all should be respected even by the king upon his throne, and that to sacrifice any human victim but a criminal was a crime sufficient to blot out the sun.

From Keeaumoku he learned that all men were ruled by their self-interest, and impelled to wrong-doing by their emulation of others. He taught that the bad men with whom we are compelled to associate should be influenced by showing our power to help them and our inclination to better their condition. But proffer not spears to timid women!

To the hopelessly bad, give a sharp spear and a fair fight for their lives, and free the state from their presence. Annihilation for one's enemies without the state was with the chief a law as unchangeable as the rock-grown hills. In this list of offenders without the pale of justice he would place all of his wife's brothers; not for any injury done to him, but for their inhumanity to one of their own blood. Thus he showed how, were he the king of Hawáii, he would deal with Keoúa, Keawe, and even Kiwalao; and thus he actually did deal, in after years, with two of these persons. Thus, though the teaching of Wailéle ever remained the groundwork of Kaméhaméha's after legislation, and rule of guidance in statecraft, yet Keeaumoku's interpretation of the ruling motives of men, and the swift, stern justice to be meted out to the incorrigibly bad, influenced the great conqueror more than all other counsels.

XXVI.

VIEW OF WAIPIO VALLEY FROM THE PÁLI.

MORNING dawned upon a busy scene. All who came forth at the dawn clapped their hands and called upon their gods, as they ran to the river for their morning plunge.

The dull thud of the cloth mallets and the stone pestles of the poi-makers were the first sounds to awaken the valley; a not unpleasant though ceaseless din, at least during the morning hours, awakening the persistent echoes of the *pális*.

Here in this Eden land of Waipio ("captive waters"), our hero was now to enter upon a stirring life, in complete contrast to any thing that he had known. A larger and less secluded valley than Waimánu, its less precipitous *pális* were daily accessible to hundreds of busy comers and goers. Governors came from the six districts to relate their dealings with their people, some of whom were unruly and rebellious subjects. Especially was this true of Kau, the southernmost district, which had long since acquired the name of "*Aina kipi*"—the rebellious land; or another and worse opprobrium, "The sepulchre of kings." Three kings had been slain there: one was beaten to death by the paddles of fishermen at Kalae*; one stoned to death at Aukukano; a priest

---

* Kalaniopuu's father-in-law, the *Alii ai moku* of Kau, was thus killed.

killed the other, King Kohao-Kalani, by crushing him with an enormous wooden idol, rolled down upon him from the *páli* of Hilea.

Keeaumoku left home soon after the morning meal, leaving his second son, Kuakini, to make Kaméhaméha better acquainted with his surroundings. Kuakini proposed that our young Alii should gain his first impressions of Waipio from the lofty *páli*, and together the two chiefs, accompanied by " Feather Mantle " and her sister, Kalakua, swam the river, and climbed the most accessible cliff near Napopo.

Seen from the lofty *páli*, Waipio was, and still is, a very paradise of beauty to look upon. Two rough, bare bluffs abutted upon the sea, one of which was nearly two thousand feet high. Surf-boards and canoes lay scattered in disorder along more than a mile of smooth sand-beach, where floundered less turbulent breakers than at Waimánu. A line of high sand-hills skirted the shore, partially protecting the valley from strong sea winds, though at times furious gusts swept into it, sufficiently strong to lift the frail houses from their foundations.

The *pális* that walled the sides of the valley were vast corrugated cliffs, mostly inaccessible, yet with not a few steep inclines that nimble climbers could conquer. Down these slopes the people coast from top to bottom, sliding upon strips of board, bunches of tough leaves, or the horny stem of the cocoa-nut leaf.

Along the river banks, near every high-chief's house, were housed large double war canoes, ready to launch at a moment's notice, for Waipio was the great naval station of Hawáii. Hundreds of fishing canoes were busy on the river, or on the large walled ponds that belonged to the king and the great chiefs. Countless dogs, pigs, and nude brown children were swimming in the river. Native gardeners and market-men were wading the stream, floating down their produce of *kalo*, potatoes, or fruits, from the upper valley seven miles away, each one crying aloud his wares or provisions from mid-river, or twisting the tail of the pig on his back, so that the creature should audibly announce himself to the hungry world as for sale.

In the upper and middle half of Waipio a river flowed along each side of the valley, joining lower down in one, and flowing along the south *páli* to the sea. The whole area of Waipio was one perennial garden of taro patches, potato fields, plantations of banana, sugar-cane, and fruit-trees. Dotting these cultivated fields, glittered the artificial ponds, all well stocked with choice fish for the chiefs. Their shining surfaces reflected the lofty *pális* and the snow-crowned summits that, rising sharp and clear above the dark green forest belt, gained the region of perpetual snows, whence gigantic Kéa flings down his sublime benediction.

Our hero was familiar with the historical events which had happened in the romantic valley, the home of a hundred generations of chiefs and kings. As he looked down upon the charming picture at his feet and caught glimpses of famous battle-fields, renowned *heiáus*, and the former homes of great kings whose bones were mouldering in the rocky tombs of *Puaahuku*,* his heart swelled and he broke into passionate utterances which made his companions look upon him almost with awe. The sympathies of "Feather Mantle" were aroused above those of others, and she crept up to the side of

---

* King Umi was deposited in a cave of the high *páli*, under the great falls of Hiilawe.

this strange chief-boy, took his hand, and drank in his mystic words as if they were oracles from the gods.

Kaméhaméha pointed out varied beauties and disclosed wonderful histories of the famous valley, wholly new to the native-born chiefs by his side. They listened to this Waimánu youth as he described the invasions of long-gone years, when every house had been burned and every fruit-tree destroyed in the lower valley by some invader from Maui, or yet more malicious chief from their own southern districts of Hilo or Puna, which were often ruled by warlike kings.

They heard this embryo warrior tell how each of the great battles had been lost, and presumptuously explain how they might all have been won. It was down the very cliff whereon they sat that most of the invaders had found entrance to the valley. Kaméhaméha showed how certain of the hills along the river should be fortified, so that the few could withstand the many. The wise boy said other memorable things, and thus they passed the forenoon, returning to Napopo in time for dinner. There a message awaited Kaméhaméha inviting him to the palace, and their afternoon excursion up the valley to the ancient *heiáu* of Pakalani was postponed for another day.

With his *aikane*, Kaméhaméha started down the river, after receiving the advice from Namahana to avoid being too outspoken about affairs pertaining to court or state matters. It was such advice as his mother would have given him upon a like occasion.

Kalaniopuu sat in the shade of the king-palms in front of the palace, his only companions being Keeaumoku and Hewahewa, the high-priest's arrogant son. Guards, a group of inferior priests, and another group of war-chiefs of inferior rank were playing *konane* (checkers) and other games on the river bank and about the palace grounds. All of them were beyond the stipulated distance of earshot, but some of these gamesters were known to be spies of Kahekili.

When the coast was clear for an uninterrupted meeting of father and son, the king made no secret of his pleasure in seeing him. He told Kaméhaméha that the Kahúna and the high-chief had been taken into confidence about his birth. But they were bound to the closest secrecy, as the king feared that Kaméhaméha would not be suffered to live should his royal birth be made known at that time. Hungry aspirants for the throne were making conspiracies against the king's own life; and a person less thoroughly protected could not live a day among the deadly intrigues.

One of the court spies had overheard a midnight interview between Kahekili, Alapai, and Kiwalao, in which the prince counted his resources in chiefs, and in the number men that each of them could bring into the field. Among the most formidable chiefs on the prince's side was Keoúa, his uncle, and Keawe, the governing chief of the Hilo district. Both of these warlike noblemen, half-brothers of the king, were jealous of Keeaumoku's ascendancy at court.

The royal councillors had deemed it best to prepare a strong army to invade Maui, as the best means of occupying the conspirators, as well as for a just punishment for Kahekili's intrigues against Hawáii. As a matter of courtesy the king asked his son what he thought of the plan, and the reply, bold, incisive, and energetic, surprised all present. This boy in years was found to be a man in wisdom, and already full of wise expedients.

Kaméhaméha's suggestions for invading Maui were novel. Instead of seeking the enemy in their own strongholds on West Maui, where Kahekili could fight surrounded by his whole resources, the young Alii advised landing an army on East Maui, to seize and fortify the mountain passes, thus occupying the thriftiest part of the island without bloodshed, and compelling the enemy to assume the offensive.

This plan, after a brief discussion among the four chiefs, was accepted by all. Then arose the question of where the fortifications should be built, it being necessary to choose strategic positions, so that small garrisons could hold the country after the army was withdrawn.

Kaméhaméha suggested that the principal point to fortify was Wailuku; as the almost impregnable hill of Kauwiki, in the Hana district, was held by Hawáii. These places were accepted as most suitable for the purpose. Then arose the question where should be the battle-field, the most advantageous place to meet the enemy, if he forced a battle.

Kaméhaméha's choice of battle-fields amazed the conservative chiefs. He proposed to meet the foe in the gigantic pass of Wailuku, where, once joined in battle, there could be no retreat for either party until one or the other was overwhelmed. To plan a deadly and decisive conflict on the brink of a *páli* 2,000 feet high, showed a grim courage wholly foreign to the slow, sure methods of the Hawáiian chiefs, who always chose their battle-ground with reference to a safe retreat. The king and Keeaumoku could not bring themselves to adopt the young chief's strategy; yet it had the effect of infusing unusual vigor into their own plans, and created a strong admiration for Kaméhaméha's boldness and courage of conception.

The proof that Kaméhaméha's choice of battle-ground was the right one is shown by the fact, as told in history, that his own subsequent battle of Iao, fought there, was the only battle necessary to win and hold Maui forever. On that day he destroyed a much stronger army than his own, damming the river Iao with dead bodies; so that the bloody contest received the name of *Kapauiwai* (stopping the waters).

The war council was soon broken up by the appearance of the prince and his half-brother, Keoúa the younger.* Kiwalao was returning from a fishing party. Landing from the river, he came swaggering up to his father, nodding haughtily to Kaméhaméha, while he filled the ear of the chiefs with his piscatory exploits. He told Kaméhaméha that he was going to give his attention to spear practice and would show him a thing or two in that line.

As the afternoon was drawing to a close, Keeaumoku rose, and accompanied by Kaméhaméha took his way homeward; entering, on reflection, more and more fully into the plan of conquering Maui.†

---

* The king had two sons named Keoúa, half-brothers of Kiwalao, by wife number five, one of whom fought against Kaméhaméha for nine years.

† The Hana district of Maui, and the strong fortress of Kauwiki, being a part of Queen Kalola's patrimony, Kalaniopuu conquered it in 1759, as rightfully belonging to his queen. Though East Maui was often assailed previous to Kahekili's time, even he did not succeed in retaking the fort until the last year of Kalaniopuu's reign.

XXVII.

SATAN CONFRONTING THE PRINCE.

BEFORE the family's simple repast of fish and *poi*, with a dessert of guavas, was fairly over one pleasant morning, Hewahewa was seen paddling up the river alone in a canoe. The unusual circumstance of the high-priest* thus coming by himself implied some matter of importance with Keeaumoku. But the fact of the haughty Kahúna's coming alone showed no wish for haste, but rather for secrecy.

Keeaumoku rose at once from his breakfast, leaving the yellow rinds of at least eight large guavas to attest his appetite, and hastened to the river-side to greet Hewahewa. After a brief time of earnest talk and energetic gesticulation, Keeaumoku called up the garden path for Kaméhaméha to join them. He took his spear and went, wondering what topic could so interest these notable men.

The beetle-browed priest greeted the young Alii more kindly than usual, for hitherto he had kept himself somewhat aloof from the new-comer. Now he invited him to go up the river to the *Puhonua*, or "city of refuge," whose priest was a great-uncle of theirs.

Gladly accepting the invitation, he stepped into Hewa-

---

* The aged Holoae was the king's high-priest, but Hewahewa now acted as such.

hewa's canoe. Eager as he was to know every thing about Waipio, Kaméhaméha was still more interested in becoming acquainted with the high-priest, the most remarkable man among all the descendants of Pàáo. His distrustful manner had previously led Kaméhaméha to observe the crafty Kahúna closely, and he had not failed to perceive a gradual change for the better. Nor was the chief wholly at a loss to explain the fact, knowing that the king had told Hewahewa about his new-found son. But it was now the young Alii's turn to become reserved and watchful, using his utmost sagacity to learn what degree of confidence could be put in the priest's friendliness, as implied by this request for a private interview.

The motherly Namahana had readily accounted for his coolness by his surprise at Kaméhaméha's appearance at court, and the disdain that he had shown for the king's guard and the priest's *tabù* restrictions. What had since happened to abate Hewahewa's distrust, she could not determine. But she feared that the change was too sudden to be of good omen, and her last words of advice were to withhold all confidence from the crafty Kahúna.

Hewahewa was the most complex character remaining at court since the departure of the Leeward kings. Rarely, indeed, is a man's nature made up of so many contradictions as his. He was a short, broad-shouldered, slightly humpbacked man. His gross, uncouth features repelled a timid nature at a glance; still more his unfeeling questions, which recalled the coarse self-righteousness with which the ancient Jesuits loved to trample on the privacy of tender souls. Such was the cold and sinister manner of Hewahewa as a priest. But more than this;

when his will was crossed he wore an expression so derisive and demoniacal that even the boldest shrank from him appalled, as when one treads barefooted upon a snake. Even in his best moods, few men cared to meet the stern glance of his deep-set eyes. Fewer yet could quite determine whether the charm of his voice in conversation was meant to cover a malediction or a blessing. He could ambush his bitterest scorn behind a seductive smile, then stab to the heart. None but the keenest could fathom his meaning. To hear the musical utterance of Hewahewa's voice without seeing the man would charm the listening ear of an angel. But how quickly the charm of his eloquence was displaced by distrust or dismay the instant one became subjected to his evil eye! Such was the monster who now sought to entice our hero into his serpent coils.

Even in his warm greeting to Kaméhaméha, with voice soft as a bird-song, the sinister expression of his face strongly contradicted the soft-worded message. His searching eye seemed eagerly questioning if the chief dared distrust his wordy welcome, while the curl of his lips disclosed a menace, should any doubt be shown.

Bidding *aloha* to Keeaumoku, and making his most courtly address to Namahana and her family, seen in the distance, the priest and the Alii launched their canoe and paddled slowly up the smooth-flowing river.

With pleasant condescension Hewahewa chatted gayly with the indolent chiefs who lounged along the grassy shore, enjoying the delightful *lomi-lomi*, or being anointed after their bath. Often they paddled among laughing groups of merry swimmers, men, women, and children, who spent hours in the soft clear waters.

At length, when the two had paddled beyond the

region occupied by the lordly chiefs, and had reached a part of the valley where only a few poor Kanákas lived,—priest-ridden people whom the lightest flutter of Hewahewa's *tabú* flag sent scampering out of the river in wild dismay—then the priest confronted his victim.

Assuming at once a sedate manner that might be deemed almost stern and arrogant, but for his usual delusive smile, the crafty Kahúna turned to Kaméhaméha and unfolded his purpose.

"Noble Alii, is it true, as the king has had the kindness to inform me, that you have been confirmed as *Kahúna maoli* of Mukíni by the gracious Pele herself?"

"Yes, it is true, Hewahewa. Pele came in person to Mukíni, and conferred the highest priesthood of the land upon me." And Kaméhaméha confronted his arrogant companion. The two sat there eye to eye, each unquailing and undismayed.

"Then, *Alii kapu*, you outrank us all if you choose to assert your right!" The fierce eyes plainly said: "Claim your right if you dare!"

"Yes. Such is the will of the supreme deity of the land," was Kaméhaméha's answer, replying more to the overbearing look of the eyes than to the guarded assertion of the priest.

"May I ask what may be the purpose of the *Kahúna maoli* of Hawáii?"

"I have chosen the *rôle* of a royal war-chief, and mean to make state-craft and the art of war my life purpose, leaving priest-craft to others for the present."

The lurid light was subdued in Hewahewa's eyes at this answer; his voice became softer and his smile more seductive than ever. But Kaméhaméha now saw that he had disclosed too much of his own plans, without learning what the priest's purpose might be, or knowing whether the wily Kahúna would deign to serve under a new political leader.

"Then Hewahewa remains the high-priest after Holoae's death?"

"Yes; provided I do not find myself compelled to assume my priesthood in order to mature my political plans." Again the storm-clouds lowered on the cumbrous brow of the priest, and his lips curled at this seeming vacillation.

"You amazed us all at the war-council yesterday. I then discovered that your mind was filled with great plans for the future, which, if matured, must place you above all your compeers."

"Then you approved of my views?"

"Yes, as far as you disclosed them."

"Tell me something of your own *manao* (thought) as to the condition of the country," said Kaméhaméha.

"I, too, have ambitions for the future greatness of Hawáii. I have sought you out this morning to learn the true bent of your schemes, that, if possible, we may befriend each other. I know not what inference you have drawn from our meeting, but it is plain that there is not room for two such aspiring souls as ours in the same career. If Kaméhaméha chooses to abjure the priesthood, then with the aid of a few great leaders like Keeaumoku and myself, the god-born of Mukíni can attain any degree of political power he may aspire to."

"Hewahewa, I am glad you have been so outspoken. The frank face of Keeaumoku won me at a glance, and has doubly confirmed my choice; but you have filled my mind with distrust of your purpose and fear of your proffered friendship."

"I read as much, and I saw that we two could make or mar each other's fortune. The kingdom of Hawáii is too small for us unless we go hand in hand. We ought to be mutual aids to the pinnacle of our desires, but we must not conflict in our aims; and our purposes must be well defined before we part."

"Most noble Kahúna, I will be plain spoken with you, as you desire. The kingdom of the "Eight Isles" is mine! I only await the proper opportunity to take my own. Kalaniopuu shall be maintained on his throne while he lives, against all the powers of priest-craft, the intrigues of the Leeward kings, and the conspiracies of Kiwalao and the dissaffected chiefs at home. Whoever comes willingly to join my upward path shall attain to the highest position in my kingdom that he is capable of filling. But I will accept aid from no man,—whether priest, peasant, or noble *alii*,—who dares to aspire to more of the spoils of my kingdom than I choose to give."

The face of Hewahewa momentarily grew more hideous to look upon as the clarion tones of the young prince rang their proud *ultimatum* in his ear, and his features became surcharged with blood as he listened to this unheard-of-assumption. Trembling with passion the priest replied in tones of withering scorn :

"Most royal chief, you speak with trumpet tones, as if the thing you aspire to were accomplished, and you were already dispensing your favors with an arrogant hand. Hewahewa has offered you the aid of the future high-priest of Hawáii, the priceless service of one as proud and fearless as yourself. I come as your equal, ready to share your exaltation or your fall. What would you more?"

"Noble Kahúna! Kaméhaméha accepts no equal among all the sons of men. Let every *kahúna* aspire to the highest priesthood of the land, and every noble chief look forward to becoming the bosom friend of the conqueror. Whoso is worthy shall have the guerdon. As Kaméhaméha was given birth by the sanction of Pele, so his mission has been conferred upon him by the gods."

"Dares the royal chief assert in my hearing that Pele has not only made him the *Kahúna maoli* of Hawáii, but has also bequeathed him the six kingdoms of the sea?"

The priest stopped paddling, with the look of Satan foiled of a victim. Wheeling furiously around to confront Kaméhaméha, his cat-like eyes, glaring with concentrated rage, hinted that his credulity was being imposed upon.

"Priest! you forget yourself. Remember you are questioning your sacerdotal chief. Bethink you a moment that the goddess can bestow all the kingdoms of the earth as easily as the superior priesthood of Hawáii. But you have barbed your passionate question by asking me if I 'dare.' That debars me from further reply."

And Kaméhaméha's eyes flashed, and his proud lips caught the trick of scorn from his companion. For once Hewahewa had found his match, one destined to be his master.

"The royal Alii must forgive me. I did indeed forget the courtesy due to a great chief. I failed to remember the homage due to my superior. But, *Alii kapu*, you surprise me by the extent of your assumptions! You are too good a historian to assert that one king has ever yet ruled over all the 'Eight Isles.' Can you soberly tell your brother *kahúna* that the great Pele, the creator of the world, has consigned all her kingdoms to your care?"

"Yes, even before she conferred the rank of high-priest upon me. But this secret must be strictly confined to the high-caste priesthood."

"It shall be respected, as coming from the gods."

"As we stood face to face on the high mountain, where the foot of man never had trod, the words of the deity were these: *Because of the holy birth of the Alii, he is loved of the gods, and shall rule supreme over the destinies of men.*"

"What proof of this can you offer to secure men's allegiance in the herculean task of conquest?" The priest's tones were now sweeter than the honey of bees, and his smile as fascinating as moonlight; yet neither dulcet voice nor winning smile could wholly cover the hate which filled his arrogant soul.

"Pepehi and Wailéle are sufficient evidence; they are my only mortal witnesses. But methinks a priest of your gifts might find means of deriving proof from the gods, as one of half your years has done for himself."

"And may I humbly ask what you have in store for your friend?" He spoke with quivering lips, and scarcely suppressed passion.

"If you serve me well, Hewahewa shall remain *Kahúna maoli* of Hawáii, and eventually become high-priest of all the kingdoms of the group. I will accept no colaborer who claims equal rewards. All is mine when I choose to take it; mine by the will of the gods, and by my power to do more and better for the people than all others who have gone before me."

"Kaméhaméha! forgive me, for my mind is yet staggered with doubt. Only the voice of deity can satisfy me that you have rightly understood the divine messages."

While yet Hewahewa spoke in the subdued voice of intense emotion, a low rumble reached the ear. All unseen a gray mist, lurid with blue flame, had suddenly gathered on the *páli*, not far from the river. The earth rocked, and the river boiled ; and while yet they looked upon the *páli*, thousands of tons of the great cliff fell, burying a small village and its inhabitants near the *heidu* of Pakalani.*

With a look of consternation Hewahewa seized his paddle to escape from the place, as the crash and roar of the falling rocks filled the whole valley with terror. Suddenly the earth was torn open beneath them, and the river disappeared in the yawning fissure. The canoe, stretching across the chasm, was grounded on either end on the black sand of the river bed. A breath of sulphur came up from below. The priest fell upon his knees and invoked the divine Pele to spare him, and forgive the iniquity of his unbelief.

Kaméhaméha sat calm and unmoved, his eyes fixed upon the blue flame above the *páli*. He strove to catch a glimpse of the goddess who had come to vindicate him against the most satanic of men. The monument of Pele's displeasure remains to this day. A ridge of black lava rock juts out into the valley almost to the verge of the river.

Slowly the mist and the pervading flame passed away. The fissure closed up beneath the canoe, and the roily waters of the river again flowed turbidly in their course.

---

*See Ellis' " Tour through Hawáii," page 353, for a description of this terrible event. " A mist was seen to gather on the summit of the precipice, with something like a lambent flame, a forerunner of Pele. A priest offered prayer, interceding with Pele ; but at ten o'clock the side of the mountain fell for half a mile, with a horrid crash."

The Priest's Consternation.   231

Hewahewa mechanically took up his paddle, and with a look of solemn contrition motioned with its blade toward the *heidu* of Pakalani; and thither the rivals paddled in silence. One was secretly triumphing over the rebuke that had been given to the arrogant doubts of the other. That other, humbled by the victory of his young rival, was also troubled because of his impiety toward the supreme god. He studied how he could make his peace with Pele; how regain the confidence of Kaméhaméha. Hewahewa was not one to evade a difficulty. He soon found a solution. As they approached the *heidu* he turned to his companion:

"*Alii kapu!* I have prayed earnestly for Pele to forgive my unbelief. I am now the third human witness of Pele's divine behest to you. May I agáin ask what you have in store for Hewahewa?"

"Remain the chief priest of the land. Check the useless human sacrifices. Seek to build up the people's belief in the coming ruler, without designating who he may be. Watch and wait patiently through the lifetime of Kalaniopuu, until he shall die in peace after a glorious reign; and band our adherents closely together under the trustiest and bravest leaders throughout the land. At the death of the king we will follow the behests of Pele, as promulgated from every *heidu* that we can win."

"Hewahewa awaits the commands of the god-born of Mukíni, and none shall be found truer to the new régime than your *Kahúna maoli*. Let us walk up to Pakalani. Nahoko is a descendant of our great ancestor, Pàáo, and he should be won to our cause as best we may without disclosing our divine authority, or making known the full extent of our plans. Age is creeping upon Nahoko; with him old-established things cannot easily be made new. Let him manage his sacrifices to his taste, for he has not a finger's weight in the politics of the outer world. We must seek your strongest adherent among the priesthoood of Waipio, to take Nahoko's place at his death. Being the priest of the city of refuge, it will be wise to cultivate his friendship in the chance of a sudden need for a place of refuge in time of peril."

XXVIII.

KAAHUMANU INTRIGUES FOR A THRONE.

THE priest and Kaméhaméha found Nahoko at the front entrance of the great *heidu* of Pakalani, where the venerable old Kahúna received them with much courtesy. Having been a contemporary of Wailéle's father, the famous Wahupu, he was delighted to make the acquaintance of Kaméhaméha. And as the young Alii sought to win every notable person in the valley to his cause, he was glad to meet this cordial reception at the ancient place of refuge.

Nahoko seated his guest beneath the historic pandanus tree where stood the house of Liloa, one of the most celebrated of the ancient kings, fourteen generations back. Liloa was father of the victorious Umi, and also of the bloodthirsty Hakau, a king who pleasured himself by beheading every *Kandka* who boasted a better head of hair than his own ; who sent out his man-killers to bring him in the best-tattooed arms of his kingdom, cleft from the bodies of their owners to minister to the æsthetic studies of the king.

The three priests, now met under the famous pandanus, were all *Moo-o-lelo* (historians), and familiar with the ancient stories of the place.

After a brief sojourn at the *heidu*, Nahoko proposed going to examine the devastations caused by the fallen cliff, an event which was unaccountable to all but the two who had been the indirect cause of it. Thousands of tons of lava rock had fallen upon the pretty village of Hepu, obliterating every vestige of human habitation, and leaving nothing but the footpaths that led to it from the river to show where the hamlet and its thrifty gardens had been. Twenty natives were known to have been killed. A large fish-pond had been filled up, and the water and fish were flung out over acres of ground beyond the ruins.

Among the people at the scene of the disaster were Kiwalao and "Feather Mantle." The priest urged Kaméhaméha to seek every opportunity of conciliating the prince, as the best means of keeping the intriguing youth out of mischief and counteracting his rebellious plots. These already promised to complicate the affairs of the kingdom at the death of the king.

In this matter Kaméhaméha fully agreed with the priest, who soon managed to join himself to Kiwalao's party. Finding the prince more agreeable than usual, Kaméhaméha took the trouble to relate some of the terrible scenes he had witnessed on Mauna Loa, which captivated the wonder-loving youth like a fairy tale. Prompted by Hewahewa, Nahoko invited the prince's party to dinner at Pakalani. This fortunately threw the two royal chiefs together for the day, and under the most favorable circumstances. Kaméhaméha's powers of entertaining were unrivalled, and a friendly impression was made upon the haughty prince ere they parted; the more easily in the absence of his low-born companions, before whom the royal scion always acted the worst that was in him.

One ever-present element of danger bade fair to prevent the otherwise possible friendship of the prince boys.

Kaahumanu was an imperious beauty; a self-willed intriguing chiefess, born to rule with an unrelenting hand, one to make or mar the friendship of the princes at her pleasure. There was but one way of inducing the connivance of this haughty girl; namely, by Kaméhaméha's disclosing to her the secret of his royal birth. Not knowing this, the ambitious *wahine* held the low-minded Kiwalao strongly in her toils, with a view to becoming his future queen; using him merely as a stepping-stone to a throne.

The intelligent princess had daily found occasion to scorn and contemn the evil doings of her flippant-minded lover, and was now hourly becoming fascinated with the strong character of Kaméhaméha, who was well-fitted to attract a noble-minded girl. Yet Kaahumanu—wise above her years—was fully capable of losing her heart to one chief and holding fast to the other, for the aggrandizement of herself and her dethroned family. She did her best to give her undivided attention to the jealous-minded Kiwalao during this interview. But the charm of the rival chief often won her smile, and brightened the glance of her elfin eyes, until her praises caused an angry frown to lower on the brow of the prince. Herein lay the insurmountable difficulty of cementing a friendship between the two royal youths. Kaméhaméha took in the situation at once, for the searching glance of his deep, dark eyes was ever weighing the dominant characteristics of every notable about the court. Like a formidable chess-player, he would forecast the moves of each, and devise his future checkmates for them all.

On the first day of his arrival at Waipio, the heart of the young Alii had admonished him that "Feather Mantle" was the only *wahine* he had yet seen worthy to become his future queen. It was therefore a sad blow to his hopes when he soon after learned that the imperious beauty was already affianced to the prince. It was not long, however, before he discovered that the heart of the maiden was as yet untrammelled. This gave him his clue to action. It was now only necessary to delay their marriage until the time should come right for him to show his hand ; then suddenly to make disclosure of his birth and win the game.

As we have seen, Kaméhaméha had already found means to touch the maiden's heart, to win the mother's affection, and to gain a strong advocate in Keeaumoku, who not only secretly despised the prince, but was shrewd enough to see the probability of Kaméhaméha's coming to a throne, whether his own or another's.

From that day the young chiefs frequently practised with spears and war clubs together, usually under the watchful eye and skilful instruction of Keeaumoku. Together they swam in the surf in friendly competition where Kaméhaméha found no equal ; being capable of standing upright on his swift-rushing surfboard as it darted forward, a half-mile course, on the front crest of the furious breakers, to the admiration and amazement of all.*

It was in the Waipio breakers that he saved Kaahumanu's life, an incident which served to bind the two in yet stronger bonds. Namahana and two of her daughters were one day passing around the stern of a fishing canoe, just hauled out upon the beach, when a huge comber came tumbling in upon them and dashed

---

* There was great rivalry at this game among the chiefs. King Umi once put to death a chief who had triumphed over him when a youth.

Kaahumanu against the canoe, bruising her head, and leaving the insensible maiden to be swept back in the undertow of the receding breakers. The only men at hand were the superstitious fishermen and the timid Kiwalao, who thinking the girl was killed, set up a wail: *Auwe! Auwe!* Dead! dead is the daughter of Keeaumoku! The beautiful *wahine* is killed, and swept away into the sea, where dwells the god Moa-alii." The heartless prince stood by wringing his hands, and would have let her drown.

Kaméhaméha was at that moment a quarter of a mile away on his surfboard, careering shoreward at a furious rate upon a mad-rolling breaker. He had seen the accident, and he now guided his surfboard toward the scene. He passed over the drowning maiden as the fierce undertow swept her seaward along the sandy incline of the bottom. Diving after her, he brought the princess to the surface, bleeding and stunned, and to all appearances wholly past resuscitation. Holding her pallid face well above the sea, Kaméhaméha swam with the girl as best he could for the shore, where, after long-continued effort, she was finally restored; this being the second time the royal maiden had been rescued from a watery grave.*

"After this event, it often happened that "Feather Mantle" found difficulty in curbing her growing contempt for Kiwalao's want of manliness and lack of courage, while Kaméhaméha was daily gaining ground in the young girl's heart. Had she not often been prompted by her father at this time, Kaahumanu would have failed to hold the prospective king in her toils.

Because of his love for the king, Keeaumoku fre-

---

* See Bingham's "Sandwich Islands" for a brief mention of this incident, p. 30.

quently assumed the thankless task of instilling courage into the heart of the prince. He taught Kiwalao heroic tales of the wars of his country; strove to make the timid prince proficient in warlike exercises, and made many an effort to awaken a noble ambition worthy of his birth.

But the cool and fearless Kaméhaméha was ever the pride of the old chief's heart. Though but twenty at this time, Kaméhaméha was of much greater stature than his effeminate half-brother, and could catch twice as many spears when flung at his naked breast; while in wrestling there was not a youth in the kingdom who could throw him, or compete with him in any athletic exercise.

The manliness of the young giant finally so won upon the love of Keeaumoku that Namahana, soon after this rescue, induced him to betroth Kaahumanu privately to the young Alii; the affair to be kept secret until after the death of Kalaniopuu.

But, woman-like, the dark-eyed princess continued to show preference in public for the foppish prince, though deep down in her heart an undying love for the rival chief was daily maturing. This was but a trait of the vanity of her sex; a girlish pride to hold in her train of admirers the chief of highest rank, even though she despised him. As compared to her love for Kaméhaméha, her feeling for Kiwalao was but a bubble, without weight or substance, the momentary sparkle of a foam-crest upon a mighty billow.

At that age Kaméhaméha was a swarthy, harsh-featured youth, and often grave and reflective in his moods, even in the sparkling presence of "Feather Mantle." Traits like these readily excite the displeasure of a young imperious beauty. In thoughtful moments Kaahumanu well knew that Kaméhaméha's heart was capable of a thousand times greater love than that of her princely admirer, who at his best was only fit for a woman's toy. Thus it happened that the child-princess was betrothed to two prospective kings.

XXIX.

THE WAR WITH MAUI.

MONTHS of warlike preparation had passed since the visit of Kahekili. Hundreds of war canoes now filled the countless nooks and havens along the Kohala shore, ready to transport a great army and its provision to Maui. The Hawáiians were going to capture East Maui, the most fertile half of the island, in revenge for the warlike intrigues and rebellious conspiracies that had been hatched by Kahekili during his recent visit.

Following the custom of those days, a public meeting of high chiefs had been called to discuss national affairs and decide upon the best method of attacking the enemy. Although the king and his privy councillors had already agreed upon the plan of campaign, yet a council served the purpose of creating popular enthusiasm by giving the high chiefs a voice in a national movement like the present.

Several days had been spent in feasting and discussing the war, when at the last hour Hewahewa and Keeaumoku cunningly contrived to arouse a general demand to hear a word from Kaméhaméha on national affairs. The popular young Naihe, his eloquent old father, and many other gifted orators, had held the warlike assembly enthralled as by a mystic spell, when this sudden call arose.

With a modest demeanor that well became the young

Kaméhaméha's War Speech.   241

Alii, Kaméhaméha took his place within the circle of noble chiefs. But the kindling fire in his dark eyes, and a majestic mien which betokened conscious rank, inspired a wild enthusiasm of cheers even before he spoke :

"My king, and you most noble chiefs, accept my thanks for your courtesy inpermitting one so young to have voice in your councils.

"Though coming from the seclusion of Waimánu, my thoughts have long dwelt upon the crying need of my country for peace. We must agree that it is a great evil to be ruled by too many kings. Six kings to eight islands are five too many. Too many masters have oppressed our people, because the constant intrigues of treacherous rulers have given them opportunity. Let us now go forth to battle and conquer the isles for our own loved king! Hereafter Maui, Molokai, and Oahu shall be ruled with even-handed justice by a single monarch. Who among you does not know the barbarous condition of the Leeward Isles?

"Maui is a land of robbers! The petty chiefs of a treacherous king infest every shore and public highway, lying in wait to kill and steal from all comers. It is a land of assassins, prompted by the murderous Kahekili. He dethroned Namahana, the rightful queen, and hunted her down with poisoned dagger and ambushed spears, until she was driven to our shores for safety.

"Oahu is a land of cannibals! Her rich valleys and fruitful groves are peopled with *Ai Kandkas*, whose chiefs spend their lives in cannibalism. Kalo of Halemanu is a monster of this kind. Kahanu and his brother Kawelao, the descendants of Newa, are also given to this vile business.* Who among you does not detest the

---

* See Dibble's "History of the Sandwich Islands," p. 135.

chief who eats his brother man? Let us go forth to slay the cannibal kings and to conquer the treacherous ones, like Kahekili, who came in friendly guise to Hawáii, and while feasting upon our plenty, conspired to set our noble chiefs at war among themselves.

"Are there any here who do not love our own great king? If so, let them hide among the monsters of the Leeward Isles. Is there any one here who doubts that honor and truth are the noblest guide-stars in the heart of man? If such there be, let him go live among the *Ai Kanákas* of Oahu, or abide in Maui, where the poisoned dagger ever follows the seductive smile of Kahekili.

"Some of you handle your daggers with a nervous grasp, and scornfully think you could defend yourselves were you there. The stoutest warrior among you all has tried it, and was glad to seek our peaceful shores in safety."

The speech was well received, and a hundred war chiefs came eagerly forward to greet this new accession to their councils.

Sometime during the summer of 1775 Kalaniopuu sent a body of troops to Maui to join forces with the garrison at Hana in a raid upon Kaupo and the surrounding country, with orders to secure all the warlike stores they could capture.

Kahekili had not yet embarked for Oahu, and with his large army was well prepared to meet an invasion. A strong body of his men were sent to resist the Hawáiians. A sanguinary battle ensued. The Hawáiians were routed and driven to their canoes, which lay conveniently under the point, and returned to the Hana district with their captured stores. This repulse was an ominous proof of Kahekili's mettle; and it led Kalaniopuu to make more vigorous preparations, that his invasion should prove irresistible.

A whole year was thus given to drilling an army. Six great *corps d'armée* were organized, to which were given the names of the six great *Alii ai moku* (district chiefs). Each brigade was under its own great leader. Kaméhaméha was commissioned to form a "Life Guard." The members of the royal family were joined with the princes and peers of Waimánu, forming a body of young chiefs of the most exalted rank. But the greatest hopes were centred upon two regiments called the *"Alapa"* and the *"Piipii,"* composed of gigantic chiefs belonging to the court circle,—nobles who were privileged to eat at the same board with the king.

These two regiments were such a band of warriors as Hawáii had never before seen. Veteran chiefs of unusual stature, with spears of equal length, their red feather war-capes glistened, and the gay plumes of their helmets tossed proudly in the wind and the sun. It was a gorgeous sight. It moved the hearts of even the timid to enlist in the ranks.

While the material resources of war were in preparation, Kalaniopuu was not forgetful of his duties to the gods. Holoae, the venerable high-priest, was zealous with prayer and prophecy, and mystic rites were held in all the great *heiaús* of the land.

Kaili, the war-god of the ancient kings, was displayed in all the camps by Hewahewa. The war-god Kaili was the special god of Liloa, Keawe, Alapai-nui, and other ancient kings, and it was averred that his crimson feathers were always erect and ruffled on the approach of war. Dreadful were the sacrifices made by Hewahewa, in the name of Kaili, at the *heidus* on this occasion.

In the meantime Kahekili, whose spies were everywhere alert, was daily informed of these efforts to enlist the spiritual powers against him. Having been an irreligious man, he had no priest adequate to cope with Holoae. But now his superstitions were aroused, and he sent a courtly but urgent message to Oahu, requesting the king, who had married his half-sister, to send Kaleopuu to officiate in his behalf.

The young king, Kahahana, was easily deceived. Having been brought up in high favor at the Maui court, he thought to win favor with the treacherous monarch of Maui, not only by sending Kaleopuu, but by going himself with a strong body of soldiers to help Kahekili against the Hawáiians. This act only briefly delayed the monstrous intrigues of Kahekili to sever church and state at Oahu, when, later, he pounced upon his young ally, seized his kingdom, hunted him and his charming queen for two years in the mountain wilds, and at last betrayed and murdered the noble young *Moi.** Though the day of retribution was cruelly delayed, it came at last, like an Alpine avalanche hurled down by the gods.

Inspired with the wisdom of an arch-fiend, the scoffing Kahekili sought to counteract the spiritual forces of his enemy by sacerdotal aid. Following Kaleopuu's instructions closely, with a view to restore confidence to his army, and modify his own superstitions—for the most ungodly are alert for spiritual aid in times of danger,—Kahekili sacrificed scores of victims, and repaired

---

* See the touching funeral chant composed by Kahahana's young queen, when her murdered king was taken from Ewa, to be sacrificed at the Waikiki temple.—Fornander's " Polynesian Races,' vol. II., p. 225.

and consecrated his dilapidated *heiáu* of Kaluli, just north of Wailuku. When all was completed, the priest, king, and a great procession of chiefs took canoe for Hana, the nearest land to Hawáii. There Kaleopuu solemnly pronounced his celebrated *wanana o make*— (predictions of death). Standing on the beetling black rocks of Hana Bay, his thin hands stretched out towards Hawáii, his long white hair streaming in the wind, the *Kahúna*, pointing ominously in the direction in which he sent his dreadful malediction, ended his awful message from the gods with these memorable words :

"*Ua koma ka ia i ka makaha! na puni i ka nea*"— like fish in the net shall they be caught, captured, and slaughtered!

Never were more truthful words spoken by man.

It was late in the year 1776 that Kalaniopuu embarked his magnificent army on the pilgrimage of death. While a part of the forces were landed without resistance in the Honuaula district, where the usual plundering took place, Kalaniopuu led the main army around by canoes, into Maalaea Bay, landing near the salt marsh of Kealia. Not a vestige of the Maui army was stationed there to resist the landing, which impressed the Hawáiians with the false hope of an easy conquest. "On to Wailuku!" became the thoughtless war-cry of the army.

Little did Kalaniopuu realize the cunning of the wily warrior he came to dethrone. As it was yet early in the day, it was thought best to send the *Alapa* regiment across the sand isthmus to attack Kahekili at Wailuku, —a hazardous expedition for even these eight hundred veterans, for they were sent wholly unsupported to the windward shore, twelve miles away.

When drawn up in battle array before the king, the

Alapa were justly proud of their noble orgrnization, their perfect discipline, and the tried courage of every individual warrior. Doubt of success was the farthest removed from their thoughts, as one and all declared they would drink the waters of the Wailuku River that day. Little did the gallant cohort of chieftains anticithe fate that awaited them.

Without offering the least resistance to their crossing over the desolate isthmus of Kamaomao, whose windblown sand-desert made a weary march for the Hawáiians, the artful Kahekili judiciously disposed his forces behind the sand-hills, ranged from Kalua to Wailuku, and there lay in ambush.

On came the *corps d' armée* with tossing plumes and glitering spears—a magnificent display. It wrung a cry of admiration from Kahekili and his chiefs, as they looked down from the tallest hill and made the signal for the hidden legions to attack.

Wild was the work of the next hour's slaughter, as one body after another of the ambushed enemy sprang out like famished wolves upon the phalanx of Hawáiians, and went down like forest-trees before a whirlwind. But as fast as one company went down another from the adjacent hillocks leaped into combat with fresh strength, until one by one the proud *Alapa*, too fearless to retreat, fell on the most sanguinary field that ever was fought in Hawáii.

Great was the joy of the stern Kahekili as he looked down on the slaughter from his sand-hill. Only one chief was made prisoner, the noble Keawehano of Hilo. He was brought to Kahekili to be sacrificed in the *heidu* to glorify the victory; but he died of his wounds before he could be despatched at the altar. Two swift runners out of the brave eight hundred were all that escaped to carry the dreadful tale of disaster to **Kalaniopuu**. One herald only, bringing such improbable **news**, would have been received with discredit, and slaughtered for **his** slanderous story. Two messengers made it so proba**ble that king and court** stood aghast with dismay, justly **deeming that only the mandate of the** angry gods could have wrought such destruction upon the noble **eight hundred.**

It was late in the evening of the day of battle, when the unexpected news of defeat was brought to Kalaniopuu, encamped with the royal family amid the main body of the army. Consternation filled the minds of all at the unaccountable destruction of the gallant *Alapa*. A wild wail rent the air as the whole army broke forth into a piercing utterance of sorrow.

A council of war was held, lasting far into the night. There were present Keawe of Hilo, half-brother of the king; Kalanimanoo of Kohala, Keawe-a-Heulu of Puna, **Nuuanu of Kau,** Kanekoa of Waimea, Nauueka of **Hamakua, with** Kameeimoku and Kamanawa, twin-born **children of Kekaulike,** and half-brothers of Kahekili *; **the generalissimo Kekuhaupio, son-in-law of** the highpriest Holoae; and the princes Kiwalao, Keoúa, and Kaméhaméha.

The council resolved to march at **dawn with the entire** army on Wailuku, and endeavor **to retrieve the ill-fortune of the previous day.**

Kahekili had been active throughout the night, stationing his detached army among the sand-dunes; the Oahu troops under King Kahahana being held in reserve. The

---

* There is more than one legend that holds to this version of their birth.—" Polynesian Races," p. 154.

ambushed men lay in a curved line that stretched from the Waikapu stream to Wailuku, sternly awaiting the appearance of the Hawáiians upon the Waikapu common. They came at length, and the great armies closed in a terrific death grapple. The battle was long and severe, ending in fearful slaughter on both sides. The final victory remained with Kahekili; but it was so dearly bought that not a man was suffered to go in pursuit of the retreating remnant of Kalaniopuu's heroes.

Again the war-worn chiefs of Kalaniopuu met in midnight conncil. Grim, stern men, their wounds dripping from the recent spear-thrusts of the victorious foe, their eyes gleamed with murderous passions at the thought of their friends thus squandered in slaughter. But the superstitions of a maddened savage are stronger than his hatred of an enemy. The wisdom of bowing to the inevitable was at length perceived; for this ill-fortune was pronounced to be the decree of the gods.

Kalola, the queen, was in council, as was her right, and was now requested by Kalaniopuu to go to her brother, Kahekili, as an ambassadress to solicit peace and promise of personal safety from the King of Maui. But she distrusted the fitful and treacherous temper of her brother, and refused to go, especially as this had been a war of devastation and conquest, not an invasion formally announced and conducted with princely courtesy. The queen advised sending her son, Kiwalao, the favored nephew of Kahekili.

The advice was accepted. Decked out with his royal *ahuula* and all the insignia which betokened his rank, and accompanied by two chiefs, Kiwalao marched to Wailuku to obtain the best terms he could for his vanquished countrymen. He passed safely through the decimated ranks of the Maui soldiers, who prostrated themselves at the approach of so high a chief.

After concentrating his broken forces for the night, Kahekili had retired to Kalani-hale, his palace at Wailuku, seeking the needed repose after two days of desperate fighting. When told that the Hawáiian heralds were announcing the approach of Prince Kiwalao, the haughty king turned good-humoredly over on his pallet of mats, with his face upward, a signal of *Iluna ke alo!* ("let him live"),* showing a kindly intention not looked for by his own chiefs.

On entering the palace, Kiwalao went directly to the couch where Kahekili was reclining, sat down on the lap of his uncle, and embraced him affectionately, wailing aloud according to the custom of the country. When the wailing had subsided, Kameeimoku and Kamanawa performed the "*kokolo*," by crawling obsequiously in to the king, and kissing his hands, according to the etiquette of the times. Kiwalao being of too high birth to open the negotiations, Kahekili commenced the conversation, and briefly defined the conditions of peace.

Hostilities were concluded; the two kings met, and after a brief interview Kalaniopuu returned to Hawáii.

Of the many heroic acts of this disastrous war, one notable event was long after sung by the bard, Keaulumoku. Among the valiant warriors of Hawáii, the legends makes honorable mention of Kekuhaupio, son-in-law of the priest Holoae, whose fame as a soldier and great leader of men stood second to none of his time.† During one of the last deadly encounters this

---

* Had he turned his face to the wall, it would have been *Ilalo ke alo!* ("let him die").

† The chief upon whom Cook's men fired, for running the blockade, and who was shot by Cook at the time of his death.

great chief became hopelessly involved among the enemy, and all looked upon him as lost; for the retreat of the army could not be arrested to save an individual. But this brilliant soldier had been the teacher of Kaméhaméha, imparting to him the most cunning arts of fence and strategy. For this kindness Kaméhaméha held the gallant old chief in high esteem. Seeing his danger, the brave young Alii shouted lustily for the royal chiefs of his life-guard to follow, and sprang to the rescue.

Beating down all opposition with his *laau palau*, and making a swath of dead foes to guide his followers, Kaméhaméha stood beside the mighty warrior in his direst need, and together they cut their way back and forth through the Maui men until they fled as from demons of destruction. Thus Kaméhaméha cemented another friendship, which was repaid with the fealty of a lifetime.

This overwhelming defeat rankled deeply in the mind of Kalaniopuu. To lessen his humiliation, the aged king, in the year 1778, gathered a large force of canoes for a marauding expedition, a common method of superannuated kings. Such plunderings of towns and pillaging of districts did not aspire to the dignity of war.

XXX.

THE COMING AND DEATH OF CAPTAIN COOK.

DAYS of equal excitement were close at hand. Shortly after the events described, two *mokus*, or "islands afloat," as the natives termed ships, had appeared off Kauai, bringing the long-expected Lono. The people on the ships were said to be volcanic gods, for fire came from their mouths. The men were white. Their skin hung loose about them, and there were holes in their sides where they kept their property, as they were seen to take out knives, beads, and pieces of iron from their pockets.

They were the two ships of Captain Cook. Mohu, a Waipio native, brought from Oahu a piece of sail-cloth made of hemp, a present from Kahana, the new king of Oahu,* to Kalaniopuu. The queen of Oahu had worn a piece of this marvellous fabric on public occasions, and had attracted much attention.

The ships were described as having port-holes in their sides from which volcanoes discharged fire and smoke, with noises like thunder. The ships had abundance of iron, the most prized of all things known to the natives. When Kapupuu, a petty chief, was sent off to steal a

---

* The last king had just been dethroned by the *Ahu Alii*—council of chiefs—and Kahahana chosen through Kahekili's intrigues.—"Polynesian Races," vol. II., p. 154.

piece of the iron, then fire, smoke, and a great noise were hurled at him, and he was killed on the instant.

The chiefs of Kauai were angry that their professional robber was killed, for stealing was Kapupuu's trade, and they concluded to take their canoes and capture the ships. But the queen said they were gods, that Lona was the chief god, and they must be won by friendship. She would send off canoes loaded with pretty *wahines* to choose husbands among them, it being the custom for girls to make the advances in courtship. The queen sent her own beautiful daughter, Lelema, who won the god Lono (Cook) for her husband, and scores of other maidens also won temporary husbands, who gave the *wahines* iron to take ashore to the chiefs. At the end of one moon the ships sailed away with all the new-made husbands, and great was the sorrow that prevailed among the new-made wives. Lono had promised to return after many moons.

The day after Mohu's arrival the whole Hawáiian fleet sailed for Maui, and took possession of the island, from Hana on the east, round to Wailuku on the north shore. A fort had been constructed years before on the great hill at Kauwiki, and now a fortified camp was made at Hamakualoa.

Kahekili hastened to gather an army at Maalae Bay, and on the night of Nov. 25th he marched across the island to Wailuku. On the following morning an engagement took place with the Hawáiians, on which occasion the young Kaméhaméha led his well-trained Waimánu chiefs in the thickest of the fight. The battle was favorable to the Hawáiians. Kahekili and his army retreated to Lahaina, and resisted the invaders no more.

Leaving the army in camp at Hamakualoa, King

Kalaniopuu and his great chiefs retired more to the east, and dwelt at Wailuaiki, in the fruitful district of Koolau. Early in the morning of the 27th Cook's "floating islands" appeared near the land. They came close in shore to traffic with the natives for food and fruit.

Great was the amazement of all to behold them. The Kanákas exclaimed: "*Moku! moku!* (islands). What are they with so many branches? It is a floating forest on the ocean. It is Lono and his *heidu* come from another world."

Kalaniopuu sent off a canoe-load of hogs as a royal present to the god. After watching the doings of the foreigner for three days the king, and several of his great chiefs went off in state to pay their respects to Lono. Kaméhaméha remained on board all night with a few of his followers, questioning about every thing he saw, examining the mechanism of the ship, and eager to understand and to possess the white man's weapons of war. He saw at once that with the weapons of the foreigner his enemies might easily be killed and all the Leeward Islands conquered for Kalaniopuu.

As Cook's ships stood off from the shore during the night, the king was in consternation about Kaméhaméha, and many wailed his loss during the whole night long. As the ships had gone suddenly away from Kauai, in the spring, there was the more reason to think that they had left Maui for good. But during the following day the vessels worked back again and landed Kaméhaméha. Cook had not known the rank of his visitor.

Standing across Upolu Sea the ships coasted to the east and south of Hawáii, trading here and there with the natives, who occasionally gained courage to approach the vessel, and anchored in Ke-ala-ke-akua Bay on January 17, 1779. It was the place where the last Spanish galleon was wrecked two hundred and fifty years before. The galleon went to pieces on Keei Point, just south of the bay. Most of the crew were saved.* The captain, "Kukunaloa," and a beautiful girl, said to be his sister, were snatched from the breakers and landed on the beach, where they both knelt down in fervent prayer to some God in the sky, whom the natives could not see. The place where the white girl knelt to another God than Pele is still known as *Kulou*, the "Place of bowing down of the *wahine haole*." These people were kindly treated by the natives, and some famous chiefs were descended from the white girl; among whom was Kaikioewa, the recent governor of Kauai.

A strict *tabú* was in force when Cook anchored. No canoes had been allowed afloat under penalty of death. But when the ships were seen approaching the restrictions were removed by the priests in reverence for the god Lono and his floating temples.

An aged hunchbacked priest named Kanina, once a famous warrior, was the foremost *kahúna* of the temple of Lono. When Captain Cook landed Kanina saluted the venerated god with great humility. After falling upon his knees before him, the priest sprang up and spread the red *tapa* cloth of a *kahúna* upon Lono's shoulders, presented a sacred pig as a sacrificial gift of welcome to the god, and made a speech of congratulation, promising further oblations at the *heiāu*. Immediately heralds were sent out to announce the coming of Lono, and bidding the multitude to gather along the way to the temple and fall on their knees in worship. So appalled were the people that they dared not look upon the

---

* This Spanish wreck took place just after a storm in 1527.

face of the dread god as he passed, but peered at him from their houses, and gazed with trembling and fear from behind stone walls, or climbed into trees and looked upon him from afar.

When Lono approached near to the multitude the people covered their faces in wonder and awe. Those very near the roadside, who could not retreat, fell prostrate with their faces to the earth. After the dread deity had passed, ten thousand half-naked men, women, and children,—creeping on all-fours, like so many quadrupeds,—followed the white-man-god to the temple of Lono. Kanina led the way, chanting and praying. Cook was formally presented to the idols, and placed in the sacred seat before the principal god, near the great altar, where a putrefied hog was deposited, a sacrifice made during the recent *tabú*.

Ten men now brought in a large fresh hog; others brought bundles of red *tapa*, with which Cook was adorned while being deified. The sacred hog was then offered in sacrifice, while many priests chanted loud praises of the new-found Lono. Next in the ceremony, Cook kissed the chief idol, after the example of all the priests present. The rites of Cook's deification were concluded by his drinking *awa*, prepared in the mouths of the priestly attendants, and allowing himself to be fed with swine-meat, previously masticated for him by a venerable priest. History records that Cook performed his part in all these rites without a word of dissent or show of repugnance.

No navigator ever discovered an unknown land under more favorable conditions to enlighten a savage people and to win them from their heathenism. For many years the priests had taught the people to expect the return of Lono, an absent king whom they had long since invested with the attributes of deity. And when Cook arrived there was not a doubt in the minds of chiefs, priests, and people, but that he was the long-venerated Lono. When he joined in their worship, and appropriated their costly peace-offerings, consisting of ship-loads of provisions and ornamental presents of great value, their belief in his divinity was confirmed beyond a doubt.

In what esteem ought posterity to hold this Christian Englishman? He not only lent himself to perpetuate the superstitions of a heathen people, but he accepted the gift of the fairest human creature in the land, of beautiful girls, proffered in conformity with the natives' best conception of deity.

Alas! it was but a selfish expedient which served his end for a while. When his ships were loaded with plunder, and his pleasure was satiated in the immolation of young girls, then the true temperament of the passionate man-god was disclosed. Tired of the delusions that he had assumed, and sated with his unmanly heathenism, the divine Lono began to practise arrogance and tyranny toward his too-loving worshippers. Cook finally suffered himself to tear down the sacred idols which he had worshipped, and plundered the temple of its costly enclosure for firewood. This godless god personally took part in robbing the very shrine at which he had been deified, and confiscated a nation's costly idols. The debasing farce ended with a heartless tragedy, in which the most friendly chiefs and priests were slain.

On the 24th of January, 1779, Kalaniopuu arrived from Maui, and at once ordered the priests to lay the whole land again under a strict *tabu*, in gratitude for his victory over Kahekili, and in honor of the coming of Lono. This *tabu* so angered Cook and his people that the officers menaced the chiefs, by firing a musket over their heads when they sought to enforce obedience to the edicts of the king.

On the 26th, the king and chiefs visited Cook in state. They went in three large double canoes. In the first was Kalaniopuu and some of his gigantic nobles, all attired in costly mantles and glittering helmets, armed with shark's-teeth daggers at their side, and shining spears held in martial array. The second canoe was filled with priests, over whom presided Holoae, the high-priest. Each priest, clad in a small crimson *mamo* and a red *kihei*, held his special idol before him, to which he chanted the prayer of his god, sung in honor of Lono. The king and the royal chiefs were adorned with priceless yellow *mamos*, and the lesser chiefs wore red capes trimmed with black. The third canoe was filled with presents, among which were many fat hogs and abundant choice fruit.

After paddling around the ships, keeping time to the songs of welcome chanted by the priests, the canoes suddenly dashed for the shore, where Cook and his officers were waiting to receive the king in a tent pitched near the observatory. With great show of reverence the king presented Lono with his own costly mantle of glistening feathers and his war helmet. He placed the beautiful *mamo* on Cook's shoulders and the gay casque on his head; in his hand he put a curious fan in token of peace. The king also gave him other cloaks of great value and beauty.

In return for these magnificent gifts from the king, upon whose bounty he was dependent, the magnanimous

Christian honored him with *one linen shirt* and a cheap cutlass at his side! This creditable ceremony was closed by an exchange of names, the greatest pledge of friendship among the Hawáiians.

During this visit the most profound silence reigned throughout the bay. Not a canoe was permitted afloat, or a person seen ashore, except a few chiefs lying prostrate on the beach. After the priests had been presented, and their religious rites ended, at Cook's earnest request the *tabú* was removed, except the restriction which forbade women to visit the ships. Kaméhaméha was a frequent visitor to the vessels, and availed himself of every opportunity to barter for weapons for himself and his followers. He purchased of Captain Clerke eight long iron daggers for a splendid feather cloak, which was worth the whole armament of the two ships. Captain King says that the young Alii, then just from the battle-field of Maui, had the most savage expression he ever saw.

Whenever Cook landed a priest awaited his coming; going before him to the *heiáu*, singing chants of praise or making eloquent addresses to the people in his honor, and calling aloud to them to bring offerings to the shrine of Lono, where the whole priesthood was assembled to bless and consecrate the gifts. At one time three thousand canoes and fifteen thousand natives were collected in the harbor, all bringing presents for the revered Lono.

For a week after the king's visit to the ships the most boundless hospitality was continued to Lono and his satellites. Their ships were loaded with every thing for which they expressed a wish; entertainments were gotten up to amuse the guests, and expeditions into the mountains were planned for them. Notwithstanding this continued bounty of the king for their maintenance and amusement, several natives were shot at for pilfering trifling articles, and one was strung up and flogged on board the " Discovery."

The fourth of February was the day appointed for the ships to go. Two days previous to sailing, Lono discarded his divine attributes. Having accomplished his ends, the false Lono began to show the hard and unfeeling character of the man.

Perhaps the most unscrupulous act of this Christian gentleman was his demand for the ornamented fence around the temple of Lono. For this he offered two iron hatchets in payment.

With sad countenance the priest submitted to this cruel desecration of their holy temple; but he sternly refused any thing in the way of remuneration. What was his sorrow, and the just indignation of the people, when subsequently compelled to witness the still greater sacrilege of losing their loved idols, taken for fuel on shipboard; and that too with Cook standing by to enforce the deed. But wishing to avoid the appearance of taking these images from the temple without remuneration, Cook again proffered the two iron hatchets for the idols. The horrified priest shrank appalled from the tempter, indignantly refusing to sell or barter the precious gods, made holy by a thousand years' worship. But Cook himself contemptuously thrust the hatchets into the folds of the priest's garment, bidding the friendly Kanina take them or nothing.*

---

* Jarves' "History," page 64. Cook gave orders to his men to break down the fence and carry it to the boats, while he cleared the way. The images were destroyed by the sailors in the presence of the priests and chiefs. Cook once more offered the hatchets, but the priest trembled with emotion and refused.

Trembling with suppressed emotion at this renewed insult to himself, his religion, and his ancestors, whom the revered idols represented, the priest stood with bowed head, overwhelmed with sorrow, and would not touch the paltry hatchets, bestowed to cover the theft of a nation's idols.

The ships finally sailed, after further abusing the natives; as when the boatswain's men beat the Kanákas with treenails for not complying with their arrogant demands while they were performing the gratuitous labor of moving the ship's rudder to the shore. The vessels lay becalmed, while off the port, until late into the night. Forgetful of the mean returns and the many indignities that the English had bestowed for his own magnificent gifts, the noble-hearted king sent off a canoe-load of hogs and vegetables, as a last act of hospitality to these voracious Christians.

A gale soon after blew up and sprung the foremast of the "Resolution," and to the consternation of priests and people both ships returned to their old anchorage on the 11th of the month. Had the vessels come back for another ship-load of food? If so it was feared that there would be a famine. The joy of the inhabitants at their departure had been of short duration. An ominous silence prevailed about the bay. The innocent trust of the natives in the stranger was giving way to the vague conviction that they had been imposed upon. Not a single canoe appeared to bid the English welcome. A boat being sent ashore, the natives said that the king was away, and that a strict *tabú* was in force. The return of the ships created suspicion of Lono's intentions.

The ships' tents were again pitched in the sacred *heidu*, which they had previously desecrated. Their storm-rent sails were permitted to be spread for repairs in the house of the insulted priest of the temple, who, though friendly in his manner, was reserved and unjoyful at the return of the marauding Christians. But no new cause for disturbance occurred until the 13th, when trouble arose about filling some water-casks at a stream. To prevent the threatened quarrel the chiefs dispersed the natives, who threw stones at the whites in return for their abuse. Hearing of this, Capt. Cook gave orders to *fire with ball* upon the natives if they were insolent.

This combative temper could not long fail to find cause of quarrel with a savage people. Soon after this a discharge of musketry was heard from the "Discovery," and a boat was seen in chase of a flying canoe, upon which the marines were firing. A theft had been committed, and the dread Lono was seen running along the beach, followed by Captain King and a marine, in somewhat undignified haste for a deity, endeavoring to head off the canoe, and to catch the thief. In their zeal for justice the thief was followed for some miles into the country.

While the white gods, with something very like human avidity, were chasing thieves, the equally zealous officer of the boat gathered up the few petty articles stolen, and in a spirit of Christian retaliation seized upon the deserted canoe with intent to carry it off. Palea, a friendly chief, and the real owner of the canoe, now came to the beach, and while denying all knowledge of the theft, objected to being robbed of his canoe. The officer refused to give it up, and a scuffle ensued over the canoe, in which Palea was knocked down by a sailor with a paddle, and left stunned and bleeding.

With showers of stones the natives compelled the

whites to give way, and swim to some rocks out of reach of the missiles. Following the Christian example of the whites, the natives now seized the ship's boat and plundered it, and would have destroyed it had not the friendly Palea rallied from the blow, and used his authority to disperse the assailants. Expressing much concern at the affray, Palea made signs for the crew to come in for their boat, which they did, every article being restored that could be found. But though the combatants parted with apparent friendship, hatred and mutual suspicion were now fully aroused.

Just after midnight, on that eventful Sunday morning, the sentinel fired at a native seen skulking about the temple of Lono. Palea was suffering greatly from his wound, which prompted him to seek revenge for these insults. He swam out through the darkness and stole one of the "Discovery's" boats, found moored at a buoy, which was taken ashore and demolished before morning for the nails and iron which it contained.

Day dawned, and the theft was discovered. Captain Cook, blinded by his self-confidence and arrogant temper, determined to seize upon the king, and to hold him prisoner on board ship as a hostage until the stolen boat should be returned. It was a beautiful Sunday morning when the ill-fated Cook determined upon this perilous measure. He ordered out three boats to blockade the harbor, and gave them the heartless order to fire with ball-cartridge upon any canoe that might seek to force the blockade from without the bay, and also to seize all canoes trying to escape from within the harbor.

The doomed Cook then embarked with the launch and two smaller boats, strongly manned with armed men, and landed at Kaawaloa, at about nine o'clock on Sunday morning. Taking the squad of marines from his own boat, under command of the brave Lieut. Phillips, Cook marched quietly, without the usual parade or music, by a circuitous route to the palace, seeking to avoid arousing suspicion of his tyrannical design.

To all appearance the town was emptied of women and children; but they could be seen peering down in multitudes from the high *páli* above. This was a signal of danger undreaded by the English. Very few men were visible as the soldiers marched through the outskirts of the town. But several hundred war chiefs, and unknown numbers of their followers, all armed, were ambushed everywhere about. The few men who were seen wore garments of black *kapa*, a well-known emblem of mourning or mischief.

The guard having surrounded the palace, Lieutenant Phillips was ordered in to bring out the king, who was sitting among his queens. When Kalaniopuu was told that the white god was without, waiting to give audience to his Majesty, a pitiful expression of sorrow and alarm swept over his aged face. He well knew what must follow if the arrogant Lono persisted in his base design. Taking the hand of the gallant Phillips, who was one to inspire confidence with all, the king arose and went out, showing respect to the stern-faced Lono,* and making a show of humiliation before the supposed deity, who arrogantly requested the king to go on board the "Resolution." As he refused, for awhile the angry god conversed with the patient monarch about the *dreadful crime* of stealing a small boat from Lono.

---

* Jarves' "History," p. 128. His look inspired consternation to the last, and not until his back was turned did he receive his death-blow.

In the brief time they were talking, as if by a touch of magic, armed men seemed to spring up from the ground; for in ten minutes the party were surrounded by two hundred powerful chiefs and countless numbers of their followers. Brave as he was, and godlike as he sought to appear, Cook grew uneasy and showed signs of alarm. Fear will lead even a dog to bite, much more an abused people. He urged the reluctant king with less arrogance, and at length persuaded the kind-hearted old monarch to go to the shore. Accompanied by Kaméhaméha and Keoúa * they went directly to the place where the three boats lay. Several of the queens also went with them. One of them, Kekupuohi, anxiously clung to the king, pleading against his going, and saying that Lono meant to kill him.

Reaching the little boat-cove indented in the lava shore, Keeaumoku and Keoúa here interposed against the king's going any farther. Another powerful chief, Kalaimano, stepped forward and seized hold of his loved king, and with a loud voice threatened Cook, if he did not desist from his purpose.

At that instant, while the enraged Lono was striving to disengage the king from the chief's strong grasp, a new commotion occurred, which hastened the final tragedy. A high chief and renowned warrior, named Kekuhaupio, rushed furiously upon Cook, exclaiming in rage and grief that Kalimu, his brother, had just been killed while they were peaceably crossing the bay. He cried aloud that he would have revenge for this foul deed. The guard held the indignant warrior aloof at the point of his bayonet; yet Cook fired upon the be-

---

* Jarves, p. 128. Captain King states that the king and his two sons were invited on board. Kiwalao and his mother, Queen Kalola, were then at Maui with Kahekili.

reaved chief with blank cartridge, thinking to intimidate him. Finding that the discharge from the " red-mouthed gun " was harmless, it only served to enrage the chief still more. He again rushed forward, demanding revenge for his dead brother. Cook then shot him in the groin. **He fell, severely wounded, and was carried off** by other chiefs. He was maimed for life.

Seeing that the enraged chiefs were now fully aroused to resist his designs upon the king, and realizing that the god-farce of Lono was ended, Captain Cook ordered Lieutenant Phillips to withdraw his marines into the boat. But the move to retreat instantly prompted the indignant Hawáiians to **attack**. Among the shower of stones thrown at the retreating guard one stone hit Cook, who saw the act and the assailant, and **instantly shot him dead.** Out of the first four shots fired that morning three were fired by the heartless Lono upon his worshippers. This imprudence on the part of the commander now drew on a general fire from all the marines in the other boats, to which the undaunted Hawáiians replied by throwing stones, killing four of the guard before they could embark.

Still holding fast with an insane courage **to the** king, Cook now savagely bid Kalaimano let go his hold of the monarch. Not being obeyed, he had the **temerity to** strike the great chief with the flat of his sword. Instantly the powerful Kalaimano seized the pigmy **Lono** in his strong grasp. He sought to restrain him, but **not** to kill him, knowing that a god cannot die. But at that moment another aged chief cried out :

" This is not Lono. He struggles in your grasp. Let me try him with my spear, and if he cries out he is not a god."

Pricking the divine Lono in the back, to the surprise

of all, brought forth a human cry for help. Then even Kalaimano became convinced, and drove his great iron dagger * clear through the body of Cook, just beneath the shoulder-blade. The other chief thrust in his spear. The ill-fated navigator fell dead, with his face in the water.

For a few moments Lieutenant Phillips, grieved at the loss of his commander, resisted the whole onslaught with his sword, filling the chiefs with wonder at his courage. Only when the last of the guards had swum to the boat Phillips also sprang into the sea, and made his way, sword in hand, to the boat, But seeing a wounded marine lying on the bottom, this brave man, though weak from his wounds, sprang into the water and brought him up, and the boat made good its return to the ships.

A memorial pillar has recently been erected on that shore. But it fails to commemorate the only noble act of that dreadful day.

Seeing the state of things on shore, springs were hastily put upon the cable of the "Resolution," and she began firing round shot among the crowd from the starboard guns. Great consternation was created by the noise of the discharge, and the havoc made among the crowd. Many were killed; and Kaméhaméha himself was wounded by a splinter struck from a rock by one of the shots. Terrified at the effects of the cannonade, Kalaniopuu ordered a retreat to the high *páli* above, taking along the body of Cook and the four dead marines. The priests took charge of these, and at once began the sacrificial rites in the small *heiáu* above the town.

---

* It was one of the numerous daggers that Cook had ordered made on the ships for barter with the chiefs.

After these religious ceremonies were over, with weeping and wailing Kanina and his priests removed the flesh from Lono and burnt it. All the large bones of the dead god were neatly cleaned and done up in a black *kapa*, laid in a wicker basket decorated with red feathers, to be sacredly preserved, and afterwards carried in religious procession from *heidu* to *heidu* over all the land. The principal reliquary for the bones was the *Hale o Keawe* at Waipio. Most of the chiefs secured some of the small bones as relics and amulets. Kaméhaméha came into possession of Cook's hair, which he kept with great veneration to the end of life. The marines were also sacrificed, and their limb bones distributed among the lesser chiefs, while Cook's heart and liver were eaten by three children who mistook them for a dog's. And so the dreadful tragedy ended. Six of the friendly chiefs and a great number of natives had been killed. The houses of the friendly priests had been fired upon and burnt, with all the gifts from the ships.

The last act of the cruel whites was perpetrated days after Cook's death. It was to fire upon a flag of truce borne by the same self-sacrificing priests who had consecrated Lono on his arrival, and who remained his true friends to the last.

The ships sailed on the 22d of February. Their late commander, who began by assuming the prerogatives of Lono and accepting the worship due only to the Divine Being, had ended by shooting down his loving worshippers and getting himself killed and sacrificed on one of the very altars at which he had been consecrated as a god.

XXXI.

QUARREL OF THE PRINCES.

THE protracted wars, together with the demands of Cook's ships, had so exhausted the provisions on Hawáii that the chiefs of Puna and Kau refused to impoverish their vassals any further by sending supplies to the court of Waipio.

This rebellious spirit admonished the king that the end of his power was approaching. Messages of recall were sent to Kiwalao and to the queen, his mother, who had remained at the Maui court after the war was concluded.

A council of the highest chiefs was convened, and Kiwalao and Kaméhaméha were made Kalaniopuu's successors, with the approval of the chiefs. Kiwalao's rank was proclaimed the highest; he was the feudal lord. Among other privileges he was to have one of those which formerly appertained to the English sovereigns—that of all the bone and ivory that should be stranded or taken on the shores.* Kaméhaméha was proclaimed second in rank and made High-Priest, with the supervision of *tabús* and the keepership of Kaili, the national war-god. The *heidu* of Moaula, in Waipio, was fitted up and newly consecrated for the special deity. Just how the kingdom was to be divided was left for the king to say at some future time.

---

* This privilege was called the *Palaoa pae*.

Having thus far adjusted his worldly and spiritual affairs, the king embarked with his war chiefs and their vassals for Hilo to subdue the rebel chief of Puna. The Kau chief, Nuuanu, had just been killed by a shark, a casualty which quieted the rebellion in his district. At Hilo, the *heidu* of Kanowa was consecrated to Kaili, and there Kaméhaméha took up his abode. The court remained at Ohela, in Waikea.

War against Puna began. The rebel chief, Imakakaloa, fought long and well. Though often beaten, he eluded capture, gathered his vassals and fought again. This so annoyed the aged king that he removed his court to Kau, his patrimonial estate and his boyhood's home. While residing at Kamaoa he built the *heidu* of Pakini for the war-god. There Kaméhaméha lived, and every thing was made ready for a public sacrifice of the rebel chieftain when captured.

Exasperated at the delay, the aged king sent the chief Puhili to ravage Puna with fire and spear, burning every village until the people should surrender their loved Alii. None would betray him. But after many villages had been totally destroyed he was discovered, captured, and brought before the king.

The rebel lord was young, noble, and manly. Though brave as a lion he was gentle as a woman. His long black hair reached to the ground and gave him something of womanly beauty. The eyes of the angry king dwelt long and searchingly upon the still undaunted chief, awed by his manly grace and noble bearing. Almost did the white-haired monarch let this young rebel go in peace. But a sudden revulsion came over the king's face—a thought of Kiwalao's inability to deal with such a subject, so haughty and self-willed, and with trembling lips and tearful eyes he turned his face to the wall. It was the fatal signal of "*Ilalo ke alo!*"—let him die!

The young noble was seized, hurried to Pakini, and slaughtered upon the altar, where he was prepared for public immolation to the god Kaili. Kiwalao was sent to the *heiáu* to represent the king. There all the great chiefs of the army gathered to witness the heathen rite of sacrificing a rebel.

It belonged to Kaméhaméha to officiate as the high-priest of Kaili, while Kiwalao should personate the king and preside as the great chief of the occasion. But with his usual arrogant manner, the thoughtless prince assembled the chiefs about the altar, and assumed the official right belonging to Kaméhaméha. He offered the baked pig, the bananas, and the bread-fruit, preliminary offerings before the human sacrifice, for which he then made ready.

Kaméhaméha stood by with a look of astonishment at this public insult by the audacious prince. Surprise gave place to anger when he saw that Kiwalao really meant to make the final oblation, and he could endure no more. With flashing eyes, and face hideous with half-suppressed rage, Kaméhaméha sprang forward to assert his rights. Seizing hold of the slain chief, he held up the body as if it were but a feather's weight. Then, in a loud voice, he offered up the human sacrifice to the god Kaili, as the only rightful priest of the deity. When the religious rite was concluded, with a brief address Kaméhaméha dismissed the assembly. Kiwalao slunk away abashed, not daring to openly resent such wrath as he had witnessed when backed by an arm of such prowess.

Kaméhaméha's daring self-assertion made a wild turmoil in the court circle. Those who favored Kiwalao—

a few would not side with an heir-apparent—loudly proclaimed it an act of rebellion. Sides were quickly taken. But Kaméhaméha was deeply versed in the prerogatives of the priesthood, and to the few courageous chiefs who adhered to his side, he explained that a priest in his own *heidu* had the sole right to make sacrifice to his especial god.

Native historians have differed about the rights of this unfortunate scene, without delving into the interior motive of the prince. It left a sting in the hearts of the royal *aliis*, and was the cause of much bloodshed after the death of Kalaniopuu. The aged king was much pained by the affair, fearing for Kaméhaméha's life among these treacherous courtiers. Calling him to a private interview, he justified his act; and after many expressions of love for him and his noble mother, the king assured him that he should soon rule in his own right, but begged him to leave now the hostile court and retire for a time to his patrimony at Halawa, or to his new accession of Waipio Valley.*

Taking his young wife, Kalola, and his god Kaili, Kaméhaméha went to Kohala, where he remained until summoned to the bedside of the dying king. His retirement was often intruded upon, for the great chiefs of his party were aggressive spirits, and had much to bear from the Kiwalao party. Knowing that the prince meant mischief, in revenge for the trouble at the *heidu*, Kaméhaméha was often urged to prepare for war, and to beware of secret assaults.

---

* Halawa was his mother's land, inherited from Pàáo, and to this ancient possession Kalaniopuu had added the whole coast-line to Waipio, together with the rich district of Kailua in Kona. As this is disputed, we give our authority.—" Polynesian Races," p. 301.

The friendly chiefs were among the most powerful of the nobility, such as Keeaumoku, Keawe-a-Heula, Kameeimoku, Kamanawa, and the renowned general, Kekuhaupio. Each one of them could easily muster a thousand spears at the blast of a conch-shell. These were his councillors, and they made a secret compact that though the half of Hawáii was already his, yet would they urge Kaméhaméha to give battle, after the custom of all new kings, and seek to acquire the whole island. To these powerful nobles Kaméhaméha owed great obligations, which he never forgot. He well knew that though they placed the united crown upon his head, it might easily, in such uncertain times, have fallen upon one of their own.

XXXII.

HAWÁII'S NEW KINGS.

FOR two years after the departure of Cook's ships Kalaniopuu held his peaceful court at Kau, the southern district of Hawáii. One April morning, after a reign of thirty years, the venerable king sent for his two sons to come to his bedside. He was dying. Taking the hands of the weeping princes into his thin, cold palms, he tried to make known his will and to impart his blessing. But his moribund tongue was speechless when they arrived, and for a while his sad eyes became as many tongues pleading for the dumb, so eloquent was his fear that he should die and leave unspoken the final bequest of his kingdom.

Hewahewa, the new high-priest, stood over him, praying devoutly to the king's idol, held aloft in his hand. The loved Keeaumoku and the intriguing Keoúa were also there, both weeping with such excess of grief that it was hard to distinguish the genuine from the hypocritical sorrow. The anxiety of all was great, lest the king should die intestate and leave the land to bitter contentions for his throne.

At length, in answer to priestly supplication and the prayers of all present, the king found sufficient voice to bestow his kingdom and to express his last wishes to the young princes :

" My sons, I wish to divide my kingdom between you.

It is the will of Pele that it should be so. Kneel and receive my blessing, and accept your kingdoms. You, Kiwalao, will be the greater king, ruling over Hilo, Puna, and Kau.* Kaméhaméha shall have Kona, Kohala, and Hamakua, and will owe allegiance to his superior. Let Kiwalao be content with the best half of my country; and you, Kaméhaméha, strive to maintain your less warlike brother upon his throne."

Pausing for breath, and looking anxiously from one to the other of his weeping sons, both of the royal *aliis* bowed in willing acquiescence to his will, and promised solemnly to obey his wishes. For a while the dying monarch could say no more, though his wan lips still moved in voiceless speech, and his deep eyes eagerly questioned every countenance, seeking approval of his dying message. In answer to the lowering cloud, seen on Keoúa's brow, and the interrogatory of surprise in others, the king strove hard for yet one more word. At length he found voice to continue, in broken, trembling tones:

"Do you, Kiwalao, respect your vassal king? and you, Kaméhaméha, pay all due homage to your higher sovereign. If you fight at the instigation of others, your warfare will not disturb your dead father in his grave, but it will lie with you two to decide your lot by force of arms. My earth-ghost will linger long over the land I have loved; my just spirit shall preside over your battles, and witness from the sky that he who first rebels against my dying words shall not win."

Both of the weeping princes again vowed solemnly to obey the wishes of the king. Kalaniopuu clasped his feeble hands in prayer, wearily closed his eyes, and calmly passed away.

---

* Kau was the patrimony of the family during the reign of five kings.

Loud was the lamentation of the two sorrowing kings over their dead father. Who shall say which shed the bitterest tears over the dead parent in that first hour of unfeigned grief? One son was known to be full of ambition, seeking opportunity to weld all the eight isles into one kingdom, yet his grief for a loved father was pitiful to behold. The other son wept most and wailed loudest over the dead parent whom he had conspired to dethrone and threatened to kill, and yet truthful history teaches us that "the grief of Kawalao was deep and profound, and could not be comforted."

Hewahewa was the first to break the wailing, by inquiring of the great chiefs:

"Where shall the two kings reside while Kau is thus polluted?"

"Where, indeed?" said Keoúa, impatiently. "You, of all men, should decide."

"Hilo and Kona," replied the priest, "are the two most suitable places; each king residing in his own kingdom. Three months is the period of mourning. Until that time has passed the near relatives must not reside in the land of Kau."

Kiwalao at once prepared to go to his beautiful district of Hilo, where fruit and flowers never cease to gladden the eye, and sunshine and showers clothe the land the whole year round in living green. Kaméhaméha and his chiefs took canoe for Kailua, to enter into formal possession of his three districts, and to put his most faithful friends in charge as the ruling powers.

A general council was held upon the arrival of the great chiefs at Kailua. All agreed upon the necessity of at once putting their whole available forces upon a war footing, as the ominous mutterings heard at the king's death presaged war at the expiration of the season of mourning. The public was still in ignorance of Kaméhaméha's birthright, the true story of Kalaniopuu's love for Wailéle being known to but few.

When the season of mourning had nearly expired, all began to wonder from what quarter the war-cloud would rise. No sooner had the will of the dead king become known than intrigues to counteract his decision were advocated by the chiefs who favored Kiwalao.

The Hilo nobles urged the necessity of obtaining Kona because of its smooth-water fishing, Hilo being on the windward shore. Keoúa expressed great dissatisfaction because his patrimonial estate was included in Kaméhaméha's district of Kohala, to whom he must pledge allegiance before he could acquire further right to his property. This he would not do, well knowing Kaméhaméha's distrust of him.

In July the intrigues of Kiwalao's chiefs culminated in a plan to deprive Kaméhaméha of his newly acquired kingdom. The plot was to embark with the late king's body for Kona, going in war canoes with a strong funeral procession. Each mourner was to be secretly armed; and they would consecrate the king's bones by further sacrifices at Honaunau. If this intrusion should be permitted without a discovery of their treachery, they would land with the royal *manes* at Kailua and there take possession of Kona. Spies from the west coast had reported that Kaméhaméha and most of his chiefs were at Kawaihae. The occasion seemed favorable. A strong band of chiefs and warriors quietly embarked. Doubling the south cape, they skirted along the calm seas of the west or leeward shore, and landed for rest and refreshments at Kahalilua. Here they were struck with consternation at meeting Keeaumoku, who had come down the coast with a double war canoe. Blinded by his grief for the dead king, whose corpse lay on the platform of the canoe, he joined his lamentations with that of his unsuspected enemies, took part in the funeral procession, and returned up the coast with the others. His suspicions, however, were soon aroused, and he inquired: "Where will you bury the king?"

They replied: "We are taking the corpse to Kailua."

Then Keeaumoku became assured that their intentions were warlike, for they were strongly armed, and were pressing on with too unseemly haste for mourners. While he pondered what to do in the emergency, a furious rain squall compelled the funeral cortege to land at Keei, where the corpse was hastily deposited in the sepulchre of Keawe, a famous tomb of dead kings.

The instant that the storm abated, Keeaumoku manned his canoe and paddled with all haste for Kohala in search of Kaméhaméha. He found him at Kehaka, ten miles beyond Kailua. A hasty council was held. It was evident to all that war was impending. Arming themselves for battle, and quickly gathering a few warriors, they sailed along the coast to Keei in search of the invaders. They met Kiwalao and his chiefs coming down from the tomb, and the two parties, as they approached each other, united in wailing for the dead king. The rival kings advanced to greet each other, and Kaméhaméha demanded a private interview. Kiwalao was the first to speak, and exclaimed with much ingenuity:

"Alas! alas for us two! Kaméhaméha, we are as good as two dead men. Here is the old Hilo chief, and Keoúa, urging me on to fight. In such a battle you and I only will be slain. A miserable plan for us."

"A miserable plan indeed. This is Keoúa's doings. Give him a piece of your kingdom and quiet the warrior."

"He wants more than I can give. One must keep a foothold for himself, being master of the whole. Aloha! I must return to Kau."

"Aloha! See that you return not to Kona again, or spears will fall thicker than stars."

Thus they separated. From Kiwalao's declamation, it would seem that he had little relish for war, but was instigated to fight by his turbulent chiefs.

Kaméhaméha's party went round into the bay and stopped at Kaawaloa. Kiwalao returned to the *heidu* of Honaunau, and endeavored to quiet the rapacity of his chiefs. But they importuned the vacillating king to wage war, and at length so fully convinced him that he would win an easy victory that he there and then proceeded to parcel out the yet unconquered country among his voracious chiefs.

Keoúa, the most warlike among them, felt himself neglected in the distribution of land, and declared that he was ill-treated and insulted by the king. This caused an angry clamor. The indignant chief quietly withdrew his followers, bent upon making mischief by bringing on the war prematurely. Marching to Keomo, he set his men to cutting down cocoa-nut trees and destroying plantations on Kaméhaméha's territory; killing whoever resisted his depredations.

These doings brought on three days of constant skirmishing, during which time the rival kings were calling forth their armies. Neither knew that the other had been making previous preparations for war; and each was surprised when he found himself confronted by a powerful force. Rude contests were carried on for four days more, during which neither party gained material advantage.

Among the great chiefs in Kiwalao's army Keoúa was by far the most notable warrior. His quick mind and his remarkable symmetry of form and beauty of face had made him a gay courtier and successful gallant from his youth; the more so among a people where the female chiefs were at liberty to express open preference for whom they liked.

But with all these advantages of rank and personal charm, Keoúa's baffled love for Wailéle early soured him and left him ill-tempered and morose. Dissatisfied with his own surroundings, he continually drew the weaker-minded chiefs around him into intrigues; and now, having been for years the chief conspirator among them, he stood boldly forth as the head and front of the war between the young kings. It was not the first time in the history of nations where a single intriguing noble has involved a whole people in war. But even now war might possibly have been avoided, had not Kaméhaméha looked upon it as Pele's providential way to teach him strategy, preparatory to making his grand dash upon the kings of the Leeward Islands. For this view we have Kaméhaméha's own testimony, given at a later period.

On the eighth day the decisive battle was fought on a tract of rough lava plain at a place called Mokuohai. Here Kaméhaméha made his first important venture in warfare, and developed the wonderful generalship which was the foundation of his power. For four days he had manœuvred to gain some advantage over the superior numbers of his rival; pressing Kiwalao's army back four miles from Houaunau. On the following morning the king and Keeaumoku had together surveyed the enemy's position from an eminence, when Kaméhaméha suggested the first piece of successful strategy recorded in Hawáiian warfare. While the king drew on the fight with Keoúa on the enemy's left wing, near the shore, Keeaumoku was ordered to outflank Kiwalao's division on the right wing by advancing some distance around and beyond their main body. This the gigantic warrior succeeded in doing, but at a dreadful sacrifice, as the left wing of his own army did not fully support his furious onslaught on the rear flank of the enemy.

Attacking the enemy with great fury, Keeaumoku soon found his small force surrounded by Kiwalao's whole division. Fighting with the utmost desperation, the giant defended himself amidst great slaughter, until his whole command was slain.

Battling on single-handed until exhausted, he became entangled by a long spear thrown between his legs, and fell to the ground. Before he could recover himself he was assailed by two warriors, Nuhi and Kahai; one piercing him with a spear, the other stabbing him furiously with a dagger. Thinking that the great chieftain was mortally wounded, his foes called out in derision: "The weapons strike the yellow-back crab"; alluding to his betraying Kiwalao's funeral deception to Kaméhaméha. Weak and faint from loss of blood, and apparently nearly dead, Keeaumoku saw Kiwalao approaching, and believed that the young king would intercede to save him, as they had been the best of friends at his father's court.

Seeing the warriors trying to despoil the wounded chief of his royal ornament, the heartless king stood by and let the new-comers stab his old friend, calling out to his men to take care of the *palaoa* and *lei*, and not stain them with blood.

Growing impatient to possess the rich prize, the king stooped down over the prostrate chief, and himself sought to untie the *lei* which suspended the costly insignia. Keeaumoku had thought himself dying; yet, when he heard the onset of his friends, rushing to the rescue, and felt Kiwalao loosening his jewel, hatred of the heartless act renewed his strength, and inspired him to live.

With a sudden spring the wounded giant grasped Kiwalao by the throat and drew him down, held as by a thousand talons, in spite of his desperate struggle to extricate himself.

At that moment Kaméhaméha and Nalimaelua rushed up. The latter thrust a spear through the body of Kiwalao, while another warrior stabbed the young monarch to the heart. The king lay dead on Keeaumoku's body, grasping the long-coveted ornament which had now cost him his life. The wounds of Keeaumoku were staunched and he was taken to the *heidu* near by, where he subsequently recovered.

In this final struggle, Keoúa stood at a safe distance, sulkily looking upon the sanguinary assault upon his king, making no effort by word or act to save him. The indignant chief had not forgotten the king's recent neglect and abuse, and would not now give the needed word to free him from Keeaumoku's avenging grasp—the same red hand that afterward dealt retribution to Keoúa himself. He was now wounded in the thigh with a spear, and when he saw that Kiwalao was dead and the battle lost, he fled with his chiefs to the shore, near at hand, swam to the canoes anchored off Keei, and escaped with his followers to Kau, where for years he maintained himself as king. Keawe, the aged Hilo chief, who with Keoúa had instigated the war, was taken prisoner and held for sacrifice, but his high rank awed his keepers. With their consent he escaped to the mountains, and thence to Hilo, over which, and the Puna district, he became king.*

Hawáii was now divided into three kingdoms, and though Kaméhaméha had shown great generalship in winning his first battle, the victory had done little more than confirm his title to his own three districts.

It was with proud joy that Kaméhaméha looked over the battle-ground and gathered up the canoe-loads of spoil left by his foe. That night he occupied the *puuhonua* at Honaunau, the recent camp of the vanquished chiefs. Namahana and her family, with hundreds of other chiefesses, friends of the rival kings, had fled to this city of refuge for safety. "Feather Mantle" was the first to greet the victor as he entered the famous *heidu*. There Naihe saw and loved the world-renowned Kapiolani, daughter of the Hilo king, who was weeping piteously at the rumor that her father and brother were dead. Naihe went over the battle-field by torch-light with the maiden, seeking among the slain ones for her friends.

Among the other notable persons at the *puuhonua* was the then unknown chief Kalaimoku, who had fought under Kiwalao. He was kindly received by Kaméhaméha, and in after years became the well-known prime minister to the king under the name of "Billy Pitt." Here also were two of the numerous widowed queens. Keku-

---

* His full name was Keawemaukili. He was half-brother to Kalaniopuu, uncle of Kaméhaméha, and father of Princess Kapiolani.

puohi, the poetess, was one. It was she who clung to her imperilled king when Cook seized him as a hostage, and who stood close by Lono when dagger and spear conclusively proved that he was no god, but a mortal. Kaméhaméha had saved her life from some of his infuriated followers after the battle, who sought to kill the frenzied mother as she wept over her step-son, Kiwalao, and railed upon those who had killed him. She was kept in honorable captivity as a state prisoner. Living to be ninety years old, she saw the entire extirpation of her once formidable race of kings.

Here, too, came the noble Keopuolani, doubly beautiful in her tears, to seek for clemency.* Being of the most exalted rank of any chiefess on the islands, the granddaughter of Queen Kalola and the elder Keoúa—before her marriage to Kalaniopuu,—Kaméhaméha determined as a matter of policy to make her his state wife. She bore him the two succeeding kings, the second and third Kaméhaméhas, and also the ill-fated princess, Nahienaena, who, after a prolonged national council on the subject, escaped the indignity of being married to her own brother, only to find a worse fate awaiting her.

In the first glow of enthusiasm the young victor cast his glittering *mamo* over the weeping Keopuolani, and thus publicly betrothed her before the multitude as his

---

* She was the daughter of Liliha-Kekuiapoiwa and Kiwalao. The discrepancy about Keopuolani is quite puzzling. A writer in the "Polynesian" speaks of her as the wife of Kalaniopuu.—(L. F. Judd's "Honolulu," page 140.) In Dibble's list of royal personages, Keopuolani's mother is queen of Kalaniopuu, which makes it doubtful about his marrying his daughter just in her teens. Other writers say she was the granddaughter of the old king. We have chosen to follow those who cite her as the young daughter of Kiwalao by his half-sister, Kekuiapoiwa-Liliha.

future queen. There was never cause for him to regret the generous act to the noble young daughter of a fallen rival.*

---

* After so many discrepancies, we would make the relationship of these two royal persons yet more clear. Their mothers, Wailéle and Liliha-Kekuiapoiwa, were half-sisters; children of Kalola by Wahupu, the high-priest, and Prince Keoúa. Thus Kaméhaméha and Keopuolani were own cousins, and both *alii pio* of equally high rank.

XXXIII.

ROYAL LOVERS ON THE MOONLIT SHORE.

THE evening of the battle of Keei was Kaméhaméha's first meeting with "Feather Mantle" since he came into possession of his kingdom. He had purposely kept away from Waipio until the maiden should have full scope to determine which of her two lovers she would accept. Kaahumanu had sent loving messages to both of her suitors, well pleased that they found other matters to attend to, until the final arbitrament of arms should decide which was to be the conqueror. Him she would accept.

But it was with unfeigned joy that Kaahumanu now greeted the proud victor, though she had wept long and wailed piteously over the corpse of the vanquished king, when he was taken to the *heiáu* for sacrifice; then to be laid by his father, whose predictions had come to pass sooner than he could have thought.

After the evening meal the lovers wandered out upon the extreme point of the bay and seated themselves upon the rock-bound shore. Never was there a more frank exchange of feelings, thoughts, and motives, past and future, than between these wise young heads. For the first time Kaméhaméha now learned from "Feather Mantle" that she had loved him dearly from their first meeting at the Feast of Kings. Yet even now she frankly declared that family considerations would have compelled her to choose Kiwalao had he alone become king. But when both of her lovers became sovereigns her heart leaped for joy; and then she would not have accepted Kiwalao before his power to rule had been fully settled by the usual gage of battle.

This honest confession of maidenly coquetry was a new attraction to a heart like Kaméhaméha's. He could not have been deceived by the usual subterfuges of women, for even at that early age he could penetrate the motives of all whom he met, reading the true characteristics of a person as easily as another reads a printed page.

So this frankness gave new warmth to Kaméhaméha's love. The full-crowned moon gave its charm to the hour; throned in the zenith it smiled down upon the royal lovers, deepening the spiritual beauty of the faraway snow-peaks that pierced the sky.

Seaward, what pictures of beauty met the eyes of the lovers! In the direction of Maui the moonbeams were flung over the Upolu Sea from isle to isle, spanning it with a floating bridge of silver on billows of gold. Nearer at hand the small waves hastened shoreward, their tiny crests flickering with plumes of moonlight, then breaking upon the sandy beach with murmurs as tender as the voices of the twining lovers. The soft trade-wind sang in the tops of the swaying palms, the sea-foam raced up the sands or leaped joyfully upon the lava rocks along the shore.

What a night was this for loving! What an hour and spot was this to tempt shy young hearts to leave their ambushed coverts and leap to their allotted mates! Both sea and wind and swaying trees sought to harmonize their melody with the jubilant heart-beats of the lovers. The witching moon pressed her benediction upon their brows, and every watchful star glinted softly down, eager to light the bridal. And at this moment love was indeed most fit reward for the victorious king. The ordeal had been passed, the battle won, the wild enthusiasm of chiefs, warriors, and the great multitude about the *heidu* had rent the air with the applause that records the fame of greatness. What now but the tender tones and ecstatic touch of one he loves could crown the glory of a warrior?

The proud, impetuous beauty twined her arms about the victor king with newly awakened pride in the object of her love. Well might the ambitious prince forget his strategy and all the toils of battle, and give himself up to the thrilling dalliance that, though it is alike in all countries, is doubly intensified by a tropic clime. We know not with what burning words they sought to impress their loves upon each other, nor need to know, for all words, in such an hour, are but throbbing wings that bring beating hearts together, as angels walk upon the stars when they approach the face that they adore. * * *

The night wore on. At last Naihe and young Kapiolani, won by the brilliance of the night and the solitude of the wave-washed point, came and sat by the king and Kaahumanu. This enamoured couple had just returned from the battle-field, where they had been searching for Kapiolani's father and brother, reported killed. They had found, instead, those who knew of the escape of the Hilo chiefs. Prompted by the moonbeams, they now sought to fathom the mystery of tender glances and pulsating bosoms,—a wondrous witchery that had served to dry the maiden's tears for the lost friends, ere they were found, and now prompted her to lend a willing ear to Naihe's admiration of her beauty.

What a notable meeting of rare maidens was this! One of these ardent girls was yet to become a renowned minister of state, the one queen among Kaméhaméha's twenty wives who should rule the affairs of a turbulent kingdom, in peace and war, after the death of the king. The other young girl was equally beautiful and imperious, though more flexible than Kaahumanu, and more reverent of divine things, whether creeds of the *tabú* dogma or the subsequent Christian revelation.

The heroic Kapiolani was among the first to forsake idolatry and break from the *tabú* creed, showing the courage of her convictions by defying Pele in her own stronghold, and descending into the dreadful crater of Kilauea, where she confronted the dread goddess before a doubting multitude, and made known to all the world that Jehovah was the only true God.

While Kaahumanu had the most logical mind, she became inert, and was often procrastinating, laboriously reasoning herself into just convictions of right before she would act. Kapiolani was intuitive and brilliant as a meteor. But having mastered a conviction, both of these noble creatures were alike immovable as the mountains of their native land.

One incident, characteristic of Kapiolani's promptness to act upon sudden conviction, is of sufficient interest to lead us to digress from our narrative.

Some days after the battle of Keei there was a great excitement at Kaawaloa. Kapiolani and a girl companion of noble birth chanced to stand by a rare banana tree whose luscious fruit tempted them to eat. "But the penalty is death," said the other. "I know it is one of the strict *tabús* against our sex, but it is wrong, and I will eat one in defiance of the unjust decree," said the impulsive princess.

A stern old priest saw the sacrilegious act. Kapiolani secreted the coveted banana in the fold of her petticoat, and hurried with her companion chiefess to the shore. With nervous apprehension the girls disrobed and swam far out from shore, where they ate the forbidden fruit, though they well knew the doom was death.

With many a furtive glance they swam back to the shore, where they were suddenly confronted by the spying *kahúna*. The priest took the girls before a tribunal at the *heidu*, where he accused them of breaking a death *tabú*. It was pronounced a dreadful sacrilege, and they were condemned to "poverty, loss of rank, and to remain unmarried through life."

Naihe, the young lover of Kapiolani, appealed to the king that the verdict should be set aside because of the youth of the *wahines*. He was summoned before the tribunal of priests, where Hewahewa presided as judge. Never was a more stirring appeal heard from the lips of man than this of Naihe; the young orator won his case, and the beautiful Kapiolani sprang to his side and fainted in his arms. They were married a few weeks subsequent to the event.

The high-priest decided that, though the dreadful desecration was worthy of death, it might be condoned by sacrificing Kapiolani's favorite page. The princess pleaded eloquently for the boy's life, and bade them take her life instead. In spite of her tears the lad was seized by the executioner and carried to the altar of Honaunau, where he was strangled, and sacrificed to the god of the *heidu*.* It was the last banana that Kapiolani ventured to eat during her whole life.

---

* Forty years after this time, the subject being alluded to, Kapiolani sent for the priest who accused her and executed the boy, and asked: "Tell me what you think of such proceedings now?"

Among the first thoughts of the young king after he came into possession of his kingdom, and had made ready to meet the expected clash of arms, was to visit Waimánu and receive the congratulations of his darling mother. It was a proud day for Wailéle when she again looked upon her son, the successful general as well as the king of all Hawáii. But there was yet many a hard battle to be fought before the surviving chiefs among Kiwalao's adherents would peacefully submit to Kaméhaméha's rule.

On his way to Waimánu, the king examined every camp of his followers along the coast, and sought to acquaint himself with the merits of the stranger chiefs everywhere he went. He also mingled freely with his native soldiers, who had just returned to their homes, endeavoring to win their love and to arouse a patriotic impulse among them; requiring every chief and soldier alike to keep himself equipped for battle.

Most happy was Wailéle when her warrior king came unannounced to Mukíni, presenting his much-loved Kaahumanu, to whom he was quietly wedded by his mother at the *heiáu*.

A sacrificial feast was prepared for the occasion, in which offerings of *ilio poli* were made to Pele, for the success of the god-born in battle; together with floral offerings to the god Lono, in honor of the new-made queen, the charming "Feather Mantle," with whom Wailéle was much pleased.

"Those were dark days to us all. We priests knew better all the time, yet it was necessary to retain power over the people."

"What did you do with my boy?"

"Strangled him and sacrificed him on the altar."

The tender-hearted chiefess hid her face in her hands and wept, exclaiming: "Oh! why did not the Christians come sooner?"—(L. F. Judd's "Honolulu," p. 98.)

Here in his native valley the king spent the early part of his honey-moon, wandering among the pleasant haunts of his boyhood with his loved young bride. Here too he organized a company of giant chiefs, for a reserve force in battle, which numbered a thousand men before the wars were over; these were called the "King's Guard," and the gigantic Keeaumoku was their leader.*

Not long could he abide in this secluded vale; for Wailéle's prophetic visions, seen in hours of fervid worship, soon warned him that yet greater preparations were to be made to resist the coming contests with Keoúa and Keawemau, the new kings of Kau and Hilo, who were organizing an army greatly outnumbering Kaméhaméha's forces. This called him to Waipio, where he was busy for months in preparing for war.

---

* The Guard took rise from the celebrated "*Alapa*" regiment of nobles led by Kalaniopuu.

XXXIV.

WAR WITH THE KINGS OF HILO AND KAU.

AS soon as he heard of the approaching death of Kalaniopuu, the warlike Kahekili attacked the Hawáiian forces which held possession of the eastern half of his kingdom. After some minor battles, the numerous outlying camps of Hawáiians were all driven into the strongly fortified camp on the hill of Kauwiki, in Hana, East Maui. Here for a time they defended themselves successfully against their besiegers. The army of Maui at length cut off their water supply, and starved out the heroic garrison, who finally surrendered upon Kahekili's promise of safe conduct to their own island. But when, weak with wounds and hunger, they marched down into the midst of their enemies, they were immediately attacked and slain. The treacherous Kahekili could not well keep a promise even with a brave foe.

Then followed one of the most inhuman acts of barbaric warfare. This whole garrison of brave warriors was prepared for baking in the earth-ovens. The bodies were wrapped in succulent *ki* leaves, and cooked like hogs and dogs for a feast.* Thus was the great victory of Kauwiki celebrated, not by the usual holocaust to the gods, but by a cannibal banquet.

---

* See Dibble's "History," p. 53, for a description of this scene.

Great was the indignation of Kaméhaméha and his army when they heard of the success of the Maui king, and of his cruel treachery. Though it was hardly prudent for him to invade Maui when his own kingdom of Hawáii was but just confirmed to him, yet so great was the rage against Kahekili for this butchery and cannibalism that Kaméhaméha feared loss of prestige with his people if he did not at once declare war. Collecting a great fleet of canoes at Kamilo and other havens lying opposite to Maui, the young king gathered as large an army as he could spare, and made ready to embark to recover his lost province. A spy from the Hawáiian court took word over to Kahekili of the intended invasion. The Maui king at once said to his brother, Alapai: "Take a swift canoe, cross the water to Kohala, land at Kamilo, and say to this young aspirant for a kingdom: Your father sends this message: '*Wait till the black tapa covers me, then my kingdom shall be yours without a war.*'

"But if Kaméhaméha still insists upon war, and will not recognize this command, then tell him: 'If you wage war upon the "Thunderer," then you and your soldiers shall die a quick death before the sun goes down.'"

Alapai crossed the Upolu Sea and landed at Kamilo. When taken to Kaméhaméha the young king asked him:

"*Alii*, what message do you bring me from the cannibal king of Maui?"

"Sire, your father, the great king and mighty warrior, sent me to bestow upon you his kingdom of Maui, saying: 'Tell my son to wait till the black tapa covers me, then my kingdom shall be his without the perils of war.'"

Kaméhaméha looked black with rage while Alapai was

delivering his message, and several of the Maui chiefs handled their weapons nervously, fearing that there would be need to defend themselves. But mastering his passion, aroused by the defamation of his loved mother, the king haughtily said:

"Go back to your treacherous king and tell him Kaméhaméha will bring his own answer in person. Begone!"

Calling a council of his chiefs, Kaméhaméha laid the case before them, and finally took their advice, which was to disperse his fleet for the time. Kahekili had too strong a force to be easily dealt with, and they must prepare to meet the new kings of Hilo and Kau, who, hearing that Kaméhaméha was about to embark for Maui, were already raising a great army of invasion. But before Kaméhaméha could organize such a force as he wished, the struggle with Keoúa was precipitated by an unexpected occurrence. Kanakoa, a powerful chief of Puna, had rebelled, and made war against the Hilo king. Being defeated, he fled for protection to Keoúa, with whom he soon after quarrelled and fought, and was slain.

A brother of Kanakoa, prompted by revenge, took up the cause and marched with all the retainers of the family into Kona, where he begged Kaméhaméha to attack Keoúa. Coming as he did with a strong body of warriors, and being well informed of the weak points of the Kau king, this great chief's aid was of value. Kaméhaméha decided to espouse his cause. A council of nobles was called. They advised war against the two rival kings.

An army was soon concentrated and marched upon Kau. Keoúa gathered his forces to meet Kaméhaméha

Battles with Keoua.

among the mountain passes, and a severe battle was fought, which so weakened both armies that the two combatants retired into camp to await reinforcements.

Keawe, the Hilo king, soon came to Keoua's aid, and together they marched to attack Kaméhaméha. This second series of battles was a long and doubtful struggle, ever after known as *Kauaawa*—the bitter contest. Beginning in Kau, these successive battles ranged northward through Puna into Hilo. They were desperate fights. Nothing but Kaméhaméha's superior generalship saved him from destruction, for his two rivals had equal bravery and greater forces. Their armies indeed were not vanquished, but they were greatly weakened and dispirited.

After one of these desperate struggles in the Hilo district, Kaméhaméha withdrew to recruit in the fruitful valley of Lau-pa-hoe-hoe, near his own kingdom. Here he reinforced his numbers, and gathered a fleet of canoes with which to outflank the Hilo army, which was intrenched upon the Wailuku River ready to receive him.

Embarking all his forces in the night, Kaméhaméha sailed southward past Hilo, and at dawn landed his army in Puna, in the rear of the enemy. A body of Puna men saw the fleet coming and gathered on the shore to resist a landing. Among these was a company of hardy fishermen. As Kaméhaméha sprang into the surf, while leading his chiefs to the assault, his foot slipped into a crevice of the coral rock, where it was held fast for some minutes during the wild confusion of battle. It came near costing him his life. Before the king could extricate himself he was assailed with great fury by the rough-handed fishermen. Pelted with stones and beaten with paddles, he defended himself as best he could. A blow from a paddle in the hands of a powerful fisherman nearly beat in his forehead; but tearing his foot from the coral, he despatched his assailant and struggled to land, barely escaping with his life.

This rear attack partly succeeded, for Kaméhaméha captured a strong body of Hilo men. Among the prisoners were a number of warriors sent to Hilo by the treacherous king of Maui; a curious proof of a "father's love" for his warlike son.

This incident newly enraged Kaméhaméha against Kahekili, and in the intervals of battle he inquired into the affair. The Maui king had previously sent to the kings of Hilo and Kohala for the loan of a large double war-canoe from each for use in his Leeward wars. Kaméhaméha did not honor the request. But Keawe sent a fine large double canoe, and in return Kahekili sent these experienced soldiers to fight against his too warlike "son." Their leader was now sent for, and asked what he had to say against the doom of death. He was a manly fellow, undaunted by his peril, and he said:

"Your Majesty! We are foreign soldiers, found fighting against a noble king. If you say: 'Hold up your heads!' we hold them up and live. If you command: 'Bow down in the dust!' we bow down. If you say: 'Die!' then we will die for having obeyed our lawful king."*

The noble nature of the young king prevailed. With Kahekili lay the blame; not with the brave warriors he sent. Kaméhaméha bade the brave chief take canoes and return to Maui; and to report to Kahekili that his treachery was discovered, and a day of reckoning was at hand. This incident finally determined Kaméhaméha to fit out his next expedition against Maui.

---

* See Dibble's "History," p. 59, for further particulars.

With a view to secure peace in Hawáii during his absence on Maui, he sought an interview with the Hilo king, and the two monarchs agreed upon terms of peace. Keawe became the tributary chief of Kaméhaméha, and agreed to furnish a quota of soldiers whenever Kaméhaméha should require them for his contemplated wars against Maui.

Keoúa had previously returned to Kau, and was therefore not present at the armistice ; but he was considered in the negotiations between the other two kings, with hopes that he too would confess the proved superiority of Kaméhaméha, and promise allegiance to him. These hopes, however, were not fulfilled. The arrogant Keoúa scorned to confess that he was beaten, and refused his submission. But the agreement between the other kings, so long as it lasted, would deprive Keoúa of all future ascendancy. This so rankled in his proud heart that he at length quarrelled with his former ally. A war sprang up between them during Kaméhaméha's absence in Maui, in which the Hilo king was killed, and Keoúa came into possession of his kingdom.

Up to this time Kaméhaméha had fought all his battles against superior numbers, and with only the rude weapons of native warfare. He had thus far maintained himself by skill and strategy superior to that of any former chief of his nation. Yet great as had been his success, he saw that ere he could conquer the entire group he must have better drilled soldiers, armed with more destructive weapons of warfare. To this he now turned his whole attention.

With this purpose in view, he now promulgated along his whole coast-line an order for the people to trade with foreign ships, only in barter for arms and munitions of war; and to befriend and protect the runaway seamen—who had hitherto been hunted and delivered to their ships for a trifle—that the white men might teach the natives the use of foreign weapons.

Kaméhaméha had already obtained a swivel cannon from Captain Douglas, of the "Iphigenia"; but as yet no one knew how to use it. From this vessel also came Kaiana, a warlike chief of Maui,* who had been to China, and was given a number of muskets, with powder and ball, for his services. So valuable an acquisition was Kaiana with these foreign weapons, that high rank and extensive landed possessions were bestowed upon him by the king; though at present the fire-arms were a trifle more dangerous to their owner than to the enemy he wished to shoot. For this dreadful weapon was, indeed, quite as likely to do execution at the breech as at the muzzle. But as the intelligent Hawáiians saw that victory must rest with those who had the "red-mouthed guns," their rapture to possess fire-arms was that of men seeking the gift of omnipotence.

A number of Hawáiian chiefs plotted to capture the "Iphigenia" as a nucleus for a navy; but Kaiana, her late passenger, informed Kaméhaméha, who forbade it and ordered the ship away. He saw that his interest lay in protecting ships and in securing the aid and friendship of foreigners. Yet his ambition must have been sorely tempted sometimes to acquiesce in some of the plots to seize a vessel. What services might it not render in transporting his army to Maui!

About this time, in the autumn of 1789, a vessel ar-

---

* One of three traitorous brothers who had previously conspired against Kahekili, and fled to Kauai; thus, erroneously, stated by Jarves and other writers as being a Kauaian.

rived among the islands whose officers and a part of their armament did more to influence the future conquests of Kaméhaméha than any other event in the history of his wars.

In February of the following year, 1790, while this vessel, the American ship "Eleanor," was anchored off Honuaula, in Maui, two chiefs from Oloalu stole a boat in the night from its moorings at the stern. The sleeping sailor in the boat was killed for giving the alarm, and the boat was broken up for the nails from which to make awls and fish-hooks. In retaliation for this theft and murder, Captain Metcalf fired a broadside of musketry and cannon among a fleet of canoes filled with innocent people, more than a hundred of whom were killed. Sometime subsequent to that event the chief Kameeimoku was subjected to insult and blows for some trifling offence on board the "Eleanor." Adopting the wretch Metcalf's plan of killing the innocent for what the guilty have done, this powerful chief vowed to be revenged on the next vessel which came in his power.

Soon after the sloop "Fair American," in command of Metcalf's son, a lad of eighteen, came in trading upon the Kona coast where Kameeimoku lived. The chief ordered out his canoes filled with trade and presents, and boarded the sloop in the guise of friendship. Overpowering the crew, he killed and flung overboard the boy-captain, and all but one of the sailors, the young mate, who was at the helm, and boldly defended himself with a pistol. Though Isaac Davis was knocked down and disarmed, so favorable was the impression he made by his courage that Kameeimoku saved his life and delivered him to the king as a warrior fit to be nurtured for future use.

The vessel was run ashore in the snug haven of Kaupulehu. The two brass swivel guns, the muskets, and the ammunition were safely landed as prizes of untold value; and with these were won all the important battles of the impending war of conquest.

News of this retaliatory piracy was hastily sent down the coast to the king, lest it should become known to Metcalf, and he should again execute a murderous revenge. Kaméhaméha was so grieved at what he heard that he shed tears over the event. But Kameeimoku was too powerful a chief to be punished at that stage of the king's power.

But the most abiding influence derived from the people of the "Eleanor" was brought about by an act of the king's. Metcalf was then lying off Kealakeakua Bay, waiting for his son to come down the coast in the sloop just captured. John Young, his boatswain, was on shore at the time with a boat and crew, and was surprised to find himself detained as a prisoner, by order of the king, when about to go on board the "Eleanor" for the night. Kaméhaméha saw the absolute necessity of preventing Young from going aboard and reporting the murder of young Metcalf. What retaliation the ferocious father would have resorted to cannot now be known.

For two days the "Eleanor" lay off the port, firing signal guns for Young's return. After the ship disappeared, Young and Davis and the crew of the boat were set at liberty. All were treated kindly. The two officers were made chiefs, and wives were given them, as well as valuable estates, in order to secure their aid and interest in the coming wars. Most efficient aid did these brave men bestow upon their noble benefactor, the king, who soon came to love *Keone Ana* (John Young) as a brother.

The two cannon stolen from the "Fair American," and the gun that had been bought of the "Iphigenia" were mounted upon three of the largest war-canoes. Carriages for land service were also made for each, and wonderful was the effect of these brass guns upon the fate of the island nations. Young and Davis trained a few *Kanákas*, with a nucleus of whites, to the use of muskets; and thus many a doubtful crisis in the coming battles was turned into victory.

XXXV.

THE CONQUEST OF MAUI.

UNTIL the year 1790 all Kaméhaméha's fighting on Hawáii had been for self-preservation, in the wars with three rival kings—Kiwalao, Keoúa, and his uncle, Keawe,—fought for the sole purpose of maintaining his newly bequeathed throne. Having gained full supremacy on Hawáii by compelling the vassalage of the Hilo king, and having so crippled the warlike Keoúa that he was powerless without an ally, Kaméhaméha was now ready to embark on a war of subjugation against the Leeward Islands, the first step in his life-long scheme for the conquest of the group. For several years he had been busy drilling and organizing his native legions. Now that the white soldiers were disciplined and well armed, Kaméhaméha believed that his war power was sufficiently formidable for any contingency.

When nearly ready to sail, he ordered the two vassal kings to send him a strong body of men to join in the expedition against Maui. Keawe willingly responded by sending a fine company of Hilo men; but the arrogant Keoúa denied all allegiance, and flatly refused. This untoward event compelled the king to leave a body of men, with Kaiana at their head, to look after the still turbulent King of Kau. The leader sent in command of the Hilo troops was Kalaimano, the great chief who killed Captain Cook. With these the fleet sailed for Maui.

Landing at Kahului Bay, in Wailuku, Kaméhaméha hastened to concentrate his whole army at the inland village of Waikapu, among the desert of sand-dunes on the isthmus of Kula, which bisects the island into East and West Maui. This position was chosen to cover the Wailuku Pass, leading to the romantic "vale of Iao." That this camp among sand-dunes was of the first military importance was evident. Thousands of bleached skeletons of dead warriors were seen half emerging from their sepulchres of sand, as if hastening forth in ghostly legion to withstand the advance of living armies.

Kahekili's spies had kept him informed of Kaméhaméha's preparations for war, and he had prudently strengthened and drilled his own army, camped among the valleys of Lahaina. A fierce war spirit was now aroused to meet the renowned young king of Hawáii in battle, for his prowess had already filled the island world with wonder. None wished to encounter the famed warrior more than young Kalani, the son of Kahekili, who was now by chance left in command of his father's army of veterans.

Obtaining prompt notice of Kaméhaméha's landing, and believing that the Hawáiians, in the pride of their strength, would follow the usual method of invaders and carelessly camp about Wailuku without present thought of an enemy, Kalani determined to march that very night by a deep gorge in the mountain that bisects West Maui and leads through the vale of Iao. He planned to debouch by Wailuku Pass at dawn, and with the spring of famished wolves to pounce upon the invaders before they could organize for a battle.

The daring conception and swift execution of this impulsive campaign was worthy of a hero. Boy as he was, Kalani had long burned with a consuming valor to meet this boasted Hawaiian king in battle. Nothing but the shock of contending armies could satisfy his kindred thirst for fame. The birth in one decade of two such remarkable geniuses for war gives the only possible color to Kahekili's claim to the paternity of both. This oft-asserted paternity led Kaméhaméha to take vengeance for the defamation cast upon his revered mother, Wailéle; while Kalani went forth to meet Kaméhaméha as his "bastard brother," in envy of his fame in war, and bitter jealousy of his suppposed birthright, and favoritism with Pele.*

Unfortunately for Kalani's well-laid plans, Kaméhaméha did not camp on the shore at Wailuku, but marched instead, with the utmost expedition, to secure the very pass from which Kalani intended to debouch and surprise him. Had each general known the plans of the other, they could not have met each other's strategy better than they did. Kaméhaméha did precisely what he once advised Kalaniopuu to do, at the secret council on the day after the "Feast of Kings." The brilliant strategy of the boy-chief was then considered a desperate scheme. It now received the sanction of the matured warrior, and won him the most successful battle of the island wars.

Leaving a strong body of canoe-men and one brass cannon to protect the fleet, the most active preparation was made for threading the pass. Young and his men were sent into the gorge to plant his battery of two cannon, so trained as to sweep the pass; while native scouts were sent on a few miles farther to give early warning should any attempt be made at a night attack.

---

* See the author's "Kalani of Oahu" for the fuller demonstration of this bitter feeling.

But Kaméhaméha had not the remotest expectation of this, for Kalani had not yet shown his genius for war.

At the earliest approach of dawn Kaméhaméha's army was put upon the march, entering the Wailuku Pass in long attenuated columns, best adapted to the rough and narrow way. Keeaumoku's Giant Guards and Young's battery and musketeers took position midway the long line of march. The sun was two hours high when the vanguard approached the vale of Iao, and to their surprise discovered the army of Maui winding down the opposite pass of Oloalu, with only the green amphitheatre of Iao separating the two armies. Each of them had hoped to steal a march upon the other.

Falling quickly back into the forest before they were discovered, the Hawáiian chiefs sent a courier back to the king, who hastened forward to plan the contemplated battle. It was agreed to fall back and keep hidden from the enemy until the whole Maui army should debouch into the valley, so that if vanquished, the whole force could be totally destroyed!

Ambushing his vanguard in the lateral ravines and dense forest overhanging the cliffs of the valley, Kaméhaméha brought some of his best fighting men to the front, taking position far enough back to permit Kalani's army to pass the ambushed division. This division was ordered not to fall upon the enemy's rear until fighting should begin vigorously in front; then, aided by the surprise, the slaughter was meant to be severe and final. Young took position as the reserve. His infantry were strongly posted, and a cannon was planted on each side of the pass, with which to rake the enemy should the Hawáiians be compelled to retreat.

The lynx-eyed Kaméhaméha and his chiefs could not

descry Kahekili's yellow helmet; but the tall red crest of tropic-bird plumes that Kalani wore was easily distinguished among the great chiefs. He was marching some distance from the front, and near him was the noted fighting chief Kapa-Kahili. Having passed the western part of the valley, the rugged roadway now led the Maui army along the verge of a precipice 2,000 feet high, below which the river Iao runs roaring down its rocky bed, encumbered with gigantic boulders fallen from the cliff above.

Between these mighty mountain peaks of Mauna Eéka, on West Maui, lies hidden the remarkable valley of Iao.* It is a solitude of singular, unearthly beauty. An open amphitheatre enclosed by stupendous *pális* (precipices), whose precipitous walls rise two to three thousand feet above the river from which it derives its name. This valley can only be reached by the narrow trail which winds across the mountain from Oloalu on the west, to Wailuku on the east. Threading this laborious footpath one climbs the mountain gorges; now delving deep down into ravines made gloomy with massive *koa* trees; now winding upward among beetling crags that crowd us upon the dizzy verge of frightful precipices, made slippery by falling waters ever dripping from still higher cliffs, where the green ferns and trailing maiden-hair clothes the crags with verdure.

Reaching this sequestered vale, we stand awed and bewildered by the novelty of the scene. Looking up from the deep defile, a delusion haunts us that we are immured forever in the donjon keep of some stupendous castle of the gods. We search with furtive glances for an apparition of the dread immortals whose haunts we have in-

---

* Pronounced E-ah-ō.

vaded. Vast rocky ramparts and vine-clad bastions loom thousands of feet above our heads. We trace turrets and towers on every hand. Foliage and flowers of supernatural beauty are everywhere festooned by unseen hands. Dim, fairy faces are seen peering down through the trailing mists that sway to-and-fro in the varying wind-gusts of the upper world. Mysterious mists! falling from we know not where, the feathery termination of far skyward water-falls, which have poured valleyward in vain for a thousand years; cascades that end in plumy vapors, so like the touch of invisible wings in the air, fanning the upturned face of the ghost-scared mortal who stands below. What wonder that one shudders with supernatural fears when groping along the fern-clad bank of the mysterious river, looking apprehensively to see the lurking demons emerge from the embowered caves in the adjacent cliff, or stalk forth with threatening mien from the echoing caverns of this dreadful vale?

Iao is a place of eternal shadows—grim, gaunt shadows which take on hideous shapes of terror, that make the blood run cold. So deep is the dell, that the tropic heat of this torrid clime never ventures within; neither the warmth nor the cheerful sunlight of the far outer-world, which we see glinting upon the cloud-capped peaks, ever reaches down to the prison gloom of the gulf below.

Such another arena of battle for men cannot be found in all the wide world. A weird place, most fit for the contentions of immortals with the demons of the place. Yet here met two great armies, led by heroic leaders —born warriors who met and grappled to conquer or die.

The vanguard of Maui passed by the ambushed Hawaiians, wholly unconscious of danger, until at length the main armies met in the forest, announced by the battle shouts as of a thousand mad demons. It was a contention of savage men who hated each other with savage fury; and the fighting soon became desperate on both sides. Kalani pressed boldly to the front and urged his men gallantly to their work. Once, for a moment, he and Kaméhaméha met in a brief tussle for a given point which both wished to secure.

But when the ambush fell suddenly upon his rear, Kalani was disconcerted, and hastily withdrew to learn the cause. The rear division of the Maui army chanced to be Kalani's best fighters. At first the ambush struck consternation among their ranks; but on account of the small space in which a body of men could be hidden from view, it was not strong enough to accomplish its work. Kalani's troops rallied and fell vigorously upon the Hawáiians. They killed every man of the ambush and hustled them over the precipice, where many of their own dead had been flung during the first of the attack.

After hours of desperate fighting at the front, Kaméhaméha was compelled to call up Keeaumoku with his gigantic Guard, a thousand such men as the island world had never seen before. The Maui army gave way slowly and stubbornly, well knowing the impassable pathway which awaited them in the rear. Falling back, foot by foot, before the furious onset of the Guard, at length the narrow fighting fronts of the two armies stood confronted on the awful precipice, down which five hundred of their number had already been hurled into the river.

The deeds of heroism performed there that day can never be told. Many of the best warriors from both armies fought on the verge of that cliff, within spear's length of the awful gulf beneath, where, weakened by their wounds, one by one they tottered and fell over the *páli*.

Gigantic chiefs sprang out from the ranks of those frenzied men, brandished war-clubs, daggers, or javelin spears ; challenging all comers to single combat. Warriors of such prestige in arms, such inconceivable prowess in battle, that the wild din of war was hushed as by a mandate to witness the sanguinary encounter between the giant gladiators.

Cheered by the two armies, and made battle-mad with slaughter, these mighty heroes fought. The victor brained his antagonist, stabbed or speared him, tore off his frontlet as a trophy, with a cry of "*Ie oho!*" as he displayed the scalp-lock of the foe ; then briefly took breath, and with hoarse bravado called on for another victim ; until exhausted or wounded, even the strongest fighter went down, and in turn was flung over the precipice after the shattered corpses who had gone down before. Chief after chief thus grappled with one another in mortal combat, seeking to win fame in the presence of the two armies. They struggled and toiled on the brink of the frightful precipice, and together tumbled over the crimsoned cliff to destruction, falling headlong downward through the air as they fought ; as contending eagles fall from their eyries with talons clenched fast in each other's breast, and beaks rending each other's plumage.

Goaded on to like desperation by the frenzied combats of their great chiefs, thousands of soldiers met in mad encounters ; thrusting their spears through each other's bodies, and clenching in the death grapple on the *páli's* brink, over which they too plunged to a frightful doom. The dead and wounded, falling two thousand feet from the battle-field in the sky, reddened the waters of Iao with a rain of blood, and dammed the swift stream with dead until it was driven from its course.

Kaméhaméha watched every move of Kalani's generals, noting their evolutions with coolness, and making his counter-moves with sagacity ; seizing the right moment to press the foe furiously, or to withdraw his own over-taxed front by a cunning feint of retreat ; or enticing the enemy to rush blindly upon a yet stronger breastwork of spears. When the line of battle wavered at some strategic point, there Kaméhaméha could be seen rushing like a lion into the thickest of the fray, his deep voice reverberating like a thunder-peal. All who came within reach of his huge war-club* were slain. Never for a moment did he lose his head in the fascination of slaughter. The fate of empires has often depended upon the courage and prowess of contending leaders in single combat. Such a dramatic episode was now to occur.

The generalissimo of the Maui army was one of the famous warriors of the age. A herculean savage, treacherous and cruel, after Kahekili's own heart, he had twice the age and experience of his young rival of Hawáii. But he had held aloof from personal encounters, as a true general should ; directing the continuous onslaught, as his army was borne back, foot by foot, along the *páli's* verge, until his hopes of success had one by one gone down with each great chief who had fallen in the front of battle.

At this moment, in the brief pause after Kaméhaméha had tossed his last combatant at the spear point over the *páli*, the young king caught the look of doubt and despair

---

* The *laau palau ;* a sort of halberd, used either to strike or thrust with.

on the war-worn face of Kapa-Kahili, and with an impulse of pity, he challenged the gigantic warrior to single combat.

With a shout of savage joy the great chief accepted the challenge. The two warriors stood confronting each other in the presence of the war-worn armies, and the thousands of women and children who clung to the crags high above the battle-field.

It was a sight above all others to rejoice the hearts of bloodthirsty men. Both chiefs were colossal in stature, and cunning in fence. At a signal from Keeaumoku, they hurled themselves upon each other. The ponderous blows of their great war clubs were given with terrific force and murderous intent.

The battle was long and fierce, for the skill of both was unequalled. But at last the endurance of the old warrior wavered, and he was crushed down by a blow he had failed to parry.

Though the king took his scalp lock, as a memento of the day, he ordered the corpse of the noble *alii* to be sacrificed with honor at the *heidu* of Wailuku, and fell back to let his warriors rush in, and follow the example he had set.

At the fall of Kapa-Kahili, the Maui army became panic-stricken. The destruction of their chiefs and best fighting men had half crushed them. On the loss of their commander the headless divisions broke and took wing like terrified birds.

Retreating pell-mell at first from the rear, fast as the narrow footpath would permit, the panic soon became general; the cry of "*Luka lua! Luka lua!* (Beaten! Beaten!) rang through the disorganized masses, closely huddled like terrified sheep between a precipice and a vertical cliff. So hard pressed were the troops of the broken vanguard that, driven at the spear point, they were at length compelled to climb the steep crags above the *páli*, where only birds could cling ; or were hustled in legions over the precipice, to fall upon the dead below.

Some brave souls turned upon their pursuers, grappled and fought until they died. One gigantic athlete, named Kaano, famed as the brutal *pepehi*, or man-killer of Kalo, the chief of a cannibal horde at Hale-manu, Oahu, thus turned upon his assailants. Goaded by spear thrusts to the maniacal frenzy of despair, he grappled and flung one after another of his armed pursuers over the *páli*. At length his wife's brother, Kahole, sprang forth to meet the giant wrestler. It was a long-sought revenge ; for Kaano had murdered his wife's whole family as victims for his cannibal feasts. They clenched in the death struggle, and together rolled over the precipice. In the fall, Kaano's huge neck caught in the fork of a tree, snapping off his head in a twinkling. Thus the two athletes were found dead below, Kahole still clenched fast to the headless trunk of the murderer of his family. A smile of revengeful satisfaction illumined his dead face.*

Seeing that his whole army was shattered and disorganized, Kalani fled in grief and shame through the Oloalu Pass, in company with a few chiefs and the broken remnant of his rear-guard. Taking canoes at Lahaina, he hastened to bear the disastrous news to Kahekili, and admonish his stern father to prepare for

---

* See Dibble's "History," p. 135, for a full account of Kaano-keewe, the man-killer, who for years furnished dead men for Kalo, his cannibal chief. The big stone platter where the dead were carved can still be seen.

The Sky-Fought Battle.   313

the defence of Oahu against the coming of such a fighter as the world had not before seen.

When Kaméhaméha saw that the Maui army was beaten, crushed beyond power of further resistance, he called off the Giant Guard, for they were too choice soldiers to be sent chasing fugitives, and embraced Keeaumoku for the heroic task he had accomplished in winning this sky-fought battle.

Fresh swarms of inferior men, but under able leaders, hastened forward to hunt down every soldier of the defeated army, for were not they the cannibal monsters who had eaten the brave Hawáiian garrison treacherously captured at Kauwiki? While these orders were being executed with relentless justice, Kaméhaméha stood on the verge of the *páli* in rapt contemplation of his surroundings.

Grand and awful was the vision of scenic beauty which met the gaze of the brooding king as he looked thoughtfully down upon the weird, wild valley of Iao, lying hushed in sunset gloom and funereal awe after the dreadful din of battle.

Everywhere green with rankest verdure, and drenched by the ever-falling mist from the mountain water-falls, the very rocks and cliffs and *páli* walls were festooned with blossoming vines, trailing ferns, and flowering maiden-hair.

From out the dusky ravine beneath Kaméhaméha there rose a vast natural mausoleum, as if reared by the gods to commemorate the new-fallen dead, a stupendous tower of hard gray trachyte rock, rising like a spindling minaret a thousand feet high. So slender and tall is this shaft of stone that one stands aghast while beside it, looking to see it topple and fall with every rude gust that bursts from out the dismal gorges.

Most horrible was the sight that met the eye of the king where lay the mangled corpses of the battle, heaped into one vast Golgotha. Dead friends and foes so dammed up the the blood-red waters of the Iao that the stream heaved and tossed the dead warriors in mocking burlesque of battle. Some were still clenched in the death grapple, and yet rolled and wrestled in the boiling flood in awful mimicry of their recent combat in life.

Not only was the eye assailed, but the ear of the brooding king was invaded by discordant sounds that harrowed the soul. Clouds of fish hawks and mountain eagles had already swooped down over the valley, impatient to gorge themselves upon the dead. Their piercing cries mingled with dreadful shrieks from the Oloalu Pass and the adjacent cliffs, where the brutal pursuers overtook the pursued, and made answer to their piteous cries by strong spear thrusts. Hateful above all human pleadings to a soldier is the cry of a vanquished coward who had paraded his glory above what was meet. Such men were never moulded for murderous warfare on a *páli's* verge. They crouched like whipped curs, and howled one last long appeal of despair.

Other sounds there were that might well arouse one's fears by their delusive cries, heard in the deepening gloom of such a place. Hoarse muffled voices burlesqued the challenges of the dead warriors. Mocking leers and derisive laughter, coming from we know not where, echoed and re-echoed over the ravine, as they will echo still for ages, calling forth and back from crag to cliff forever,—supernatural creatures! before whom the battle was fought, who gloat over the strife of men, and still gather in legions in their native haunt when the setting sun deepens the cathedral gloom of the sepulchral valley where fought the mighty and fell the brave.

XXXVI.

BRILLIANT NAVAL VICTORY OF KOHALA.

THE battle fought in the vale of the Iao gave to Kaméhaméha immediate possession, not only of Maui, but of Molokai and Lanai as well. After confirming his conquest of Maui the king divided his army and took canoes to secure the strategic places on the two latter islands.

While tarrying among his new kingdoms for the purpose of distributing his newly acquired possessions among his dependent chiefs, Kaméhaméha took occasion to send an insulting challenge of battle to Kahekili, at Oahu, with hopes of drawing him into an engagement at Molokai. The following message was borne to him by a courier:

"Kaméhaméha, king of all the Windward Islands, to Kahekili of Oahu. Send your best *ulumaika* to your superior at Molokai." (A sort of bowling-stone used in games of chance.)

To this Kahekili replied, smothering his towering rage, partly in defiance, but more in his oft-repeated moan about death, for he seemed to believe from the first that Kaméhaméha was god-born and ever under the protection of Pele:

"My son! I am the only *ulumaika* by which you can sweep the whole track. Wait until the black *tapa* covers me, then Oahu shall be yours."

Fortunately, perhaps, for the fame of Kaméhaméha, he did not succeed in extending his war of conquest at that time, for, by the delay, his final battles took place under more favorable conditions, and word was soon brought that disastrous fighting was going on at Hawáii.

Keoúa had quarrelled with Keawe, engaged in war, and slain the friendly Hilo king. Elated with his success, the infatuated Keoúa determined to invade Kaméhaméha's kingdom during his absence. Marching to the fruitful valley of Waipio, he cruelly destroyed every vestige of fruit and growing food, including food plants which required years to mature; and committed wanton outrage upon property, killing old men, women, and innocent children.

On hearing of these outrages, Kaméhaméha sailed at once with his whole force for Kawaihae. Keoúa and his army were glorifying over their conquest at Waimea, some twelve miles inland. Discovering the fleet from his elevated camp, Keoúa hastily marshalled his army and marched down toward Paahau. He did not try to prevent the landing of Kaméhaméha, who disembarked and hastened inland to meet the invader. The two armies met and joined in battle on the uplands, when Keoúa, after a brief engagement, finding his forces too hard pressed, manœuvred to withdraw, and retreated over Kohala Mountain in the direction of Hilo, camping for the night at a place called Koapapa.

This event gave an auspicious opportunity for Kaméhaméha to display his generalship. Hastening his army over the mountain by a flank movement, by a shorter route that he had discovered years ago when as a boy he mapped out his future campaigns, Kaméhaméha intercepted the retreating army of Keoúa. A fierce and bloody battle took place. "Lopaka," the only one of Young's pet cannon which had yet been brought into action, made such havoc among Keoúa's ranks that his ablest general, Kaiaiea, made a desperate assault and captured the dreadful gun; though it was of no use to them, as they knew not how to serve it. The king led a brilliant charge and recaptured the gun, with frightful carnage on both sides.

Kaméhaméha's front ranks, wearied by their rapid march, were now completely overtaxed by the stubborn resistance of Keoúa, and soon gave way and were routed. The battle seemed lost. Keoúa pushed his advantage to the utmost, little knowing the fertile resources of him whom he fought.

Young, with his well-armed reserve of foreigners and native musketeers, was always in position for just such a crisis. As the routed army swept by the phalanx of musketeers, and reformed in their rear, the onset of Keoúa was met by a deadly volley of muskets at short range. Appalled at the havoc made by the bullets and terrified by the unaccustomed noise, the enemy wavered, halted, let fly their spears at random, and fled. The tide of battle was turned into a slaughter. Keoúa and the remnant of his army fled to the mountain fastnesses of Hilo, broken in strength and humbled in pride.

Kaméhaméha now took up his residence at Kawaihae; Waipio, the king's valley, having been desolated. The army was distributed in camps over the fruitful district of Kohala; and active preparations were made to finish the war with Keoúa before renewing the conquest of the Leeward Islands.

At this time Hewahewa the high-priest and other influential *kahúnas* asked Kaméhaméha to build a massive *heiáu* to Pele, in deference to the wishes of the goddess, that religious observance and strict *tabús* should follow all successful wars. While Kaméhaméha hesitated about delaying his conquests to forward the affairs of the church, Keao, King of Kauai, becoming alarmed at the growing power of the "Conqueror," as Kaméhaméha was now called, hastily collected a well-armed fleet and sailed to Oahu, where he aroused Kahekili to the certain danger awaiting them all.

Uniting their fleets, the most formidable armament of these warlike times, they sailed for Hawáii full of proud hopes. Among the novel means of warfare adopted by this army of invasion was a pack of fierce bull-dogs, trained to attack men with wolfish ferocity. Much was expected from them. Kahekili's gigantic dog was named Boki, derived from the foreign name "Bose." *

Landing at Waipio, the two kings found means of destroying property by cutting down more fruit-trees, after their usual wanton methods of warfare.

The first Hawáiian to escape from the valley hastened overland to Kawaihae to inform the king. Collecting a canoe force with the utmost dispatch, Kaméhaméha followed along the coast of Kohala to meet the invaders. The three brass swivel-guns were mounted on three of the largest double canoes, in charge of Young, Davis, and other well-tried foreigners. The cannon were well supported by the company of musketeers; while Kaméhaméha and his most warlike chiefs centred about this nucleus of foreigners, knowing that in a sea-battle of this kind every thing depended upon their courage and skill.

Keeping to the calm waters of Kohala so that the can-

---

* From this dog the famous chief, Boki of Oahu, was named.

non could be brought into most effective use, Kaméhaméha's flotilla of canoes was soon met by the magnificent fleet of Kahekili and Keao, which came bowling around Waimánu Point, numbering ten to one of the Hawáiians.

Great was the surprise of the two vain-glorious kings to see the fearless advance of Kaméhaméha's diminutive fleet as the two navies met off Waimánu Valley near the great *páli* of Hilaana. It was agreed between the invaders that the utter annihilation of such an insignificant navy would be insufficient to wipe out the deep disgrace of "Iao."

But when the Hawáiian navy got fairly into action at short range, and the cannon and musketry were brought into full play, the result was manifest at once. The foreigners did most marvellous execution, striking terror to the invading fleet, and filling the hearts of the arrogant kings with such consternation that they set the example of retreat. At once the combined fleets of two nations were scattered in wild confusion.* While the canoes bearing the two vanquished kings fled in dismay across the Upolu Sea, many of their fleet were sunk or captured during the brief but brilliant engagement. This naval battle was called *Ka-pu-waha-ula*, the war of "the red-mouthed gun."

On their arrival at Maui, Kahekili, now greatly dispirited by events, bestowed that kingdom upon Keao. He and his followers hastened on to Oahu, full of superstitious fear that the dread Conqueror was following upon their track, and glad to place his younger brother, who was less depressed, between Kaméhaméha and Oahu.

---

* Kahekili had an Italian named Marc ———, with some sort of gun.

Soon after these events Kahekili died from sorrow and shame at the disastrous termination of his naval expedition. He left his kingdom to Kalani. This young hero took fresh hope and at once began to re-organize the broken army, courageous to the last, though in daily expectation of the Conqueror's following up his naval victory. And thus ended Kaméhaméha's fourth campaign.

XXXVII.

THE TRAGEDY OF KEOÚA AND HIS ARMY.

KAMÉHAMÉHA had good cause to be elated after his three last brilliant victories, battles fought with such renowned commanders and their different armies. But his religious convictions were now too fully aroused to go on with his conquest until some monumental work should be built in commemoration of Pele's love for her worshippers.

Hewahewa had seriously impressed the king with the necessity of building a great *heidu* and making a human sacrifice of unusual magnitude to Pele, lest the dread goddess should forsake his cause for lack of religious zeal, before his final conquests were accomplished.[*] Ten thousand men were therefore set to gathering material, while the skilled workmen among them erected the massive temple to be called Puukohala.

This famous temple was built on an eminence overlooking the sea, a barren hill in the southern part of Kawaihae Bay. It was a massive structure of stone laid

---

[*] This was in accordance with a previous prophecy, for when Kaméhaméha sent his challenge to Kahekili from Molokai, he also sent the venerable chiefess Hoaloa (Namahana's mother) to solicit a prophecy about his conquest from the aged priest Kapoukahi. The *wanana* advised building a great *heidu* to Pele, and predicted Kaméhaméha's supreme rule over Hawáii.—" Polynesian Races," vol. II., p. 240.

without mortar, 224 feet long by 100 feet wide, having walls 20 feet high on the three land sides, while along the cliff next the bay the sea-wall was eight feet high and six feet thick at the top, where it was paved with smooth flat stones, making a promenade for the priests and chiefs. The entrance to Puukohala was prison-like; it was a long, narrow passage between high walls, easily defensible by a few resolute men. Here the man-killers dragged their victims to the altar.

The high upper terrace in the middle of the temple was also paved with smooth stones brought from a distance. At the southern end of the terrace, within an open court, was erected the *anu* or holy-of-holies, a lofty obelisk of open wicker-work, five feet square at the base. Within the *anu* was kept the national idol, Kaili, the king's favorite war-god, while numerous other great wooden idols of hideous aspect were placed in the sacred court.

Kaili was carried to the battle-fields by Hewahewa and his attendant *kahúnas* as the divinity held most sacred by all. This idol was an image about five feet high, made mostly of wicker-work closely covered with red feathers. Its face was of hideous expression, to terrify the enemy; the mouth was adorned with triple rows of shark's teeth; great eyes of mother-of-pearl glared in their sockets; the head was crowned with a lofty helmet of great beauty. Its crest was formed of long black tresses of human hair, among which were locks taken from the head of Captain Cook, and held as the most sacred of all.

Within the *anu* the high-priest immured himself when seeking wisdom from the gods, while without, round about the court, stood the king and great chiefs soliciting oracular utterances upon great events ; to which questions the wise *Kahúna*, inspired like the weird sibyls of the classic ages, answered directly, though with sufficient ambiguity to puzzle all who were not imbued with sacerdotal craftiness.

Just without the sacred court stood the sacrificial altar where human sacrifices were offered to the gods. On the day that Kaili was placed in the *anu* eleven human victims were immolated to the god, together with hundreds of hogs and dogs, sacrificed upon an altar at the opposite end of the *heidu*. On that day the place was a pandemonium too dreadful to be described.

During these days of sacrifice, and during all strict *tabú* periods, the king remained in his own sacred house in the middle of the terrace. The houses of the priests were at the north end of the terrace, where the venerable *Pepehi* and other famous visiting *kahúnas* were entertained during the service of consecration. None but priests and sacred chiefs were ever allowed upon the terrace.

During the long and laborious task of building the *heidu*, the war-chiefs about the court organized and drilled a new army for coming days of conquest. The foreign war being thus necessarily delayed, an army of the untried soldiers was sent to battle with Keoúa, rather with a view to test their quality than with a hope of breaking up that troublesome kingdom among the mountain fastnesses of Kau. Kaiana and his warlike brother Namakeha were given command of the expedition. Keoúa was at Hilo when he was informed of the invasion of Kau. At once he set out with his army toward the scene of action, taking the overland route that leads past the great active crater of Kilauea, near which they camped for the night.

The volcano was comparatively quiescent at the time, and the night was calm and cloudless. As if in idle derision at the general superstitions about the fiery home of the goddess, some irreverent chiefs amused themselves casting stones down upon the smouldering lava-sea. This heinous insult to Pele could not pass unreproved.

In a recent interview with the dread goddess, Pele had promised Kaméhaméha that Hawáii should soon be freed of his enemies; but as yet none knew what form her malediction would take. It was, however, in furtherance of the divine decree, "Whom the gods would destroy they first make mad," that the chiefs were induced to invade the *tabú* grounds and cast stones into Pele's palace of fire.

During that eventful night Keoúa's fated army lay in peaceful slumbers, when suddenly the volcano burst forth into terrific eruption. It threw up large stones to a great height. Fountains of red lava leaped into the sky, and blue flames made the midnight lurid with ghastly glare. Shrieks and groans were heard; and loud detonations that shook the earth. It was such a night of terror, that in the morning Keoúa and his chiefs were afraid to march, lest the offended goddess should destroy them for the impious acts of the previous day. They thus spent the day in penitence and prayer, while the priests offered sacrifices in hope of appeasing the angry deity. But the second and third nights were as full of horror as the first, which filled both the priests and the chiefs with perplexity. When the third day dawned bright and beautiful, the king ventured to order an advance, the army marching in three divisions along adjacent paths leading toward Kau.

The first division had not gone far before a terrific

earthquake occurred, accompanied by an astounding noise exceeding the loudest thunder. The surrounding surface rose and fell; the rocky ground was torn into awful chasms that yawned among them; hundreds of men disappeared, with frenzied screams, where they stood. The whole mountain shook and shivered as with ague, rocking to and fro like a ship in a tempest. The terrified soldiers reeled as if drunk with *awa*, staggered and fell to the earth. The ground heaved beneath them like ocean billows. Bottomless fissures multiplied on every hand, threatening to engulf all who tarried, and yet locomotion was denied them, for they were hurled to the ground by the awful earthquake shocks as fast as they could rise.

A new volcanic eruption now took place. Dense clouds of black sand and burning cinders were hurled aloft from the crater, until the sunlit day was excluded, and the darkness of midnight mantled the earth. The darkness was made more terrifying by the lurid glare of jetting lava and the flashing blue flame of burning gases. The soldiers of the first division were now scorched to death by the hot cinders, or suffocated by the sulphurous fumes that poured upward from the earthquake chasms. These stupendous phenomena produced such electric effects that a furious thunder-storm broke from a cloudless sky. The lightning ploughed up the earth, rent the rocks, and splintered the trees. Several chieftains were torn to pieces by these awful bolts.

The rear party, which remained at the crater with the priests and king, offering their last supplications to Pele, had experienced similar earthquake shocks and electric storms; but the shower of hot sand and burning cinders passed over their heads and not one of their number was killed.

When the awful tumult was over, and the day became bright and clear, the men of this division sprang up and resumed their march, dazed with terror at the infernal scenes they had beheld. Rejoiced at their escape from death, and supposing that they alone had been exposed to peril, they pressed rapidly forward to overtake their companions.

They were soon confronted by an appalling sight! Every man of the second or middle division lay dead upon the volcanic plain. Out of four hundred human beings not one was alive.* Some lay as if asleep; others seemed reclining at their ease, as if musing over the recent wonderful phenomena. No look of terror could be traced on their faces. Other warriors were sitting up, as if soothing their wives or children in loving embraces, while they exchanged the national salutation with face pressed to face of their darlings. Some appeared so lifelike, so unconcerned at what had happened, that they had to be touched before the mocking delusion of life was broken. But in all that division of armed men not one was left to tell the tale. The only living creature that survived the sulphurous gases and hot cinders was a solitary hog, found rooting affectionately among the dead, and striving to awaken his companions from their seeming travesty of death.†

So appalled were Keoúa and his men that they stayed not an instant to bewail the dead, but hastened on until they overtook the forward division, many of whom also had been killed.

It required several days' rest in camp before Keoúa and his chiefs could gain courage to join in battle with Kaiana's army, which had impatiently awaited his com-

---

* Jarves' "History," p. 146.   † Dibble's "History," p. 66.

ing at Kau. Though they skirmished and fought for several days, and won a final battle that was worthy of Keoúa's renown, yet so disheartened was the brave king by his superstitions, and especially by his belief that Pele had forsaken him for his rival, that in the end he was unsuccessful, and prepared to retreat to the mountain fastnesses.

These equally ambitious kings had contended for nine years for the supremacy of Hawáii. While the one was yearly augmenting his resources, his rival was weakened by every battle. But aside from the discouragement of a never-ending war, Keoúa was now convinced that Pele had doomed him to destruction; and he resolved to yield to his fate with dignity becoming his royal rank and military renown.

One night, in the interval of battles, two noble chiefs appeared before his camp bearing *ki* leaves in their hands. They were Keawe-a-heulu and Kamanawa, two of Kaméhaméha's principal councillors. They approached the enclosure about the royal *hale*, where they lay prostrate, waiting permission to enter, according to the usual etiquette of the times.

Kaieiea informed the king that Kaméhaméha's ambassadors were without and asked permission to kill them, as they were two of the wisest and most cunning of their enemies. But Keoúa refused, saying that Keawe was a near relative of his father's, and bade his general ask them to enter. When admitted, the two chiefs performed "*Kokolo*," by crawling up to Keoúa and embracing his feet, uttering a piteous tale of woe.

"Why are you here?" asked the king.

"We come to the son of our late lord to induce him to be reconciled with Kaméhaméha, that you two noble kings may rule in peace together."

"Perhaps I may agree to it. To-morrow I will decide. Is this the true wish of Kaméhaméha?"

"It is indeed the dearest wish of our noble king."

"Go, eat, and rest. We shall march to the mountain, and there hold council with our chiefs."

The chiefs did not find it hard to impress Keoúa's mind with Pele's enmity to himself, and the deity's well-proved love for Kaméhaméha.

Retreating to Hilo, while he was deciding upon his future conduct, Keoúa returned to the scene of the disaster. His dead warriors still lay in mocking attitudes of life, untouched by other marks of decay than hollow cheeks and sunken eyes. In mortal fear of again angering Pele the bodies were left unburied, almost unmourned. Forty years after their bones were still seen bleaching in the torrid sun.

This awful dispensation of the gods so dispirited the brave Keoúa and his chiefs, in council, that they concluded to disband the army and surrender to the clemency of Kaméhaméha. Returning to Kau with his principal warriors, Keoúa and Pauli, his brother, obtained permission to pass through Kaiana's lines, when they embarked in canoes. Coasting around South Point and along the west coast toward Kawaihae, where Kaméhaméha and his great war-chiefs were encamped, Keoúa took the precaution to send a message in advance ; and he again received solemn assurance of present safety and future protection, the generous amnesty purporting to come from the king himself.

During the voyage to Kawaihae, it seemed to his mournful followers as if Keoúa really trusted the smooth speeches of Kaméhaméha's treacherous ambassadors. But his motives and his thoughts can only be guessed ;

for in marked contradiction to such an implied trust, on that fatal morning Keoúa bathed and anointed his own body for the sacrifice, and quietly selected from among his chiefs his *moe-pu* ("companions in death"), seven men willing to die with their heroic king.

When ready to leave the last stopping-place, Keoúa gave his feather cloak and other valuables to Keawe to dispose of; and stepping lightly upon the platform of his own canoe, he smiled upon all, and saluted his twenty-four oarsmen. His seven chosen *moe-pu* followed him, together with Uhai, his *kahili* bearer. When the word "Push off!" was given to the paddlers, the king said, "Aloha!" with a parting wave of the hand to those whom he should see no more.

The party left Kekaha with a long procession of canoes; that of Keawe and Kamanawa keeping close in the rear of the king's. The canoe of Pauli Kaoleioku, the king's half-brother and loved companion in arms, led the fleet. The thoughtful Keoúa would not permit Pauli to be one of his *moe-pu*, as being a natural son of Kaméhaméha, he feared it might seem like an attempt to awaken sympathy for himself to have the gallant Pauli in their midst.

When off Puako point the harbor of Kawaihae burst upon their view. The new *heiàu* frowned down upon them from the hillside, waiting to be consecrated by the sacrifice of some notable victim. Did Keoúa ask himself who that victim would be?

A great fleet of war-canoes formed an ominous looking semicircle around the bay. An opening yawned at its centre to receive those who would never pass out again. Keoúa saw that crowds of chiefs were gathered about the king; and the whole shore was lined with warriors as if for battle. All seemed to present an appearance too warlike for the reception of one who came but to surrender his army, his throne, and if need be his own young life.

So thought Keoúa. Turning to Keawe, whose canoe was near his own, he sadly exclaimed: "*Ino uka!* It looks bad ashore. The clouds fly most unfavorably for me."

To which lament Keawe replied:

"Whence should evil come on so fine a day?"

"The clouds fly unfavorably for me," was Keoúa's only answer.

When Keoúa's surrender was first made known to Kaméhaméha, he was importuned by his chiefs to destroy the troublesome king and his most warlike followers. They argued that one of such energy and ambition could not long remain at peace, as the old adherents of Kiwalao would continue rebellious so long as such a leader was living.

It is sad to think that the noble son of Wailéle could be brought to adopt this line of argument against a submissive foe. The subtle philosophy taught him by Keeaumoku cropped out upon this, as upon other direful occasions of his reign. The measure proposed was murderous; its incentive was to make the most of the opportunity thus thrust into his grasp. Kaméhaméha proved himself human. He was probably induced to give Keeaumoku, though reluctantly, the secret instructions he desired.

The gigantic warrior at once took the lead in the treacherous act which followed. Soon the royal canoes were seen approaching the beach of "Boiling Sands" at the head of the bay, with intent to land within the ominous shadow of the newly-completed *heidu*. A great

Assassination of Keoúa.

concourse of chiefs stood waiting to greet the renowned warriors on the shore. The king stood aloof in the background, with folded arms and face full of commiseration for his victims.

As Keoúa's canoe approached near the landing, the crew visibly hesitated, so awed by the instinctive irresolution which often appalls the bravest, when suddenly confronted with death's invisible presence. Keeaumoku stepped courteously forward to the beach and invited them to the shore, while a line of armed men made a girdle of spears about them, excluding them from all others. Seeing Kaméhaméha and the high-priest standing aloof from the crowd, Keoúa called out cheerfully to the king:

"Here I am!"

Kaméhaméha replied: "Aloha! Rise and come ashore that we may know each other."

And the gallant young king rose up, gathered his mantle about him, and prepared to step ashore.

But before the canoe could touch the sand, Keeaumoku sprang into the shallow water, dagger in hand; his savage face grown black as a tempest. Wading with long strides to meet Keoúa, he fell upon him and stabbed him through and through,—muttering revengeful imprecations about the cruelties inflicted upon himself at the battle of Keei. Clutching the cruel dagger, the death-stricken king wrenched it from his breast, staggered, and fell dead.

Driving his reeking weapon through the other seven submissive chiefs in rapid succession, Keeaumoku then signalled to his encircling spearsmen to end the work.

They rushed upon the crew and slaughtered them to a

man, ere the death-freighted boat could grate upon the shore. Maddened by the scent of blood, the enraged giant would have inflicted like injustice upon those in the other canoes, headed by Keoúa's brother, had not Kaméhaméha sprang forward and interfered with great vehemence to prevent further slaughter.

Judging from one fierce imprecation addressed to Hewahewa by the king during the assassination, a revengeful invective connected with his sainted mother's name, one cannot but believe that a deadly feeling of revenge against Keoúa was at the bottom of this dreadful act.

The bodies of the eight chieftains were taken to the new *heidu*, Puukohala, and there sacrificed on the altar of Pele, Hewahewa and a score of other *kahúnas* presiding over a strict *kapu kane* of a month's duration, preparatory to renewing the conquest of the Leeward Islands.

Thus fell Keoúa, the hero of many a hard-fought battle, together with his seven brave *moe-pu*, who gladly became the king's "companions in death." It was a cruel act, a foul deed ! and no voice has yet justified the crime. It is not known that Kaméhaméha sanctioned or justified it. Let us hope, for humanity's sake, that his sceptre was not stained by the deed. It was symbolic of the barbaric times in which he lived, when many an obnoxious chief was "put away" secretly or publicly, and no voice was raised against the cruelty, if but the hand which inflicted the blow was strong.

Kaméhaméha was ambitious to consolidate the group and civilize the land, and Providence did not provide him with saintly hands to accomplish his task. To reform a barbaric nation—whether by pious Puritan or savage pagan—seems to require that most of its hearts should be pierced. When the stately edifice is reared, few question too closely whether it was reared by prayer or founded in blood.

XXXVIII.

THE TIME OF THE GOOD VANCOUVER.

MOMENTOUS events occurred during the five years prior to 1795. The avenging Pele inscribed the pages of Hawáiian history with a ruthless hand, and warlike kings flashed with meteoric splendor across the arena of battle.

The smoke of sacrificial offering ascending from the new temple of Puukohala—a cruel holocaust of royal *manes*—had not disappeared from the sky before a wail went out over the land for the dead mother of the king. Was it divine retribution for the transgressor coming from another God—the real God, rather than Pele?

Wailéle, the loved priestess of Mukíni, died of grief at the last ruthless act of her son. While kneeling at her altar, on the evening of the day in which she heard of the assassination of Keoúa and of his chieftains, the bursting heart gave way. If the beautiful Wailéle had not loved the handsome king of Kau when he laid his heart at her feet, she had not yet forgotten his beauty and bravery, nor his undying affection, and she had often prompted her god-born son to be lenient and generous with his rival, in whom she recognized great nobility of soul.

The death of his mother was a source of lingering grief to the king. He visited Waimánu and mourned over her tomb, and made new vows for the future. In all the coming years of warfare and state-craft no other act cast such a shadow over his reign. The loved Wailéle was never again forgotten. Her precepts were ever upon his lips; her love for her fellow-men served to soften the hard lot of the defeated and the lowly in all the land.

Pemilani, the king's favorite priest-girl at the *heidu*, was appointed priestess of Mukíni, and soon after became one of Kaméhaméha's subordinate queens. She lived, however, at the *heidu*, his birth-place. Other wives were added to Kaméhaméha's list of queens about this time. An obnoxious chief having aspired to the hand of Kalakua, "Feather Mantle's" sister, the king paid her brief court and wedded her himself, much to the indignation of Kaahumanu. Not long after, in fear that a still younger sister, Namahana, should be improperly mated, the king added this third beauty from one family to his queens. She was then a delicate young beauty, but later in life she acquired a quite undue corpulency.*

Kahekili, like many other ruling chiefs when deeply grief-stricken, became addicted to the use of *awa*, which soon brought on premature decay. He did not long survive the destruction of his fleet and army at the battles of Iao and Kohala. Grieved by his death, even the warlike Keao became depressed by the lowering shadow of coming events. Deserting his new kingdom of Maui, the recent gifts of his dead brother, the aged king embarked with his ill-disciplined army for his more remote kingdom

---

* I would like to send home, as a curiosity, one of Lydia Namahana's green kid gaiters. Her ankle measures eighteen inches, without exaggeration"—(L. F. Judd's "Honolulu," p. 11). This was in the year 1828.

of Kauai. He departed with something of unseemly haste, seeking to put more islands between himself and the conquering king of Hawáii. The rebellious land of Maui had been so devastated by repeated wars that Keao's half-starved followers could not be depended upon to meet the trained forces of Kaméhaméha.

Tarrying for a time at the remote end of Oahu, awaiting favorable weather to continue his voyage, the fractious old monarch found excuse to quarrel with his nephew, the boy-king of the island. Though Kalani was its rightful ruler by the death of his father, and though the conqueror daily threatened to overwhelm all their kingdoms, yet the savage old Keao suddenly turned his forces upon his young nephew, and sought to wrench Oahu from his rule. The first battle was fought at Punahanele, where victory leaned to the old king's side. Kalani was forced to retreat for a time, with the loss of several foreigners who had done good service in his ranks. Encouraged by his success, Keao injudiciously followed up his advantage, when a final engagement took place at Kalauao. There the old king was killed, and his whole army surrendered to the heroic Kalani, who now turned his attention to organizing from the wrecks of battle a new army with which to resist the coming invader.

Notable among the contemporary events of this period was the arrival of Captain Vancouver, from whom, more than any other, Kaméhaméha derived instruction in war; and from whom he received efficient aid in building a vessel and fitting out his war canoes. The last of Vancouver's visits occurred just before the king embarked on his final expedition of conquest.

Being absent on his first Maui expedition during Vancouver's first visit, Kaméhaméha did not see the English captain at that time. Kaiana, who, as we saw, was left in charge of an army to keep Keoúa in check, met Vancouver in Kealekeakua Bay, in March, 1792.

Going on board the "Discovery," this arrogant chief sought to impress the foreigners with his growing importance; representing himself as having equal share in the government with Kaméhaméha. This false representation induced the English to salute him with four guns. From this gratification of his vanity came the subsequent disaffection of this Benedict Arnold of Hawáii.

After a brief visit the ships sailed for the northwest coast. Returning to Hawáii early in 1793, they anchored in Kewaihae Bay, while the king was at Kailua, farther to the south. On the 19th of February Vancouver landed a California bull and cow, as presents for the king. This aroused the jealousy of Kalaimoku, chief of the port, and he refused to lend his canoe, the only one suitable to make the landing, until he was bribed, although he had already received presents suitable to his rank. This event showed the growing avarice of the ruling chiefs, to whom the king alone was superior. These cattle were the first of several herds brought to Hawáii, the wild progeny of which fairly overrun the mountain regions in after years.

Weighing anchor, the two ships coasted along the shore to the south, trading for the provisions needed for the cruise. When the "Discovery" was off Kailua, Kaméhaméha boarded the ship accompanied by Young and several minor chiefs, his personal attendants, such as the "fly brusher" and the "pipe lighter." The first of these ever remained near the king, waving his long feather plume or *kahili*, whether his master was standing, lying, eating, or sleeping.

Vancouver was surprised at the agreeable change which had taken place in the formidable warrior since he saw him at the visit of Captain Cook. The savage expression then attributed to Kaméhaméha by Captain King was gone. The ferocity of those days had given place to a calm and resolute look, and dignified carriage. His majestic mien betokened the nobility of soul that ever after distinguished him. His eyes were dark as a tempest, and piercing as an eagle's. They could be soft as a dove's, when touched by affection, but lurid as lightning when ablaze with anger in the mad hour of battle. He read one's thoughts at a glance, penetrating the most secret designs of those who approached him; and his glance was so commanding that the most arrogant of his chiefs quailed beneath a look of rebuke from Kaméhaméha.

Vancouver found him frank, generous, and cheerful; but the obtrusive presence of one of his overbearing chiefs at once made his height more towering and his tones more commanding; while his dark eyes acquired a sinister, greenish tinge that was fearful to see. In bodily frame and stature he was a herculean savage; and his soul was as great. He was wise, sagacious, and benevolent; a man whose noble traits the most enlightened would be proud to acknowledge.

While Vancouver's benevolent counsel could not in the least repress the king's ambition for power and national aggrandizement, yet it greatly served to foster his courtesy to strangers, and confirmed his protecting policy toward foreigners who resided in the land. And more than this, it gave to the ripening intellect of the king broad and humane views of government, and clearer perception of the effects of religion and statesmanship in moulding the commercial policy of other lands. Kaméhaméha long felt the elevating influence of his noble English friend. He became a better man and ruler from this brief contact with one of nature's noblemen. Vancouver's character formed a benign contrast with that of the egotistic and quarrelsome Cook, whose vanity led to his being worshipped as a god, and whose tyranny and arrogance brought about the tragic end of his great career.

Kaméhaméha visited Vancouver's ship, taking with him Kaahumanu, his "love queen," as " Feather Mantle " was called from the ardent affection with which she inspired him. Several of her pretty court ladies also followed the king on board. Vancouver represented the young queen as being agreeable and beautiful; a plump, voluptuous *wahine*, of whom Kaméhaméha seemed most fond and proud. A number of high-chiefs also made their appearance, and Vancouver took the opportune occasion to distribute foreign presents among those of high rank. Kaméhaméha received a military cloak of scarlet trimmed with gold lace and adorned with epaulets. He was much pleased, and paraded the deck with a martial air of mock gravity, much to the delight of the queen and her followers.

The ships lay off and on during the night, anchoring in Kealekeakua Bay on the following morning. During the day Kaméhaméha made a visit of state to the ships. He was arrayed in his gorgeous feather *mamo*, glittering like burnished gold; so ample was this magnificent robe that it trailed from his colossal shoulders to the deck. This cloak was the work of nine generations of kings, under whom thousands of bird-catchers had toiled in the mountains of Hawáii. Its value, as represented by this immense labor, was inestimable. On his head the king wore a plumed helmet adorned with red and yellow feathers. He looked every inch the conquering monarch that he was.

Embarking in one of his largest war canoes, manned by thirty-six huge paddlers, one might well deem he was among a race of giants. Ten other great canoes followed the king, each laden with nine fat hogs of the largest size as presents to Vancouver. Stepping on board with great dignity, Kaméhaméha took the slight hand of the English captain in his gigantic palm, and covering him with his deep, dark eyes, said :

" *Aloha oe, Kapene ! Oe he hoa aloha* Kaméhaméha ? " Thus translated by the interpreter : " Love to you, Captain Vancouver. Are you friend to Kaméhaméha ? "

Vancouver responded warmly : " Yes, King George and I will always be your best friends."

" *Maikai ! maikai !* " (good, good !) exclaimed Kaméhaméha, for Vancouver's answer needed no interpretation to the keen-eyed monarch, who saluted the Captain with a warm embrace. Considering the massive nose that gave emphasis to the greeting, it might have been regarded as a dangerous degree of frictional affection.

Four helmets of beautiful fabrication were then tendered Vancouver as presents, followed by the ninety great swine in the ten canoes, together with prodigious quantities of fruits, fowls, and vegetables brought in a fleet of smaller canoes. All of these were deposited on deck to the amazement and delight of the Englishmen.

Although these vast quantities of food could not be used before they took hurt, nothing was allowed to be returned.

Responding as best he could to this unexpected hospitality, Vancouver then presented to the king five more cows and a number of sheep, which were sent ashore. Kaméhaméha promised to give attention to their care; while Hewahewa tabued them for the space of ten years, with the proviso that the women as well as the men should then be allowed to eat of the *puaa-bipi* or " swine-beef," as they called the cattle.

These presents were all made to the king. This circumstance aroused some appearance of jealousy among the chiefs, as at Kawaihae Bay. It did not fail to attract the keen-eyed monarch's attention, and soon after brought down upon the offenders a terrible reprimand. Kaiana coming on board just then, Kaméhaméha's austere look showed to all present the growing disaffection which already existed between him and some of the arrogant chiefs. He had already heard of Kaiana's false representation of his power in the land; but policy prevented Kaméhaméha from coming to an open rupture in the present condition of his affairs. But from this hour was dated the deep-laid conspiracy of Kaiana to conquer the kingdom for himself.

When Kaiana's presents came to be accepted by Vancouver—who still believed in the exalted rank of the false chief—then the gigantic Keeaumoku became angry because his presents had been declined, while yet he was by far the more exalted in rank.

The king sat black and silent until he could contain himself no longer. The quarrel between the chiefs and the arrogant part played by Kaiana compelled the indignant monarch to assert his prerogative. In reply to the noisy bravado of the latter, Kaméhaméha sprang to his feet and said in a voice of thunder :

" *Malie! Oe Alii naaupo*—Hush ! you dark-hearted chief."

In an instant the stormy elements were stilled by his mandate and overpowering presence. He then declared with great force and dignity to Vancouver and to the turbulent chiefs that there was no need for the English to accept gifts from any one but himself, saying :

"I am the king and master here! Captain Vancouver, do not receive pig, potato, or banana from the mightiest chief who visits you. These brawling *aliis* are all subjects of mine. Every foot of the land and all it contains is the rightful property of the king; and Kaméhaméha is King!"

The flashing eyes and terrible look of the monarch emphasized what he said, and among the twenty enraged chiefs within hearing of that passionate utterance, sitting with heads bowed in sullen acquiescence, none dared say nay. They sat sulking with lowering brows, their muttered maledictions serving as timid echoes to the outburst of the king's resonant voice, which was alike appalling to friend or foe. From that moment Vancouver grasped the situation with which he had to deal. He saw that if Kaméhaméha did not already possess absolute authority he would soon acquire it by his greatly superior force, both of mental acumen and physical prowess; and to the king he henceforth paid his principal court.

After the ships had been cleared of all but the royal guests, Keeaumoku being the only chief who remained, Vancouver asked permission to erect an observatory on shore in order to correct his chronometers.

This request recalled the tragic difficulties with Captain Cook. While Kaméhaméha assented to Vancouver's wishes, he demanded authoritatively that certain rules of strict discipline should be observed by both parties.

He urged that no foreigner could be permitted to infringe upon the *tabús*, enter the *heidus*, or violate any of their religious observances.

On his part the king promised not to allow any but chiefs of rank to visit the ships, and if theft occurred, he would be responsible for both the thief and the stolen property. An occasion soon came to test his sincerity. A woman was induced by an officer to swim off to the ship in the night. On returning she committed some thefts. The stolen goods were promptly restored, though on board the ship they were not known to be lost.

Vancouver's good judgment and good-will led to a lasting mutual respect. It rendered his visit beneficial, and his final departure was equally sad for the English and the Hawáiians.

At the last hour before sailing, Vancouver exerted himself to make peace between Hawáii and the Leeward Islands. This elicited a flash of eloquence from the king and chiefs. All listened with profound deference to Vancouver's argument. The interest the English had shown in them increased their vanity and strengthened their wish for conquest. In Kaméhaméha's reply he said:

"Captain! You ask me to make peace with the Leeward kings. We agree with you that peace is the true policy of our Eight Isles. But how can there be peace among many rulers? King George makes war on other lands because he is not their king. A king does not make war on his own peaceful subjects.

"It is plain there can be no peace among so many kingdoms. There must be but one kingdom, one king. Who shall be king? Who shall make conquest of all the isles and give peace to the people forever? It cannot be the cannibal kings of Maui, for Hawáii never was conquered since it was a small egg floating about on the sea. Who then shall go forth and conquer the isles from Maui to Kauai, and make a peace that shall smile over all the land, make good laws until "old men can lie down in the by-paths and not be robbed?" There is but one, he whom the gods have most favored among all the sons of men; it is Kaméhaméha!"

Keeaumoku said:

"If the English chief would have peace, let him help Kaméhaméha to conquer the base kings of the Leeward Isles. He has fitted our war canoes with sails; let him now mount them with swivel-guns. Give us muskets and daggers, and the conquest is made easy; and there shall be no more war forever. Will the *haole* give us the powder and guns?"

The hush which followed this ingenious appeal to Vancouver was broken by one mystic word, a cabalistic reply, which silenced all further importunity on the subject:

"TABÚ to King George!"

Sailing that day, Vancouver anchored for a while at Maui, March 12th, where he met Kahekili and Keao. He recommended his pacific policy to the two aged kings, who were so humbled by their naval defeat at Kohala, that peace at any price would have been welcomed, such was their growing dread of the young conqueror.

Sailing upon a cruise, the ships returned for the last time June 1794. The vessels appeared off Hilo Bay. The wind being unfavorable for entering, the king, who was residing at Hilo, went on board the "Discovery," where he was urged by Vancouver to go round to

Kealakeakua in the ship. At first Kaméhaméha refused, for it was the *makahiki* or New Year's festival, a month of wild saturnalia in which the king took conspicuous part, and he did not wish to break the religious observances to which he was strongly wedded.

At the *makahiki* it belonged to the king, or in his absence to the highest chief of the place, to embark in a canoe before daylight, landing at sunrise at some appointed spot where a renowned warrior was stationed to receive him with a shower of spears when he landed. The first spear was to be caught in the hand; with it the others were to be warded off, and when the assault was over the king carried the spear, point downward, into the nearest *heiáu*. After this began the games, dances, and sham fights, which opened the *makahiki* festival for the assembled multitude. During the days of festivity crimes went unpunished, wars were discontinued, and no person could leave the place until the expiration of the holidays.

When solicited by Vancouver to accompany him, the king urged the necessity of obtaining the priest's sanction to his absence. But Keeaumoku and Vancouver both replied that the king was exalted above all social or religious rules. He acquiesced, and a canoe was sent ashore to announce that the king would not take part in the games. During the passage a number of chiefs came off, much surprised to find the king on board, but were satisfied when he made known that it was his own choice.

In part payment for Kaméhaméha's boundless liberality of provisions on this and previous occasions. Vancouver directed a vessel to be built for him; and on the first of February, 1794, the keel of the "Britannia" was laid, the first vessel built at the Islands. She was built by the ship's carpenters, and fitted by the seamen with a full suit of sails, anchors, and cables.

He rendered the king a service in love as well as in war. Finding that Kaméhaméha had been estranged from his loved Kaahumanu, owing to an alleged intimacy with the treacherous Kaiana, Vancouver invited the repentant queen on board. By an innocent artifice he also induced the kings to come off, and confronted the indignant monarch and his spouse. The tears of a beautiful woman were too subtle for his anger. The royal pair embraced and were reconciled. But "Feather Mantle" begged Vancouver to induce the king to promise to forego the usual beating when she got ashore,— this discipline being then a part of a Hawáiian queen's domestic training.

Perhaps Kaméhaméha the more easily believed in the infidelity of his favorite queen when he remembered the coquettish maiden, already betrothed to Prince Kiwalao, who had flirted with him, a stranger, at the Feast of Kings.

XXXIX.

THE INVASION OF OAHU.

VANCOUVER sailed, beloved and regretted. Immediately after his departure, preparations for the final expedition of conquest were resumed. An army of 16,000 men was fully equipped, carefully disciplined and fitly marshalled by experienced chiefs of great military renown. These, together with a company of foreign and native soldiers, armed with muskets, drilled by Vancouver's officers, and commanded by Young and Davis, gave the Hawáiians such advantage over the ill-assorted forces of the Leeward kings as to leave little doubt of Kaméhaméha's eventual success.

With an army of such size and skill, led by a warrior of indomitable energy and superhuman prowess, well might his own followers deem Kaméhaméha sent from Pele. What wonder that the benighted barbarians of the Leeward Isles should shrink from encountering such a demigod,—appalled by the tradition of his supernatural birth, his wolfish ferocity, and his unprecedented valor in the hour of battle.

While the famous shell trumpet * called *Kiha-pu*, was

---

* Many a weird tale has been told by the gossips of long ago of the wonders of this *kiha-pu*. This shell trumpet was said to have had power to call up the *kini akua* (gods and genii). When properly blown, its ringing notes could be heard from Waipio to the mountain town of Waimea. It was composed of a singular nautilus shell, seldom found on Hawáii, and richly inlaid, after the ancient custom, with the

being blown by Keeaumoku, Kaméhaméha, and a group of his chiefs stood on the ever-verdant cliffs overlooking the Upolu Sea, where he could watch his great canoe fleet gather and form in the still waters along the Kohala shore. Emerging from every inlet and haven that indented the coast-line for fifty miles, the canoes flashed into view, grouped into diminutive fleets under appointed leaders of the districts, but gathering like flocks of white-winged birds in dozens and scores until a thousand full-armed vessels were concentrated beneath the eye of the king, where he stood by the great temple of *Moa-alii* on the beetling crags of the Kohala shore.*

Hewahewa had recently presided over a great sacrifice at the new *heidu* of Puukohala, where human lives had been offered up without stinting. Every temple of Pele in the land had borne its dreadful oblations to the goddess to insure success to the army.

The aged Pepehi had sacrificed his bleeding holocaust, and sent his last prophetic oracle to the king. He had also sent his poison-god, Kalaipahoa, to adorn the new temple of Puukohala, lest at his demise the dreadful idol might fall into hands unfriendly to Kaméhaméha,† and untold evil might occur. His last message to his nephew was brief, but one to stir the soul of the conqueror and to confirm his convictions of success:

---

teeth of war-chiefs slain in single combat by King Kiha. It was exhibited at the Paris Exposition in 1865, and may still be seen in the museum at Honolulu.—"Polynesian Races," p. 72.

* The costly statue of the king represents this occasion.

† A small idol similar to the great poison-god was made for Kaméhaméha, and carried about with him everywhere, being placed under his pillow when he slept. When the king died Pepehi's old poison-god was divided and distributed among many great chiefs. (See Ellis' "Hawáii," p. 61.

"All hail! Kaméhaméha the Great, King of the Eight Isles! Though mine old eyes are blinded with age and natural infirmity, a wondrous vision of glory yet rises before me, following the most red-handed victory that shall be known among all the contentions of men. Be humane as you are brave, be just as you are noble; and the name of Kaméhaméha the Great shall never be forgotten in the history of the world. Aloha! my son. Herein receive the last god-given oracle from the dying priest of Puukeekee"

This message from his uncle affected the king to tears. It renewed his grief at the loss of his loved mother, and awakened his regrets that Wailéle could not have lived to partake of the crowning glory that awaited his coming.

When the final sacrifices to *Moa-alii* were completed—human oblations proffered for safe passage over the intervening seas—the king descended to the adjacant harbor where the "Britannia" was anchored, with sails hoisted and colors flying, awaiting his coming.

Embarking amidst his fleet of a thousand canoes, Upolu Sea was made gay with sails and fluttering flags; while the roll of drums, the shriek of fifes, the intense resonance of conch shells, created a martial din sufficient to awaken valor in the least combative. Kaméhaméha's great heart must have thrilled with just pride and exultation in contemplating his invincible armada, and dreaming of universal empire on that eventful day. Yet history relates that he whose mandate had convoked this vast array, and whose fertile mind had presided over every detail of discipline and organization, was the calmest and least exultant person among that assembly of renowned chiefs.

The newly launched "Britannia" led the fleet in the direction of Maui, gay with pennons and glittering with four brass cannon, three of which had already achieved such wonders, and were yet destined to batter down the ramparts of the foemen, and lay low the one black traitor in that exultant army.

Kahekili and Keao, the two kings who had fought the Hawáiians for seventeen years, were both dead. The one, of grief because of his ill success against the new-comer; the other while seeking real or imagined cause for war with Kalani, in a time of peril to all, and falling before him in the second of two desperate battles just previous to Kaméhaméha's invasion. Koalaikaui, the young brother of Kalani, had been left to govern Maui. When the unwarlike prince beheld the great fleet of invaders about to assail his shores, he gathered a few of his followers and fled to Kauai, tarrying at Oahu just long enough to report to Kalani what he had seen. But he had not sufficient patriotism to join in resisting the invader.

This campaign began in February, 1795. About two months were taken up in overrunning Maui, and securing the conquest of that and the neighboring islands. Leaving a thousand of the less valuable warriors as a garrison to hold Maui, the whole available army was at length concentrated in Sandy Bay, at the east end of Molokai.

Early upon a bright morning in May, Kaméhaméha manned his canoes and weighed anchor for the long contemplated invasion of Oahu. Going in person with the first division and the Giant Guard, the king led the way across the Kaiwi Sea in the "Britannia."

The trade-winds blew gently from the east, making the usually rough waters safe for even the smallest canoe.

The day bid fair for a good landing, even should the enemy concentrate in force to resist them. A few hours' pleasant sailing brought them abreast of the black cliffs of Koko Point. Doubling the rocky cape the fleet rounded gaily into Waialae Bay, where the army disembarked, and rapidly occupied all the strategic points along the Kona shore, surprised that the active Kalani was not there to resist the landing. But the wise young king knew his inferiority of force and its discordant elements, and had sagaciously concentrated his mixed army in Nuuanu Valley, in the rear of Honolulu. There he would fight and fall, battling nobly for his loved isle and his beautiful Kupule.

Kaiana, the Maui chieftain, was left in command of the rear division on Molokai, with orders from Kaméhaméha to follow on later in the day. This turbulent leader had a force of three thousand men, mostly Puna soldiers whom he had commanded during his later campaign against Keoúa. He had won sufficient control over his men from the "rebellious land" to enable him to carry them with him in his contemplated desertion to Kalani.

The time was now auspicious for Kaiana to put his base conspiracy into force. Making choice of some Oahu men, soldiers taken prisoners at the battle of Iao, Kaiana embarked them in a swift canoe, with directions to follow Kaméhaméha's fleet and to make a wide detour when the army landed, if it were not too dark to prevent discovery. Keeping on their course, the messengers were to land at Honolulu and inform King Kalani that Kaiana would join him in the morning with three thousand men; and together they would destroy the proud Kaméhaméha, and divide his great kingdom of Hawáii.

It was a strange infatuation which led this able general and warlike chief to think he could overcome, through treachery, such a natural leader as Kaméhaméha, backed as he was by a force that possessed novel and decisive elements of advantage over the whole combined armies of the islands. But such was Kaiana's hatred of his noble benefactor, who had taken the exiled Maui *alii* into his court and council, and had been to him as a brother, that the deluded chief made no doubt but that his traitorous conspiracy would meet with success, and redound to his honor by leaving him King of Hawáii.

When the last sail of Kaméhaméha's fleet had dipped down over the blue horizon, the war-conchs about Sandy Bay were blown for Kaiana's army to embark. Steering out on a N. E. course and availing themselves of the favoring easterly trades, with a view of not being seen by Kaméhaméha, they doubled Cape Mokapuu, which led them in the direction of Kaneohe Bay in the Koolau district. Hence the rebellious army could join Kalani's forces on the following day.*

---

* Nahiola, another of the three treacherous brothers, was with Kaiana, while Namakeha, the third one, got up a conspiracy on Hawáii during Kaméhaméha's absence.

XL.

BATTLE OF NUUANU—KAIANA SLAIN.

AS day began to close over the Hawáiian camp, surprise and indignation were written on every face at the unaccountable delay of the rear division under Kaiana. Keeaumoku had previously sent up one of his keen-eyed guard to the top of the Kona cliffs, with instructions to signal if the laggard division could be discerned.

The sagacious Young now went out on Koko Point, with an anxiety about the matter which he dared not express. He was soon followed by the king, and together they scanned the glittering waters of the Kaiwi Sea without discovering the gleam of a single sail in the slant rays of the setting sun.

After a searching look over the wide expanse of sea, the questioning eyes of the English sailor met those of the irate king, and each interpreted the unspoken maledictions of the other regarding this basest of military crimes.

With a low gutteral laugh, almost demoniacal in its expression of hatred for the subject of his thoughts, the king broke the painful silence which was becoming unbearable to both:

"*E hele mai, púna hele!*—Come hither, bosom companion." The two took their seats upon one of the black lava rocks facing the vacant sea. "*He pilikia nui keia!*

—This is a great difficulty"; and the king's eyes flashed, and his full lips curled with a sneer that insured a terrible punishment for Kaiana, should time ever bring the opportunity.

"Does your majesty think Kaiana has deserted to the enemy?"

"I think just as you do. The scoundrel has gone to join Kalani?"

"What is your *manao* (thought) in this dilemma?"

"John Young! there shall not be an hour's delay. We will rather march all the earlier, to show our contempt of this *pilikia*."

"Should we not make some new disposition of our forces for the night?"

"You are right, my *puna hele!* Train one of your guns to cover the landing, and to protect our canoes. Mount two of your cannon in the gap yonder through the Kona hills, lest the cunning *Alii* seek to surprise us in the night."

The two walked silently back to meet Keeaumoku, who was seen coming to make his adverse report from the look-out on the high Kona hills.

"Well, noble *Alii*, where is our rear division of the Puna men?"

"I hope my king will not care if Kaiana has deserted. Better that it should happen now than in the presence of the enemy."

Again the same low, diabolical laugh grated upon the ears of the two commanders, fit expressions of the king's hatred of Kaiana's perfidious act.

Keeaumoku was ordered to station the Guards upon the rising ground in the direction of *Leahi* (Diamond Head), in case the Oahuans should contemplate a night attack from that direction.

But the night passed in quiet without anything occurring to disturb the repose of the slumbering army. The shore-watch, belonging to Young's battery, reported a few canoes seen in the offing about midnight, spying upon the Hawáiians to report any night movement of their forces.

Some hours before dawn all were astir in the camp, partaking of an early breakfast of fish and *poi*, preparatory to marching up Nuuanu Valley. There the returning scouts reported that Kalani's army was encamped, mostly behind a fortified position, three miles in the rear of Honolulu.

Orion was dipping his yellow sword-belt in the western sea, and Venus, the *hoku aloha loa*—the universal love-star—sung her morning song from out the pearly orient to the broadening dawn. The Hawáiian army, twelve thousand strong, emerged from the whispering palm groves of Waikiki, in full view of the deserted homes of Honolulu. All was silent there; not even a rooting pig or a yelping cur remained to greet the invaders.

Deploying into the plain as they passed the frowning hill of Punch Bowl, which yet cast a grim shadow over the early morning, the army halted along the banks of the small mountain stream that runs valleyward to the sea. During the hour of refreshment a guard was placed over the canoes in the harbor.

The great chiefs clustered about the king after their simple repast. Kaméhaméha waited for another report from the reconnoissance sent up the valley, ere announcing his line of march and order of battle.

Word was at length brought that the Oahuans had retired behind their fortifications, where they quietly awaited the Hawáiians. The army corps of deserters under Kaiana was stationed on the left wing, in position farthest up the valley. The combined army of Oahu numbered about eight thousand men, and was marshalled under three leaders from as many different kingdoms.

As the sun burst over Waolani, and lit up the far-famed vale of Nuuanu with his welcome beams, Kaméhaméha gave the order to advance. The Hawáiians marched in three lines of four thousand men each. As they neared the entrenched camp of Oahu, Kaméhaméha took pride in displaying the discipline and soldierly bearing of his army.

Ordering a halt, the whole army was simultaneously deployed into a new order of battle, previously agreed upon. Forming his centre into a huge phalanx, flanked with double line of spearsmen and slings, the king with his staff of war chiefs and the battery of four cannon, with Young and his artillery-men, were enclosed in the great hollow square. Keeaumoku and his one thousand giants formed the front of the phalanx, the colossal warrior commanding the central division.

The right wing was commanded by Kalaimoku (Billy Pitt), a relative of Kalani and brother of Boki. A sagacious statesman and successful warrior, he was soon after made premier in place of Kaiana.

Kameeimoku commanded the left wing, a formidable and ferocious warrior. It was he, as we have seen, who captured the "Fair American"—an outrage which led to Kaméhaméha's detaining Young, whose aid in this conquest was more important than that of any of the great war chiefs.

Thus formed, the Hawáiian army marched close up to the rampart wall of coral rock, behind which Kalani, Kaumualii, and Kaiana had marshalled their three com-

combined armies from the three islands of Oahu, Hawáii, and Kauai.

When called to a halt, Naihe, the national orator and court diplomat, was sent forth to offer peace and agree upon terms of surrender. The smooth-tongued courtier bore a *ki* leaf, as flag of truce, and advanced into the open space between the armies until met by Boki, the commander-in-chief under Kalani. Each chief introduced himself with great ostentation, though they were well known to each other.

"*Aloha, alii kiekie!* (love to you, noble chief!), I am Naihe, the great orator of Hawáii, and councillor to my king. Kaméhaméha, king of all the Windward Islands by right of conquest, requests me to speak kindly to your young king about surrendering Oahu."

Boki bowed politely and replied: "*Aloha, alii kiekie!* The warrior before you is Boki, commander-in-chief under Kalani, and councillor to the mighty king. If Kaméhaméha comes to request our recognition of your Windward conquest we shall be glad to entertain him royally, but if you seek another kingdom you surprise us. If you come for war, you amaze us, for when did the king of Oahu ever decline the pleasure of a battle?"

"Most noble Boki, you are a man of wit and eloquence. Nuuanu is indeed a pleasant place for a *kauaawa*—bitter contest. It must remind you of the dreadful 'Vale of Iao,' where we dammed the waters with dead Oahuans."

"Whoever comes to take Nuuanu will see a worse *paniwai*—stopping the waters—than at Iao, where there were more dead Hawáiians, if I remember rightly, than of our people."

"Noble Boki, how fleet a thing is memory! Have

you also forgotten the lost battle of Kohala where we destroyed your fleet and set your king a-running?"

"Some little misfortune did happen there, owing to your three cannon, stolen from the foreigners. Strange that you should still remember that little affair."

"We have a fine day for a little brush, and as your people are at home there will be nothing to call you hurriedly away from battle, as on the two previous occasions."

"Be sure, Naihe, we will entertain you well to-day."

"But the morning passes. What shall I say to my king about your surrender?"

"Say to the mighty Kaméhaméha that, rather than surrender, we will die to the last man, fighting for our fair isle of Oahu."

"Must I take back this message to Kaméhaméha? The wrath of the 'Lonely One' will be dreadful." There was no response. "Then *aloha!* Come and join us in a calabash of *poi* after the battle."

"*Aloha!* Naihe. If your wounds are troublesome after the fray, our doctor, Koleamoku will dress them for you."

With smiles and bows the courteous chieftains parted and returned to their respective kings. Ere the sun went down that day one of them was cut to the ground by a fearful sword-stroke, inflicted by his diplomatic brother of the morning.

Kaméhaméha frowned till his massive forehead was like the corrugated flank of a volcano. He towered with yet more awful might and majesty as he listened to Naihe's version of Boki's ironic reply. A savage ferocity spoke in the king's angry gestures as he gave his orders in a terrible voice that reverberated from crag to crag like distant thunder. This display of savage frenzy made an impression upon Kaiana and his Hawáiian deserters that boded no good to Oahu's cause.

Though Kalani was incapable of personal fear, yet his face was flushed and his eyes ablaze as he saw the frightful mood of his rival. He enjoyed the terrific vehemence of his foe, and his excitement was that of a born warrior, impatient as a leashed hound for the coming clash of arms.

Not in all his army of heroic men was there a figure so noble, a presence at once so elegant, so commanding, and so brave, as Kalani's. Descended from the Spanish cavalier who was wrecked on Pele Point, at Hawáii, centuries before Cook's rediscovery, he sprang from a long line of warrior kings; and his wavy hair had the graceful terminal curl of his ancestor, the proud hidalgo of long ago.

Kaiana stood sullen and savage beside the Oahu king. His seven feet of stature gave him a little the advantage of Kalani. The traitor chief was arrayed in a sumptuous red *mamo;* it made a strong contrast to the radiant gold of the king's yet more costly war cloak. No one could envy Kaiana his situation of public shame. How his burning thoughts must have seared his brain as he stood there, a traitor and a deserter from the highest place of trust in the gift of his benefactor, confronting his late lord and king! How he must have cursed his lack of military sagacity as he saw the Oahuans confronted by such odds in number and discipline. He well knew that the battle could only end in destruction to his army and death to himself.

Kaumualii, who commanded the left wing, was pallid as his olive complexion would permit, for it was an open secret that the effeminate king of Kauai was no lover of war. Seeing Kaméhaméha in such ferocious mood—for even in that age it was Napoleonic for great leaders to show rage before their enemies—Kaumualii plucked the rare *iiwi* feathers from his royal *mamo*, as a rejected lover tears the petals from the rose that his love has refused.

All was now ready to begin the battle. The front of the square was thrown open by deploying to the right and left, and positions were taken convenient for again closing up the phalanx in case of a strong sortie from the fort. This movement discovered the battery of four cannon to the Oahuans stationed along the ramparts. Kalani and his chiefs had previously seen the guns from the hill-side, where the king had taken an elevated position to overlook the battle.

Kalani was arrayed in state on opening the battle, as was his gigantic rival opposite on the green knoll. He wore his splendid *mamo*, and from his helmet a small crimson plume waved in the freshening trade-wind.

Kaméhaméha wore his magnificent war cloak. His head was adorned by a lofty helmet, elegantly woven with *oo* feathers and decorated with strings of choicest seed-pearls, the rarest gems that Hawáiian divers had gathered for a thousand years.

Towering above his herculean chiefs, no one could look upon the colossal king without a thrill of admiration. Such ease and grace and symmetry in one so huge, such an intellect in a body so powerful, awed the beholders.

Young was now directed to open the battle by concentrating the fire of his cannon directly on the coral wall of the rampart, in the line of Kalani and his group of chiefs on the hill above. The distance being short, every discharge of the plunging shot told heavily on the porous coral, until stone by stone was knocked away and a breach was readily made.

Ordering up a column of spears from each wing to be in readiness to receive the first spear-cast of the Oahuans, before the real attack was made, the effect of the cannonade was watched with eagerness by the Hawáiians. At this stage of the battle the king called Young to his side, leaving Davis in charge of the battery. Drawing his long two-edged sword, with smothered rage Kaméhaméha pointed his ponderous blade where stood Kalani and his chiefs on the hill-side, saying :

"My *puna hele* (bosom friend), look at that beetle-browed traitor!"

"Ay, sire. At the right hand of Oahu's gallant king."

"It enrages me to look at the villain. Kill me the troublesome fellow, if you would be made an *alii kapu nui* on the spot."

"I 'll try, my king; but would you risk harming the noble Kalani?"

"Kill me Kaiana! and let the gods protect Kalani," exclaimed the furious monarch.

Returning to his battery, Young loaded his favorite piece with care, and elevated the gun to its utmost lift, high up over the rampart wall and the mass of heads and spears beneath. Kneeling on the grass the English boatswain trained his cannon with the utmost precision on the royal group, freshened his priming, swung his portfire to impart a better glow, and fired.

Mingled with the long-drawn reverberation was heard a crash as of splintered rock. For an anxious moment the result could only be guessed ; for the smoke gyrated curiously over the scene ; now swayed to one side by the glad shouts of the invaders, now recoiling slowly back before the wails of the afflicted Oahuans.

At length the sulphurous cloud lifted majestically over the rampart wall; it rose slowly over the glittering spear-points of the soldiers, over the grassy hillside and gray lava rocks, and revealed Kalani sadly contemplating the traitor weltering in his gore. He was dead on the very day of his iniquity. Not another chief in all that group was harmed.*

Wild were the shouts of ten thousand Hawáiian warriors, made joyous because Kaiana had fallen; the great soldier who had deserted his general in the hour of battle.

As a black storm-cloud may shine with quick lightning in the hour of its wrath, so the grim visage of Kaméhaméha gleamed with a smile of sardonic delight. He unbent his savage frown and brandished his glittering sword in the morning sun as the preconcerted signal for the assault, shouting to Keeaumoku:

"*E hele, Hawáii!*—Advance, Hawaii! Who wins yon breach the battle wins!"

The hoarse voice rang loud above the clang of battle, as his lusty chiefs sprang to the front and led their spearmen into the ragged opening through the rampart wall. A thousand wolfish men pressed on to enter where not fifty could pass in line.

While yet the mad columns were rushing into the breach, the king failed not to remember the divine interposition of Pele. He turned his flashing eyes in the direction of Loa's far-off flame of volcanic blue, and made a reverent oblation in the savage gladness of his heart.

---

* Young's field-piece knocked the stones about their heads, killed Kaiana, and so disordered the men that they broke and fled. (Jarves, p. 181.) Kaiana's footprints, still kept visible by others standing in them, are yet shown in the lava rock where he stood to cast his last spear.

Next to Pele there was another deserving thanks. Flinging off his saffron-colored mantle upon the greensward, and shaking his ponderous blade hungrily in the air, Kaméhaméha called lustily for Young.

As Young advanced he exclaimed with pride:

"A chiefdom! Sire, I 've laid the traitor low!"

"*Hele mai, puna hele!*—Come here, bosom companion! Killed as well as our good blade could do it! Pele sent the missile there, but yours is the glory and you shall receive the reward. Kneel, good foreigner! Though time is brief we name you *Keone Ana*, the noble chief. Now up and batter down more wall."

The sudden death of the traitor made a most favorable opening for the Hawáiians, and cast such dread over the allied armies of Oahu that every one of Kaiana's deserters broke ranks and fled over the far end of the rampart, up Nuuanu Valley to the giddy precipice at its head. These cowards were quickly followed by thousands of Oahu's panic-stricken soldiers, terror lending utmost speed to their flight. Grief and indignation filled Kalani and his chiefs as they beheld the cowards run before a blow had been struck in their ranks. But as Keeaumoku hurled his spearsmen through the breach, they were met with fiery ardor by the great chiefs of Oahu, who loved the clash of weapons.

For long hours a terrible conflict took place. It mattered little how impetuously the disciplined Hawáiians leaped into the breach, or scaled the rampart walls, they were everywhere met by equal bravery and equal skill. The rude shelter behind which the Oahuans fought, made available their lesser number, and they successfully resisted the ceaseless onset of the attack.

At times the trained Hawáiians surged through the

breach with an overwhelming fury that bade fair to carry all before them. Then Kalani's voice was heard, cheering on his chiefs, his orders ringing like bugle notes along the front of battle. Not often was his skilled sword needed in the ever-varying fight, but when a foeman especially worthy of his steel slashed his way through all opposition, then Kalani's *mamo* was flung off, and wild were the deeds of daring the valorous king accomplished.

When once the breach was freed, Kalani sheathed his dripping sword and resumed his *mamo*, falling back to a position where he could watch the defence and send reinforcements when needed. Once Keone Ana and Kalani thus fought for a moment. Young, exulting in his newly-attained rank, had hewn his way through the breach against all opposers. But these great swordsmen were forced apart against their wishes, for the chiefs of both sides became alarmed for their leaders, and pressed forward with such haste as to separate the combatants.

Young was recalled by Kaméhaméha and ordered to plant his battery opposite the extreme right wall of the rampart, Keeaumoku being left to assail the breach. Kaméhaméha himself commanded the assault, showing that it was intended to break through the ramparts instead of being the feint that Kalani supposed.

Kaumualii, the young king of Kauai, commanded the right wing of the Oahuans. He was now reinforced by all his Kauai men, and left to meet the emergency as best he could. After an hour's cannonade the artillery breached the rampart, when a furious assault was made by the Giant Guard, led by Kaméhaméha in person, over-riding all resistance in an instant. Wild were the yells that rang from the breach? Kaméhaméha's ponderous battle-axe crushed all who opposed him, as he flamed like a thunder-bolt at the head of his Guard, himself the hugest warrior among them all. The "Lonely One" taught the swiftest blows to heart and head. His very shouts appall! casting a sudden palsy over the already wavering men of Kauai. Suddenly they fell back in unmanly confusion, crying out like cravens: "*Luka lua! Luka lua!*—beaten, beaten!"

Kaumualii was slightly wounded at the close of the attack, and was taken prisoner by Kaméhaméha himself, a consummation quite to the liking of the timid young chief. Before night this effeminate warrior contrived to escape to Kauai, where he lived to rule over his island kingdom.*

When it was known to the wounded remnant of Oahu's army that the dread Kaméhaméha had broken through the rampart to the right, and was leading his Giant Guard down upon their rear, other thousands of Oahu's timid serfs broke ranks and ran for their lives, and thus the battle of Nuuanu was lost through the feeble resistance of its right wing. When Kalani saw what had happened, he steadily withdrew his remaining warriors, retreating by a left flank movement up the valley.

There yet remained to Kalani four hundred invincible chiefs, greatly attached to their king, warriors who loved the clang of battle as the breath of life, together with nearly a thousand other fighting men. These were now

---

* Kaméhaméha subsequently organized 7,000 men to take Kauai, but a sudden pestilence broke up the expedition. Kaumualii finally came to Oahu and ceded his island to the conqueror, by whom he was reinstated, ruling in fiefdom under him. Kaméhaméha II. afterwards abducted Kaumualii and married him and his son to the arrogant Kaahumanu, thus keeping him a state prisoner for life.

called off from the breach and led along the mountain path, with design to reach the *Páli*. This precipice, with the deep gorge between the mountains, was the spot previously chosen by Kalani for his last stand. It was an inaccessible pass, where the few could withstand the many, and sell their lives dearly. The Hawáiians, not apprehending Kalani's resolute design, were left to press through the deserted breach and take possession of the camp of Oahu, thus losing their opportunity to head off the retreating enemy from their stronghold at the *Páli*.

It was not supposed that Kalani would retreat far up the valley, but that he would cross the western mountain instead, into Waialua, where he could take canoes for Kauai, as did several of the noted chiefs of Oahu. The brave king's plan had, however, ever been to fall back upon the *Páli* of Nuuanu, and there fight unto death, defending the last rood of his dear vanquished land.

XLI.

BATTLE OF THE PÁLI AND DEATH OF KALANI.

WHEN Kaméhaméha saw that Kalani had withdrawn his forces along the narrow mountain path, where not more than three abreast could follow, he sent on Keeaumoku with a division two thousand strong to harass the retreat and crush the Oahuans when brought to bay. The remaining Hawáiians were suffered to occupy the camp of Oahu, and partake of such food as could be found for famished men. But while they sat devouring their food with avidity, what was their surprise to see Kalani's army leave the western mountain path and cross the Nuuanu Valley in the direction of the *Páli*, which, they at once surmised, had been previously fortified and provisioned for a siege.

Kaméhaméha was angry and annoyed at his misconception of the foe. The Hawáiians were quickly called off from their half-eaten dinner, reformed, and sent up the valley with orders to overtake the fugitives and give battle, with hopes of crushing the war-worn force before they could reach the mountain pass.

Kalani had debouched into the valley through a narrow gap in the hills, easily defended by a small rear-guard; thus Keeaumoku was held in check, while the Oahuans crossed the Nuuanu River on their way up to Waolani's sheltering gorge.

Kaméhaméha, Keone Ana, Hewahewa, and a large

group of chiefs remained behind with the Giant Guard to finish their dinner; for all believed that the main fighting was over, and that Kalani only designed to secure a mountain covert from which to make better terms of surrender.* Even the conqueror deemed the day was won, and remained in camp, leisurely smoking and relating the incidents of storming the ramparts, little dreaming that hundreds of his best warriors must yet fall before Oahu's heroic king was subdued.

Kalani saw the Hawáiians leave camp on the double-quick, endeavoring to cut him off, and feared for his rear-guard, which was still holding Keeaumoku at bay. Halting in a strong position which covered his retreat to the *Páli*, he sent back orders for Boki to withdraw, and fall quickly back while the main army awaited him; choosing to risk a battle rather than the safety of his loved commander.

When the Hawáiians pressed on too heedlessly on his retreat, as if following the rout of a panic-stricken foe, Kalani planted himself in the fore-front of his column of chiefs and hewed his way into the thickest of the mêlée, smiting many a daring chief who leaped from the Hawáiian ranks to cross swords with Oahu's gallant king. Many a noble warrior went down in that hour before the resistless blows of the finest sword-fighter upon his isle. Few chiefs had yet acquired the skilled use of this new weapon of war.

Like a row of monstrous gladiators stood the great chiefs around their loved king. He was cool and wary in that hour of slaughter, wasting no strength in random blows. Wherever he struck, the leaping crimson ran.

At length Boki joined them with the rear-guard, while

---

* As a previous king had done when Kahekili conquered Oahu.

Keeaumoku was pouring down through the mountain pass with his superior force, which could easily overwhelm the Oahuans in an open fight. Worn and wounded, **Kalani and** his chiefs withdrew to the *Páli ;* their footsteps dyed the green grass and mountain flowers **as they** retreated.

The Oahuans stood at last in Waolani's **rock-ribbed pass, weary and hopeless to win the day ;** though still **devoted to** Kalani with a barbaric love that surpasseth the wish **for life** or the love of woman. It was a sight **to** draw tears from the bare lava rocks to see the gnarled old warriors, through all the sickening slaughter of that **memorable day, so** devoted to their Alii, the image of their dead king.

Once safely within the cool gorge **at the** *Páli*, Kalani formed his forlorn hope of chiefs into six lines **of** fifty men each, in a pass where fifty war-loving braves could easily keep a thousand at bay.

Seeing the strength of the position, made unassailable **by the jutting** crags **of** Waolani towering above and behind the Oahuans, the Hawáiians fell back to reform and organize for **a swift** succession of assaults, which Keeaumoku saw would be required to win the day ; well knowing their fierce king would suffer no rest, until the last of the brave Oahuans were dead or routed.

Wearily lifting his dark eyes up to the rough crag which leaned with savage friendliness into the gorge, Kalani discovered Kupule, his loved queen, the god-born daughter of his hated rival. At the beck of the king, the queen **and** her maidens, with other *wahines* who had husbands and brothers below, descended with water, fruit, and provisions for the famished warriors. **Not** one among these heroes but was wounded and needed more or less attention.

Kneeling in a pool of blood, Kupule supplied food to the king, who had cast off his *mamo* and flung himself down in the crisp shadow of the beetling crag, where the strong trade-winds blew merrily through the gorge. Manona and Lelu, the queen's *wahines*, soothed the king's wounds with *ti* leaves, while Kupule tore up her own *tapa* garment to bind them and those of his chiefs.

Weary, haggard smiles were the best Kalani could bestow upon his darling. It was an hour of voiceless sorrow to all. The queen was so crushed by her grief, she could only press her fond kisses upon the dear hand that patted her cheek and stroked her tresses in token of heart-broken agony.

An hour of rest and refreshment was followed by a furious clash of arms, too confused and chaotic to be described.* At length there came a pause in the long-continued battle. The demoralized Hawáiians were called off to prepare for some more concentrated effort to save the day.

Kaméhaméha determined to press the assault, and sent forward the Giant Guard to finish the long-delayed work. The retardation of his hard-earned victory had at first amazed him. It now aroused his anger. The stubborn defence not only delayed the conquest, but was fast depriving him of the best warriors in his army. He now called upon the cool, sagacious Young to save the day, and also the life of Kalani, if compatible with immediate victory. Yet the king's orders were peremptory to capture the pass, at whatever cost of life.

"Keone Ana! take the Guard and win the pass, or never come back again."

---

* See the author's "Kalani of Oahu" for a fuller description, at p. 377.

The reply of the burly boatswain was prompt and to the purpose :

"Aye, aye, my king, it shall be done. Shall I save the gallant king, who has fought so well, or shall I bring his head upon a spear?"

"Ah! brave man, you know my heart ever warms for the brave. What a hero is Kalani! He is the husband of my Pelelulu.* But away, and win me the battle, or come back no more."

Young bowed in silence, put himself at the head of the Giant Guard, and gave the word "Forward!" None better than he knew the almost womanly tenderness of the monarch's heart. Often had the king folded him to his breast for some heroic act or kindly deed. Yet, as his mighty warriors swept past up the valley toward the defile that led to death or victory, there was a look of savage resolution on his face that was dreadful to look upon. It awed the chiefs before him as he repeated his fierce orders to each :

"Lead your men against yon beardless boy and win the pass, or leave your carcasses among the slain."

"Aloha, Moi nui!"† was the cry of the thousand warriors. But three hundred of them were left dead in the *Páli* before the "boy king" went down on that memorable day.

A brief hour passed, then a wail for some royal dead smote on the ear, rolling down the valley like a funeral knell, announcing the fall of Kalani. The shock of a sudden earthquake ran quivering through the kingless land. Instantly Kaméhaméha turned his reverent eyes toward distant Loa, uttering his glad oblation to Pele, the divine author of all his successes. He little knew

---

* The previous name of Queen Kupule.   † Love to you, great king.

that he might have been a vanquished king that day had not Kalani rejected Pele's proffered aid.

Hewahewa fell obsequiously upon his knees, bellowing forth his loud-mouthed prayer to the goddess. The king and priest had paced the bank of the mountain stream in unspoken agony, for Loa had long burned a red-flamed torch for love of Kalani, as if Pele had deserted the Hawáiians, and the god of battles had decreed that Oahu should win at last.

Calling upon his chiefs to follow, with long strides the black-browed king led the way to the *Páli*, curious to behold the place of strife where the few had found it possible to slaughter so many.

They were met by Keeaumoku bringing down the costly *mamo* of the dead king, hacked and pierced by a hundred cuts and stabs. This, with the cleft plume of the slain monarch, was brought as hard-earned trophies of victory to Kaméhaméha, who gazed with momentary interest upon them, and passed the royal emblems to Hewahewa for safe-keeping in the temple of Waikiki.

Climbing over his dead soldiers, heaped from crag to crag across the rocky pass, Kaméhaméha's rough face began to look more furrowed than ever, so saddened it was at beholding these loved chiefs among the dead.

Descending from this ghastly rampart into the ravine beyond, there, over the fallen king and his dead queen, stood brave John Young, leaning on his red-bladed sword above the royal pair, fallen in their strength and their beauty. He was weeping with bowed head over the cruel deed that he had accomplished.

Not until that moment did Kaméhaméha know that Pelelulu had died broken-hearted, clinging there fast to her heroic king—both gone forever from earthly sorrows. As the conqueror picked his way down over the dead Hawáiians, and beheld the fallen hero clasped in the dead arms of his queen—lying beautiful as a flower, even in death,—the pride of his might gave way and he abandoned himself to a fond' father's grief over his much-loved daughter.

Long and loud wailed the "Lonely One" over his dead child, whom he loved with something more than parental affection because of her kinship to Pele. Dropping upon his knees beside the royal pair the grim warrior kissed them both as they lay embraced so tenderly in death. He covered his giant head with his feather mantle, to hide his sorrow and the loved dead together. The king and savage warrior sobbed aloud in agony, weeping like a tender child who is orphaned by sudden death.

Kneeling with his bare knees in their blood Kaméhaméha prostrated himself in utter abandonment. At length the loud-voiced grief of the crowd ceased to be heard in the gorge, where only the subdued sobs of a more bitter anguish rose and fell beneath the *mamo*.

Then a murmur of discontent arose among the chiefs, because the king's grief was not more considerate of circumstances, for the sun was near his setting. None of his own chiefs, however, dared intrude upon him, lest in a moment of frenzy he should cut them down with his sabre. As Keone Ana was becoming too powerful, too much beloved by the king to be in good savor with the more ambitious chiefs, he was prevailed upon by some who loved him least to adventure upon the dangerous task. Readily did the English sailor undertake the sad office. Kneeling tenderly down beside Kaméhaméha, Young lifted the *mamo* and found the rough cheek of the savage warrior pressed lovingly against the dead daughter's, and clasping the cold sword-hand of Kalani in his own.

But how is this? The two war-worn veterans are again sobbing aloud over the royal pair. The king has drawn the English chief under the *mamo*, and together they weep as over a new-found sorrow. Kaméhaméha well knew that this was the only man who could appreciate his loss and the motives of his sorrow. For it was the thought of both in that hour that it were better to have left Kalani to rule over his beautiful kingdom, and to enjoy the love of his darling queen, than that both should lie there dead, as the price of Hawáiian victory.

Young whispered to the king that the day was nearly done, and some disposition should be made of the royal dead before darkness shut down.

Instantly Kaméhaméha rose up to find himself confronted by curious eyes, eager to witness a warrior king weeping like a *wahine* over the results of his conquest. The Giant Guard had just returned from their work of slaughter at the *Páli's* brink, where they had hurled a thousand warriors over the awful cliff, and they now stood arrayed in line waiting to receive their king's praises for having won the pass, killed Kalani, and slain every Oahu soldier.

Kaméhaméha frowned upon them all as if they had done him some grievous wrong. He saw that their faces were full of savage exultation at their deed. With his heart full of sorrow, the king was in no mood to glorify soldiers who smiled while he was weeping for his loved dead.

Turning away from his favorite soldiers Kaméhaméha took off his feather mantle and spread it tenderly over the royal pair. Speaking aloud, that all might hear, he bade Young take charge of their bodies, and permit none to look upon them while they should be removed to the palace for the night.

At that moment a sorrowing maiden, almost as beautiful as the dead queen, leaped down from the crag, prostrating herself at the king's feet, while almost frantic with grief she clasped his knees. The wondering king bent down and raised the grief-stricken *wahine*. She pleaded piteously that she might be the *Moe pu* of the queen, and die with her loved mistress.

Looking down on the sweet vision before him, the piercing eyes of the king read the maiden's heart like a printed page, and for a moment he joined tears with hers. Learning that the chiefess was Manona, the *puna hele* of the dead queen, the huge monarch stooped and embraced the beautiful girl, kissed her tearful eyes, so like his Pelelulu's, and bid her take up her abode at the Nuuanu palace.

"Manona, keep with the dead queen. Follow her down the valley and make your home in the house of the *wahines*. You are henceforth the queen of Kaméhaméha. It shall be death to whomsoever abides not by this mandate!"*

Lowering his resonant voice to a hoarse whisper that echoed ghost-like among the crags, he continued:

"*Wahine Moi*, cross not the path of Kaahumanu, lest she tear your dark hair, as a mad tempest claws the sea. My "Feather Mantle" is jealous when I bestow affection upon another. But fear not, little darling, for I will protect the bosom friend of my daughter."

Recalling his imperious soul to martial affairs, the king now gave his orders brief and fast:

---

* More than one great chief was killed for not heeding a warning like this.

"Ho! Hewahewa."

The high-priest elbowed his way from the crowd of chiefs and stood with assumed humility before his arrogant master.

"*Kahúna*, take charge of Hawáii's dead chiefs and give them all noble burying."

"Hewahewa will do your utmost bidding. What may be your pleasure about Oahu's gallant dead?"

"Cleave off their heads to awe the yelping crowd on the mountain. Feed their headless bodies to *Moa-alii*— the dread sea-god,—and impale the chiefs' heads upon their spear-points, planting them thick as palm-trees about the Waikiki *heidu*."

"What is your will about the royal dead?"

"Keone Ana has charge of the brave Kalani and my dead daughter. Render their remains the utmost honors due. She is a Hawáiian princess—an *Alii pio;* he, the noblest warrior-king of his martial isle."

"A *kapu kane* should darken all the land."

"Yes. To-morrow a hundred living victims bleed. Make sacrifice of an untold holocaust to Pele, the much-loved deity, who has remembered us to-day. Make your *tabú* most terrible to look upon, lasting from moon to moon. But hark you, priest! Leave Nuuanu and the adjacent sea untouched, unterrified. We who have fought and won must feast and make merry to express our joy to Pele. But make your wailing at the *heidu* long and loud. Bid every *kahúna* tear his hair and beat his breast, for boundless sorrow and prayer are due the noble dead."

"Hewahewa has heard the wishes of the king, and——"

"Away! Have done with that. Keeaumoku! Where is the noble *Alii?*"

"Here, my king."

"*Alii nui!* Deploy your guard to watch the sneaking mountain foe, lest the cowardly serfs steal canoes and escape to Kauai. Bid Kalaimoku camp the war-worn army behind the ramparts in Nuuanu, where food and shelter may be found for the night. Let tender hands remove the wounded Naihe to the palace if his spear-pierced body will permit. Send Hoapili with a squad of the Guard to patrol the palace grounds. *Aloha!* noble *Alii.*"

"*Aloha!* my king. It shall be done."

"Come, chiefs, companions in arms; let us be gone. The day is waning, and a feast of *ilio poli* awaits us in Nuuanu's pleasant vale."

XLII.

CONCLUSION.

THIS final victory at the Nuuanu Páli was decisive; war never again defiled the fair isle of Oahu. The conqueror now came into possession of all the group but Kauai and the diminutive island of Niihau. To complete his conquest Kaméhaméha soon after embarked seven thousand men for Kauai, the recruited ranks of his shattered army, for he had lost six thousand of his brave Hawáiians during the recent conflict.* A furious gale compelled the expedition to return. It was not necessary for it to set out a second time; for Kaumualii subsequently came to Honolulu and voluntarily resigned his kingdom, which he governed thereafter as a vassal to Kaméhaméha.

The authority of Kaméhaméha was made absolute by the conquest. By the ancient usage of Hawáii he now became the sole lord and proprietor of the soil. He dispensed favors with an affluent hand, apportioning estates and districts among his faithful chiefs, according to their rank and deserts, on the feudal tenure of rendering military service and contributions from all the revenues of their holding.

Each large island was allotted its governor, who ap-

---

* See Jarves' "History," p. 182. Kaméhaméha lost 6,000 of his troops, and the enemy's loss was far greater.

pointed the head chiefs, tax-collectors, and other petty officers, subject to the approval of the king. The islands were divided into districts, districts into towns and villages, and these, in turn, were subdivided into farms and plantations, each being duly apportioned with mountain, valley, and forest land, with fair allotments of sea-shore and fisheries for all the people. Governors and councillors were chosen from the most trusty of his warriors. A regular cabinet and a minister of state were appointed, and merit more than rank was the passport to favor.

The gigantic Keeaumoku, who had rendered the most distinguished services of any of his chieftains—and who was also the father of three of his queens *—remained chief councillor and head of the army. Kalaimoku, the most sagacious statesman among the nobles, though he was of inferior rank and descended from the Maui kings, was proclaimed *Kuhina nui*, or premier, and retained his office long after the death of his benefactor.

Keone Ana was made Governor of Hawáii, assuming his office immediately after the rebellion of Namakeha, brother of the traitor Kaiana, and held it to the satisfaction of Kaméhaméha and of his successors to the day of his death. Kameeimoku was made governor of Maui, while Kananawa, Hoapili, Naihe, Kekuanoa, Kuakini, and his brother, the younger Keeaumoku, were greatly distinguished for faithful services. Several " wise men " of great talent, though of inferior rank, were selected to assist in organizing laws best adapted to the minor affairs of the kingdom.

Kaméhaméha had not only the intuitive perception of character which enabled him to choose efficient men for every department of government, but he also possessed

---

* Kaahumanu, Kalakua, and Namahana.

the faculty of inspiring others with his own generous sentiments; and thus he secured hearty coöperation in his wise undertakings. Famine, caused by the destruction of fruit-trees and vegetable foods during the long successive wars, bore heavily upon the oppressed people for a time. Natives starved to death, or sometimes were burnt alive by their chiefs for stealing food for their starving families.* Yet in no way did the king show his humanity and administrative ability more conspicuously than by the example which he gave of tilling the land with his own hands, and raising his own sustenance during the famine.†

In public affairs he consolidated his power, and brought order out of chaos. Turbulent and seditious chiefs of the old dynasties, whose ambitious views threatened to disturb the new order of things, were withheld from their hereditary estates and retained about the court, being compelled to follow in the king's train wherever he went. With these refractory nobles—most dangerous men to deal with after their training in murderous misrule—the king affected a more haughty mien and greater state. The most arbitrary customs of the ancient kings were revived and rigidly enforced,—humiliating ceremonies, which were intended to increase the awe of his peaceful subjects and humble the unsubmissive chiefs.

It was proclaimed that heads and shoulders must be bared whenever the king passed, or when one approached the palace or other abode honored by the sovereign for

---

* See Jarves, p. 182.

† See Jarves, p. 201. He labored for his own food, and compelled his followers to work likewise. The spot he tilled is at Halawa, on Hawáii.

the time. The penalty was death for crossing the shadow of the king, or of his house. To assume a position above where he was standing was the highest crime; and for paying too special attention to Kaahumanu, a chief of high rank and a priest both lost their lives.* By this uniform system of despotism Kaméhaméha broke the power of the petty lords and greatly ameliorated the oppressed condition of the people. Though chiefs were permitted retinues suitable to their rank, they were forbidden to overtax or overwork their tenants, or to maintain bodies of armed men. By suitable rewards the king encouraged skilful artisans among the various handicrafts. Nothing was too trivial for him to investigate; nothing that affected the welfare of the people escaped this lynx-eyed man.

Never, indeed, was there more urgent need of the iron hand of a despot to weld together the conflicting elements of a conquered people. Having assumed the headship of the Church as well as of the State (much to the annoyance of Hewahewa), Kaméhaméha held both the scheming priests and the refractory chiefs to an equally strict account. He maintained the tenets of the *tabú* creed to the last, though he confessed to foreigners his unbelief in the divine origin of his heathen gods. But alas! it was his misfortune never to commune with a mind of sufficient religious ability to convince him of his error and show him evidence of the one true God. For him idolatry was a subtle power by which to govern a superstitious people, and priestcraft contained for him more of policy than of piety.

---

* Jarves', Honolulu edition, p. 48. Kaméhaméha strangled the high chief, Kanihonui, and executed a priest for this offence, even at the risk of a rebellion. This was in 1809.

But the stern bigotry of the king was often overmastered by his humanity, as in the case where Hewahewa doomed a fine boy for sacrifice on a certain day. The lad fell sick in contemplating his cruel fate, and was likely to die from terror before the allotted time. Shocked at such an insult to the gods, the priest ordered his man-killer to strangle him upon the altar at once. The king heard of this decree, and ordered the *kahúna* to bring the sick boy to the palace. With his own hand Kaméhaméha cared for the lad, and he recovered, remaining one of the royal family until the king's death. Possibly this act of humanity was meant for a check upon the priestly arrogance of Hewahewa.*

Peace and good laws were at length everywhere established, and so complete a change was brought about that a truly golden age dawned upon the once rebellious land. All open opposition to Kaméhaméha's rule was completely subdued, and the only secret conspiracy known to the government was personally suppressed by him in a characteristic way.†

Knowing that the powerful chiefs of the old dynasties would lose no opportunity of plotting against the new régime, the sagacious monarch would not trust the suspected *aliis* to collect the taxes, or other "sinews of war," on their own estates. In such cases female chiefs were appointed tax-gatherers. They were also made secret detectives in the pay of government, with instructions to spy secretly upon the doings of all the seditious nobles. Wonderfully well did some of these chiefesses perform their detective duties.

---

* See Jarves' "History," p. 197.

† Compare this method of subduing a conspiracy with Kahekili's "*waipio kimopo*" (general assassinations) of a whole community of nobles, innocent as well as guilty.

One day the king was about to sit down to his evening repast when a spy, one of the chiefesses, claimed private audience. Trembling at what she had to disclose—for some of her dearest friends were involved—she reported a formidable conspiracy against the king. Fifty of the powerful old-line chiefs of Ewa, **Waianai, and Waialua** were to meet in secret that night at a lonely house in Puùloa (Pearl River) to concert plans for an immediate rebellion. Quieting her fears with a promise of dealing fairly **with her friends,** Kaméhaméha dismissed **the** pretty chiefess, and bade her paddle home in her canoe as she came.

Though a sumptuous repast was **spread** in the eating-house of the king, and numerous chiefs **of the** old and new dynasties were present, waiting to **grace the evening** meal, the stern monarch was too full of **the sudden** disclosure to remain. It was necessary, however, **that the** old-line chiefs should be kept from following him, **or** learning the cause of his absence.

Bidding all present to be seated, and appointing Keeaumoku to preside over the feast until his return, the king excused himself on the plea of important business of state. He permitted none of his attendant chiefs **to** accompany him. Taking down his ponderous war-spear from the roof-tree of his sleeping-house, he started alone in the darkness for **the place of** secret meeting fifteen miles away.

The gloom following a tropic twilight had just ushered in the stars, and the sea-gulls were at roost upon rock and reef along the shore, as the black-browed king left Puláholáho. His rapid walk could be traced by the crowd of screaming sea-birds that rose **with** a startled cry over the beach as he strode by, **trusting to the** awe-inspiring might of his military renown to quell a rebellion of savage chieftains.

When the beach failed to lead in the direction he was going, he chose a pathless track across the wilds, delving into deep ravines and swimming, spear in hand, over lagoons and rivers. It was nearly midnight when he reached the desolate moor and stealthily approached the lonely house. There he saw fifty ferocious chiefs of the conquered land, assembled in secret conclave and plotting treason.

Listening attentively until the conspirators had fully unfolded their plans, chosen their leaders, and fixed time and place for immediate action, the angry monarch tarried just long enough to thrust his huge spear, point downward, in the sand of the bleak moor, about four feet from the only door of the house, and departed.

The spear was the well-known *Ihe nui* of the king, the beautifully carved souvenir which Kalaniopuu left with Wailéle before Kaméhaméha was born, the most costly weapon in the land. There would be no mistaking as to who had given the mysterious warning of death.

Kaméhaméha strode homeward beneath the midnight stars, with longer steps and greater vehemence than he came. He had listened to treason declaimed by nobles who had fawned about his court with such a profusion of friendly professions that he had made generous restoration of their estates, adding.

"Go, and be faithful. Remember that the all-seeing eye of Pele is upon you, and the '*Ihe o Kaméhaméha*' will find you out in the evil hour."

When the king reached the palace he dismissed the wondering guests without a word of explanation, for none had dared disobey his command by leaving the eating-house before his return. He retired as if nothing unusual had occurred, and the noble chiefs were not enlightened about the indignity put upon them until the next morning.

The treasonable meeting at Puùloa broke up soon after the departure of the king. The first of the conspirators to leave the secret conclave was the newly chosen leader, Kanéonéo, a haughty chieftain of the treacherous race of Kahekili. As the *tapa* curtain was flung from before the door, a glare of light from the candle-nut torches within flashed out upon the shining spear-staff. The nervous conspirator, already startled by his own black shadow standing gaunt and grim in the night-gloom before him, stood aghast with awe at the sight. Then, with a look of consternation, he plucked the great spear from the sand, rushed back among the assembled conspirators, who were still in earnest discussion, exclaiming in a voice hoarse with terror:

"The ear of the dread Giant has listened at the door. This is the '*Ihe o Kaméhaméha!*' Our plans are known to the king; we must die!"

"Yes, it is the *Ihe nui* of the Hawáiian king," echoed many voices from the groups of savage men.

"Who has done this foul treachery? Who has betrayed us?" bellowed a ferocious chief, maddened by the thought of treason within treason, as he sprang out from among his fellows, flourishing his long-bladed dagger, glaring about among the fear-stricken faces, and ready to take vengeance upon any suspected one.

"*Alii!*" exclaimed the leader. "It is none of our number. It is the dread Pele who has disclosed our secret to the Hawáiian, and we are as good as dead men."

"*Auwe! Auwe!*" was the doleful exclamation of all.

The pallor of death was upon every face. Each warrior grasped spear or dagger, and glanced furtively into dark crannies and toward the door, aghast with the expectation of seeing the Giant stalk into their midst and execute the stroke of death upon them all. Each chief among them was a strong, brave man, ready to risk his life in any warlike enterprise; but there was something dread and supernatural in finding the black *Ihe* at the door of their secret rendezvous. They were appalled and terror-stricken, for they believed it to be the work of invisible hands. With whispered messages and brief farewells most of the terrified *aliis* dispersed to their homes; while others fled to the mountain wilds, or took canoe for the distant island of Kauai.

After brief reflection, the most sagacious among them bethought them of the well-known humanity of the conqueror; and at early dawn, in accordance with an ancient custom, many of the conspirators approached the palace of the king, crawling upon their hands and knees, and crying: "*E ola au! E ola au!*—Let us live! Let us live, most noble king!" The gigantic leader, with greater humility than his fellows, crept close up to the monarch and laid the ponderous spear at his feet, bowing his head upon the ground, and patiently waiting the death-stroke he justly deserved.

But the wrath of the king was abated; while in furtherance of the supernatural fears of the conspirators, he briefly addressed the cringing nobles before his door:

"Base men, treacherous *aliis!* Who among you thought to hide his evil doings from the all-seeing Pele? Begone! away to your homes, and beware of evil ways, for the god-born of Mukíni has possessed himself of your lands forever."

The repentant conspirators failed not to keep fealty with their liege lord. They remained faithful to their allegiance all their lives long, and went to their graves in the unfaltering belief that the "*Ihe o Kaméhaméha*" was placed at their door by the agency of the gods, in dread league with the king.

As the savage's highest conceptions of deity are ascribed to physical attributes, what wonder that the Hawáiians deified and adored their warrior-king for his surpassing strength, courage, and deeds of prowess? He was a very demi-god to his people!

Whether we view Kaméhaméha's perfected work by the light of his military renown, or contemplate his strongly centralized government, welded together from many lesser despotisms, we can but marvel at the genius which conceived and matured such an enterprise in youth, which organized and maintained a stupendous army, and which handled it with the strategic ability of a born general.

In boyhood, as we have seen, Kaméhaméha acquired the name of Puhi-kapa, "strangler of sea-snakes." So completely did he strangle every rebellion among the old dynasties, that his government was established more thoroughly than the mailed Norman's in Britain, or the still greater Corsican's in Gaul.

* * * * * * * * *

Since the conquest of Oahu, the Nuuanu Valley has been deemed classic ground by all true lovers of the Hawáiian Islands. It is a most romantic spot, justly held dear for its precipitous cliffs, jutting crags, and romantic gorges. Its picturesque beauty and matchless view of surf and sea, its lakes and groves and flowery meadows, together impart a charm which fascinate the resident and stranger alike.

What an arena of savage grandeur is the Pali for the final Thermopylæ of Hawáii! What sacred memories flood the mind when we recall the tragic incidents of that dreadful battle! The heart thrills as we contemplate its life-like visions of historic drama come and go before our wondering eyes.

Here bare the head and bless the hour for what you see to-day, for, towering like an eagle's eyrie, the *páli* now overlooks a paradise of Christian homes, a bewitching panorama of peaceful lands, bounded by land-locked mountains and enclosed by a surf-lashed shore. These are Nature's best balm to dispel our sadness and assuage our tears after sorrowing over a nation's bereavement, when standing where a once martial kingdom was lost and won.

Stand with us on the dizzy brink of the precipitous *páli*, over which the Giant Guard spear-tossed a thousand defeated soldiers into the plain below. Hark to the wild clang of that long-gone battle of savage men! It rings down the century as if it were fought but yesterday. Its final clash of spears still echoes among the wooded crags above us, where the screaming tropic-birds circle about their nests to-day as on that day of battle.

Here, on this bare black rock, Oahu's youthful hero fought and fell. And here Love still lies bleeding upon her dead king, as when their loved island was made a kingless land. Look through your blinding tears and see his golden *mamo* stabbed through and through by a score of daggers.

There, above you, hangs the beetling crag where Kalani's newly-wedded queen crouched among her maidens, watching through her tears to see her royal lover fight and fall; then leaping like a wild antelope from the high crag, in answer to his dying call, Kupule died broken-hearted on the pierced breast of her dead king, in the first flush of her beauty and in the dawn of her love.

A HAWÁIIAN GLOSSARY.

The ancient language had but twelve letters, in the following order :

A, E, I, O, U, H, K, L, M, N, P, W.

The vowel sounds are uniform, varying only as they are long or short. A, has the sound of a in father ; e, of a in fate ; i, of e in me ; o, of o in note ; and u, of oo in good.

Neither words nor syllables ever end in consonants. Most syllables contain but one or two letters, never more than three. Words are mostly accented on the penult, and are pronounced, in spelling, as O-á-hu, A-ló-ha, and Ho-no-lú-lu.

A'-a, hard lava, or pumice
A'-e, an assent, yes
Ai, to eat
Ai-á-lo, privileged to eat with the king
Ai-Kanáka, man-eater, cannibal
Ai-ká-ne, friend of same sex
Ao, a cloud, the day
Ao-kéa, white cloud
Ao-úla, red cloud
Ao-úli, blue cloud
Aó-le, no, not ; a universal negative
Au, the time
Au-móe, time to sleep
Au-wé, alas ! oh !
A'-hi, fire, fiery
A'-hu A'-lii, Council of Chiefs

Glossary.

A'-hu Úla, red feather cloak ; the color worn by chiefs
A-ké, to tattle ; to tell lies
A-kú-a, God, the Deity ; any supernatural being
A'-lii, a chief
A'-lii Nú-i, a great chief
A'-lii Ká-pu, a tabu chief, a priest
A'-lii Pio, chief of high rank
A'-lii Ni-aú-pio, the highest rank, born of *brother and sister*
A-lii wó-hi, chief of rank next the king
A-ló-ha ! love to you ; a greeting or a farewell
A-na-a'-na, praying to god Oúli to kill
A'nu, a sacred enclosure. The " Holy of Holies "
A'-pu, a cup made of cocoa-nut shell
A'-wa, a plant ; an intoxicant made from its root
A-la-pái, path to justice. An ancient king

'E, yes, synonymous with A-é
E-á, the spirit, the breath, the life
E'-e, distant, out of sight
E-lé-le, a herald, an embassador
E-le-é-le, dark, black, brown
E'-pa, false, deceitful

I-á-o, name of a noted valley and river on Maui
Ia-lo'-a, to embalm the dead
I-i'-wi, a red bird, from which chiefs' cloaks were made
I-ó-le, a mouse ; iole núi, a rat
I'-he, a spear
I-lé-na, a general burial-place
I-lí-o, dog ; I-li'-o pó-li, breast-nursed dog
I'-mu, a baking-place, an earth-oven
I'-no, bad, sinful
I-nú, to drink, to be drunk
I-pú, a gourd cup

O, of ; also an imperative prefix
O-á-hu, to split. The island
O'-e, thou, you
O'-o, a royal tabued bird
O'-he, bamboo, a hollow reed

Glossary.

O-hé-lo, whortleberry
O-hé-lo pá-pa, strawberry
O-hí-a, a red apple, the tree
O'-ho, hair, scalp-lock
O-hú, fog, mist, smoke
O'-le, no, not ; used after a noun, as Aó-le is used before it
O'-li, joy, pleasure
O'-li-o'-li, to sing joyfully
O-lú-lo, shipwreck
O-mó, to nurse
O'-no, sweetness
O'-pu, the belly, which is deemed the seat of thought ; the soul
O-wái, who ? what person ?

U, the breast, breast-milk
U'-a, to weep, to mourn
U-áo, a cat, to mew as a cat
U-há-ne, the soul ; a spirit, a ghost
U'-la, red, color of a flame
U'-lu, bread fruit
U'-mi, keep the secret ; hide your emotions. Name of several great chiefs
U-pó-lu, name of a cape

Háe, a flag, a banner
Ha-ó-le, a foreigner
Há-ku, lord, master
Há-le, house
Há-le a-ka-lá, House of the sun. Crater on Maui
Há-le màu-màu, House of everlasting fire. The crater
Ha-ma-kúa, gap in the ridge. A district on Hawáii
Ha-wái-i, the island
Hè-le, go, move on
Hei'-au, a heathen temple
Hé-le mái, come here
He-ó-ha, scalping the dead
Hé-wa, sin, wrong
He-wa-hé-wa, "crazy." Kaméhaméha's high-priest
Hí-lo, new moon, to twist
Hii-lá-we, to "carry in arms." The famous falls of Waipio

Ho-á-no, sacred, holy
Ho-áo, marriage to test the affections
Hó-e, to row, to paddle
Ho-ku, a star, the young moon
Hó-pe, or Ho-pe-na, the end, finish
Ho-no-lú-lu, a "calm spot." Town of
Hoo-pá-lau, single combat, betrothed
Hú-a, fruit, an offspring
Hú-a oo, ripe fruit
Hú-hu, to be angry, to offend
Hu-la-á-na, "to swim round the cliff." The great *páli* of Waimánu where the naval battle was fought by the three kings
Hú-la, music, dancing, singing
Hu-na-ké-le, hiding the dead chief's bones

Ká, definite article, but spelled Ké before nouns beginning with K
Kà! exclamation of surprise, anger, a profane curse
Kài, the sea
Kai-kóo, high surf
Kai'-ko, constable
Ka-i'-li, the king's war god
Ka-ó, a peace-maker
Kaù, the season. Name of a district
Kaù-ai, fruitful season
Ká-u, mine, to me
Ka-hú, guardian, nurse
Ka-hú-na, priest, a professor
Kà-lo (taro), an esculent root
Ka-pú (tabú), sacred, holy, forbidden. System of heathen worship
Ka-pú we'-la, "prostrate or die," "bow to the chief or be burnt"
Ká-pa (tápa), bark cloth, a garment
Ka-pú Ká-ne, human sacrifice
Ka-pú hú-a, fruit sacrifice
Ka-pú pu-à-a, hog sacrifice
Ká-ne, a male. The god
Ka-ná-ka, a common man
Kau-lúa, double canoe
Kaù-wa, a servant
Kaù-la, a prophet

Glossary.

Ka-hí'-li, fly brush
Ké, article *the*
Ke-á, white. Name of the mountain
Ke-i'-ki, a child of either sex
Ke-lá, that
Ki' (ti), a shrub with sweet root and healing leaves
Ki-ài, a guard
Ki-ai-pòo, King's guard during sleep
Ki-ú, a spy, to spy
Ki-ha Pú, the shell trumpet to call up the genii
Ki'-hei, a tapa cape
Ki'-lo, a magician, a judge
Kii, an idol, statue, picture
Ki-mó-po, plot to assassinate, a secret rebellion
Kí-pa, a rebel, a revolt
Ko, sugar, sugar-cane
Kó-a, the great canoe tree
Ko-i', an adze, an axe
Ko-há-na, naked, destitute
Ko-kó-lo, to creep or bow down when saluting the king
Koó-lau, falling leaf
Kó-na, S. or S. W. wind
Kú, right, proper
Ku-kú-i, candle-nut tree, a torch
Kuú-la, the god of fishermen
Ku-lí-a, a beauty, desire for beauty
Ku-kú-ni, to burn in sacrifice
Ku-loù, to bow in grief

(LIST OF IMPORTANT NAMES AND THEIR MEANING.)

Ka-mé-ha-mé-ha (Kah-may-hah-may-hah), "The Lonely One"
Ka-lá-ni, "heavenly." The last king of Oahu
Ka-lá-ni-o-pùu, "budding heaven." Last king of Hawáii before the conquest
Ka-he-ki'-li, the "Thunderer." Last king of Maui
Ka-pi-o-lá-ni, "Captive of Heaven." The heroic wife of Nai'-he
Kai-á-na, "sea of trouble." The traitor chief who deserted to Kalani
Ka-lai-mó-ku, "quiet the land." The premier, Billy Pitt

Glossary.

Ka-lai-má-no, the shark. Chief who killed Captain Cook.

Ka-lai-pá-hoa, the poison god, made from the Niói tree

Ka-ló'-la, "neglected." Queen of Hawáii, and mother of King Kiwaláo

Ka-ló'-le, "woven cloth," a chiefess

Ka-lá-ma, "torchlight," Queen of K. III.

Kaa-hu-má-nu, "Feather Mantle." The love-queen of the Conqueror

Ka-la-kú-a, "way of the gods." Sister of Feather Mantle and wife of K. I.

Ka-ó-lei-ò-ku, the "secret garland." A natural son of K. I., who was spared at the assassination of Keoúa

Kai-lú-a, "two seas." Place where the old king died

Ka-la-káu-a, "day of battle." The present king

Ka-mee-i-mó-ku, the pirate chief who captured the "Fair American"

Ka-mà-ne-wá, this, and the last-mentioned chief, were the "Maui Twins," sent by Kahekili to guard Kaméhaméha in his youth

Ka-wai-háe, "torn waters," Town of

Kee-au-mó-ku, "swim to the ship." The giant chief who did most to establish the Conqueror. Father of "Feather Mantle," and two other wives of the king. Who killed Kiwaláo at the battle of Kećí. Who assassinated Keoúa and seven companion chiefs after they had surrendered

Ke-o-úa, "rain-food." The warrior-king who resisted Kaméhaméha for nine years. Pele having destroyed 400 of his army, he surrendered and was assassinated at Kawaiháe

Ke-ku-hau-pi'-o, "captive winds." The renowned general whom Cook shot in the thigh, while protesting his brother Ka-li'-mu's death by Cook's boats. He who taught the art of war to Kaméhaméha

Ke-ò-pu-o-la'-ni, "clouds in the heaven." Kiwaláo's widowed queen. State queen of K. I. Mother of K. II. and K. III.

Ke-á-we, ancient king of Hawáii

Ke-áo, a "legend." King of Kauai

Ke-kau-li'-ke, to "hang even." An ancient Maui king

Ke-ó-ne A'-na, John Young, the white chief

Ke-ku-pu-ó-hi, a queen and poetess

Ke-éi, town where the king fought his first battle

Glossary.

Ki-lau-è-a, "shooting fire." **The active** volcano
Ki-wa-lá-o, "rebellious." Left as joint king with Kaméhaméha
Ko-ni-a, "disobedient," wife of Paki, and mother of Mrs. Bishop
Ku-a-ki'-ne, Gov. Adams
Ku-pú-le, "prayerful." Kalani's queen

Lá, the sun
La-aú, trees
La-è, **a cape or headland**
La-è lóa, **long cape**
Laù, a **leaf, an herb**
Lau-á, dual, they **two, we two**
Lau-há-la, the Pandanus
Lá-ni, heaven, heavenly
La-pù, a night-coming spirit
Léi (lae), a wreath, necklace of beads, **shells, or flowers**
Le-hú-a, the first slain ; to be sacrificed
Le-à-hi, "wreath of fire." Diamond **Head**
Lé-le, an altar, to leap
Le-pà, the tabú **flag placed** to guard sacred places
Li'-li, jealousy
Li-li'-o, gluttonous
Li'-lo, lost, gone, taken
Li-li'-ha, "fat of hogs." A chiefess
Ló-a, long, a measure of time or distance. The mountain
Ló-mi, or lómi-lómi, to rub, knead the body
Ló-no, the god of fruit and flowers
Lu'-a, to kill **by breaking the bones**
Lu-à, a pit
Lu-à Pé-le, a volcano
Lu-ku, beaten, slaughtered **in battle**

Mà, at, by, in, through
Ma-à, a sling used in battle
Maa-lé-a, cunning, **crafty. Bay of**
Má-i, come
Mai-à, banana
Mai-kà, a stone used in bowling
Mai'-kai, good, handsome, correct
Mai-kó-la, **worthless, contemptible**

Ma-ó-li, true, pure
Mau-na, mountain
Ma-ú-ka, inland, from the sea } terms in constant use
Ma-kái, toward the sea
Ma-hé-le, to cut, divide, circumcision
Ma-hí'-na, the moon
Ma-hó-pe, behind, after
Ma-hú-a, to mock, to deride
Ma-ka'-po, blindness
Ma'-ke, death, to die, the dead
Ma-ka-hí'-ki, New-Year
Ma-li'-e! hush, be quiet, be calm
Ma-li-hi'-ni, a stranger
Má'-lo, a strip of tapa cloth worn about the loins
Ma'-mo, the yellow war cloak of royalty. Red cloaks were worn by the chiefs ; black, by the priests
Ma-ná-o, a thought, plan, purpose
Ma-ná-o lá-ni, a heavenly thought
Ma-ná-o la-nà, a floating thought
Mè-a, a thing, a person
Mé-ha, alone, lonely
Mé-ha-mé-ha, "Lonely One"
Mé-le, a song, to sing
Mé-le i-nò-a, to chant one's pedigree
Mi-o-mí-o, sloping. A companion of the king's
Mi'-hi, to eat poi with the fingers
Mi'-lu, Hell, the place of departed spirits
Mo'-a, a fowl
Moa-á-lii, the sea god to whom sacrifice was made
Mo'-e, a bed, to sleep
Mo-e-pu, companion in death
Mó-i, the sovereign chief, the king
Mo-ó, a lizard
Moo-o-lé-lo, history, tradition
Moò-ka-hú-na, historian, or history-making priest
Mo-hái, to sacrifice
Mo'-ku, an island, a ship
Mu'-ki, to kiss
Mu-li-wài, a river

Glossary. 397

Mo-ku-a-wéo-wéo, a "red crack in the land." Crater on Mauna Loa

Mo-lo-kái, "parting the seas." The island

Mo-ká-pu, broken tabú. N. cape of Oahu

Ná, the plural sign placed before nouns

Na-au-aò, a teacher; a person of enlightened bowels

Na-aú-po, dark-hearted

Ná-lo, a fly

Ná-lu, the surf, a billow

Na-ná, to bark

Ná-ne, a pedigree told in allegory

Ná-ni, glorious, beautiful

Ni-ó-i, poison tree of Molokai

Ni-hó, a tooth

Ni-ho pa-la-ó-a, an ivory tooth

Ni-ú, cocoa-nut, the tree

No, of, for; same as O or ko

No-à, to release from tabú

Nó-ho, a chair, a seat

Nó-ni, a plant used to sanctify the dying

Nú-i, large, great, much, many

Nu-ú-lu, a shade, an umbrella

Nai'-he, "the spear." The great national orator

Na-ma-há-na, "warm-hearted." The Maui queen; mother of Feather Mantle and two other wives of K. I.

Na-ma-ké-ha, "puffed with pride." Brother of Kaiana, also a traitor to the king

Nuu-a-nu, "even temperature." The valley

Pá, a wall, an enclosure

Paá, keep secret, be silent

Pá-áo, the "guard wall." The renowned priest, and first white man known to Hawaii

Pa-é, to land, to go ashore

Pa-é-pu, roar of the sea

Pa-hé-lo, to throw a spear

Pá-hi, sword, edged with shark's teeth

Pa-hó-a, a dagger

Pa-hú, a drum used at the heiáus

Pa-í-na, to eat
Pá-ki, a ti hedge
Pa-kí, to divide the water. The chief
Pa-kú, a curtain
Pa-la-ó-a, an ivory ornament. Insignia of rank
Pá-li, a precipice
Pa-pú, a fort
Pa-ú, a tapa petticoat
Pau-á-hi, "consumed by fire." The chiefess Mrs. Bishop
Pé-le, the fabled goddess of volcanoes; the dominant deity of Hawáii
Pe-pé-hi, "man-killer." The priest
Pé-po, black. Pepehi's assassin
Pi-li-kí-a, trouble, difficulty, danger
Pí-o, a captive, a prisoner
Pó, night, darkness; in distinction to Aó, day. Nights are named after three phases of the moon
Pó Hí-lo (first phase), new moon, seen on the west side of the island at eve.
Pó Mo-há-lu, moon at quarter, seen over the islands at sunset
Pó Hó-ku, full moon, rising at sunset
Poe-hò-e-hó-e, satin lava
Pó-i, food made from taro, potatoes, bread-fruit
Pó-la, platform of a double canoe
Pó-li, the bosom, the breast
Po-ló-lu, a long spear
Pó-no, good, right, proper
Poo-lú-a, a bastard
Po-wá, to rob, a robber
Pú, a shell horn, a gun
Pú-a, a blossom, a flower
Pu-á-a, a hog
Pu-a-li, a life-guard, company of soldiers
Pu-à-wái, flowing from. The "Punch-Bowl" crater at Honolulu
Pú-ka, a door, a gate
Pú-ka pa-ká-ka, private door, sacred to the king.
Pu-ko-ha-la, "the gun begets sin." Heiáu built by K. I.
Pú-le, a prayer; to pray
Pú-lu, the silk of fern trees

Glossary.

Pú-na, coral
Pu-na-wái, a spring, a well
Pú-na hé-le, a bosom friend
Pu-pú-le, insane
Puu-ho-nú-a, "City of Refuge." A retreat during **war**
Pu-wa-lú, tapa flag of war canoes

Wá, private talk, gossip about others
Wa-à, a canoe
Wái, fresh water; distinct from kái, **sea-water**
Wai O'-ha, holy water
Wai-o'-li, singing water
Wai-ú, **breast-water or milk**
Wai-ki-ki, spouting water. Town of
Wai-lé-le, leaping water, water-fall. **The Priestess**
Wai-lú-a, two waters
Wai-lú-ku, destructive **waters**
Wai-lú-lu, shaking water
Wai-má-nu, water bird. **The valley of**
Wa-hí-ne, a woman, a wife.
Wa-hú-pu, "reason without anger." The priest, father of **Wailéle**
Wa-ná-na, prophecy; **the** will of God
Wai-pí-o, **captive water.** The valley of
Wí, famine, destitution
Wí-ki, quick
Wí-ki wí-ki, quicker, **hurry**
Wi-wó, timid, modest
Wi-wo ó-le, **fearless**

FINIS.

www.ingramcontent.com/pod-product-compliance
Lightning Source LLC
Chambersburg PA
CBHW022117290426
44112CB00008B/705